Cultural Critique

29

Print and cover design: Nora Pauwels

Cultural Critique

Cultural Critique (ISSN 0882-4371) is published three times a year by Oxford University Press, 2001 Evans Road, Cary, NC 27513, in association with the Society for Cultural Critique, a nonprofit, educational organization.

Manuscript submissions. Contributors should submit three copies of their manuscripts to Abdul R. JanMohamed, *Cultural Critique,* Department of English, University of California, Berkeley, Berkeley, CA 94720. Manuscripts should conform to the recommendations of *The MLA Style Manual;* authors should use parenthetical documentation with a list of works cited. Contact the editorial office at the address above for further instructions on style. Manuscripts will be returned if accompanied by a stamped, self-addressed envelope. Please allow a minimum of four months for editorial consideration.

Subscriptions. Annual subscription rates are $28 for individuals and $52 for institutions. Outside the United States please add $11 for normal delivery and an additional $5 for air-expedited delivery. Subscription requests and checks (payable in U.S. funds) should be sent to Journals Customer Service, Oxford University Press, 2001 Evans Road, Cary, NC 27513.

Back issues. Single copies of back issues are $9.95 for individuals and $21 for institutions. Outside the United States the price is $15.50 for individuals and $25 for institutions. Copies may be obtained from the Journals Fulfillment Department, Oxford University Press, 2001 Evans Road, Cary NC 27513.

Advertising and permissions. Advertising inquiries and requests to reprint material from the journal should be directed to the Journals Department, Oxford University Press, 2001 Evans Road, Cary, NC 27513 (fax: 919 677–1714).

Indexing/abstracting. *Cultural Critique* is indexed/abstracted in *The Left Index, Alternative Press Index, Sociological Abstracts (SA), Social Welfare, Social Planning/Policy and Social Development (SOPODA), International Political Science Abstracts, MLA Directory of Periodicals, MLA International Bibliography,* and *Periodica Islamica.*

Postmaster. Send address changes to Journals Customer Service, Oxford University Press, 2001 Evans Road, Cary, NC 27513. Postage paid at Cary, NC, and additional post offices.

Photocopies. The journal is registered with the Copyright Clearance Center, 222 Rosewood Drive, Danvers, MA 01923 (fax: 508 750–4744). Permission to photocopy items for the internal or personal use of specific clients is granted by Oxford University Press provided that the copier pay to the Center the $5.00 per copy fee stated in the code on the first page of each article. Special rates for classroom use are available through the CCC or by contacting the Journals Department, Oxford University Press, 2001 Evans Road, Cary, NC 27513. Requests for permission to photocopy for other purposes, such as for general distribution, resale, advertising, and promotional purposes or for creating new works, should also be directed to Oxford University Press at the same address.

⊗ The journal is printed on acid-free paper that meets the minimum requirements of ANSI Standard Z39.48-1984 (Permanence of Paper), beginning with Number 1.

Arab Women Arab Wars

Miriam Cooke

Venturing out into the street for the first time alone, Cherifa adjusts her veil so that the seeing eye should not be seen. Heedless of propriety, she crosses the medina to warn her dissident husband that he is in danger of his life. Meanwhile, Touma in a bar in the French quarter tries to look casual in her strange new clothes and the even stranger environment. Family and friends condemn her as a prostitute.

***

Nuzha, the "prostitute," watches incredulously as the young men climb the walls to their death. The Israelis are not going to run out of bullets. Another way must be found to penetrate into their stronghold. She offers to lead the combatants into the compound through a secret underground passage that can be accessed through her kitchen.

***

In a paroxysm of pain, a woman tries to prevent her child from being born, while her husband at the front tries to survive mortal wounds. They are both struggling to keep the promise that he should be the first to see their son. The dead infant is placed on the dead man's chest.

***

© 1995 by *Cultural Critique*. Winter 1994–95. 0882-4371/95/$5.00.

Three vignettes from three Arab wars: the Algerian Revolution, the Intifada, the Iraq-Iran War. Glimpses snatched (by this reader) from stories women wrote while their people were at war. Assia Djebar (*Les Enfants du Nouveau Monde*), Sahar Khalifa (*Bab al-Saha*), and Aliya Talib (*Greening*) each recorded in fiction some of the roles women played in an event generally considered to be the preserve of men.

***

The way we talk about an event affects the way we will experience or perceive our experience of a later analogous event. We all collaborate in this shaping of history. Some events like war are so existentially important for their communities that they demand a greater degree of collaboration in the construction of the narratives than of the counternarratives. Differences of perspective and in sociopolitical roles that are acceptable in normal times become intolerable in war time.

In *Writing War,* Lynne Hanley deplores the disputes that have so often arisen between those who have chosen to write about war and their critics. She says that

> a rigid distinction is drawn between the act of producing and the act of interpreting a literary work, and a battle ensues over which is the more essential enterprise. And because such battles for supremacy are premised on the validity of the categorical distinctions upon which they are based, the bellicose literary mind is always vexed by writing and writers who refuse to stay in their proper place. (8)

She urges war writers and their critics to work together without striving to set up hierarchies of value and "truth." Her contribution to this cooperative project is a volume that alternates short stories and literary essays. Hanley's project is both creative and critical, and its janus-like ambition has helped me to situate my own work: I do not see myself as simply criticizing or dispassionately describing and analyzing what Arab novelists and short story writers have penned on the wars they have experienced. I conceive of my work as part of a broader literary intervention: to explore possible causes, to expose probable effects, and then to imagine alternatives.

The premise of this paper is that attention paid to literature that emerges out of the very entrails of war may change the ways in which we experience and express war. During the anger and chaos of war, many write; most will quickly be forgotten, if they are ever noted. Yet, many of these women and men who write, even those who are paid, do so because they hope, however forlornly, to intervene in the situation and thus make a difference. Such writing is an integral part of the war endeavor, and as such it has new and often surprising things to say. If we wish to approach the dynamic of war and not just to repeat canned tales of heroism and victimization, we should listen to these writers' words and make others listen. It is this literature, much more than that written out of the comfort and safety of postbellum panelled studies, that can teach us about war, about the ways in which people negotiate violence, and about the construction of counternarratives.

These narratives cannot be invented ex post facto. They have meaning and power primarily when they participate in the action itself. To locate and recognize these oppositional stories, we must take seriously the immediately encoded war experience. Yet few until recently have accorded such writing any worth. In general, the only war literature to be taken seriously was that which emerged after the passion of war had subsided. In *Wartime*, Paul Fussell reiterates a commonplace of literary criticism when he condemns military men's recording of life at the World War II front as "gush, waffle, and cliche occasioned by high-mindedness, the impulse to sound portentous, and the slumbering of the critical spirit" (251).

However, in the 1990s there are two problems with such an attitude. First, debates about the literary canon have revealed that blanket statements about literary production enable a kind of knee-jerk censorship—don't bother to read any European war fiction published between 1939 and 1945 or any Iraqi war novels and short stories that came out during the Iran-Iraq War of 1980–88. They're all rubbish. With so much fiction published, the judicious reader will not open the maligned books. Thus, works important possibly for literary and certainly for political reasons will become effectively censured. A second problem is still more crucial. It concerns the interface between war and social values that fiction uniquely elicits. The unthinking rejection of fiction written during war makes it difficult to understand how war today is fought other than it was during and at any time before World War II. War today does not always feel like war. The front that had conveniently marked a space as other and appropriate for killing and dying has in may cases come home. As we in the West watch our world as we knew it crumble, we recognize that the Cold War was cold in the West only. Hot war pervaded and continues to shape the lives of others. Now war as a condition of militarized alertness has become endemic to our daily lives. We realize that it is as hard to separate armed, organized conflict from unarmed, disorganized violence as it is to distinguish between combat and noncombat.[1] Yet, we have few guides to thinking anew about war. Fiction is one such guide. For writing that we had thought to be about peace time may also relate to war. In fact, it may not be so different and certainly not so easily separable from that which was once only written about an event clearly labelled "war."

* * *

Since the outbreak of the Iran-Iraq War in 1980, Iraqi critics, such as Abd al-Sattar Nasir, Salah al-Ansari, and Latif Nasir Husayn, have debated whether this war was the first to have produced what they have called "war literature" (al-Hamid Hammudi 95). They use the term to specify literature written during war that is not transparently propaganda. Of course, in the absolute sense of the term, this is not true—Homer himself was surely not the first to turn fighting into writing. But then again, these Iraqi critics may be at least partially right. It is only in the 20th century (perhaps, as Gareth Thomas suggests, since the Spanish Civil War), that war literature has been discussed and self-consciously produced as a constitutive part of a war effort (Thomas 18–29). However, this literature in war, even when not rejected out of hand, remains at best controversial.

When I met the Lebanese male writer Taufiq Awwad in the summer of 1982, he told me that it was not yet time to write the *War and Peace* of the Lebanese Civil War nor to paint its Guernica. Time was needed, he assured me, to see the contours of this chaos more clearly. Yet, many women and some men in Lebanon had by that time written libraries of books and painted galleries of paintings, and what they had produced could not be so easily dismissed as mere journalese and photography, in other words, as a form of unreflective recording that can respond to the unexpected. Awwad was nostalgically calling for Wordsworthian reflection or what the Iraqi critic Basim Abd al-Hamid Hammudi in 1986 called *takhzin* (storage). However, Hammudi does not use this word in the sense of Wordsworth and Awwad. He rejects such storage as damaging because it does not permit the authentic war text to be constructed. In his enthusiasm to tout the war writer's, and incidentally the critic's, importance, Hammudi goes beyond Hemingway's advocacy of the "true" transcription of the experience of great events[2] to assert that literary merit *derives* from the documentary function. In effect, he claims that glorious events spontaneously unfold into glorious texts.

Even if I do not agree completely with Hammudi, I do believe that the novel, poem, short story, or painting that emerges directly out of the war experience (whether this be at the front or in a war-like situation analogous to civil war or to social anarchy) does have a unique and important story to tell, and not just about Iraqis, but about all present-day communities at war. This is a story that challenges the Homeric myth that divides itself between men fighting and women crying. These war texts may also have a unique and important role to play, because they not only reflect but may sometimes interact with the events and mood of the conflict. By retaining and perpetuating the dynamism of the experience, they can project a space in which changes can be imagined. This envisioning is possible because the final form has not been fixed and now, thanks to such texts, might never be. The experience that is immediately encoded retains the play of the conflicting discourses of war time. In his poem "War Poet," the British soldier Donald Bain captures the dynamic between a harrowing experience and its immediate narration:

> We in our haste can only see the small components of the scene; / We cannot tell what incidents will focus on the final screen. / A barrage of disruptive sound, a petal on a sleeping face, / Both must be noted, both must have their place. / It may be that our later selves or else our unborn sons / Will search for meaning in the dust of long deserted guns. / We only watch, and indicate, and make our scribbled pencil notes. / We do not wish to moralize, only to ease our dusty throats. (qtd. in Fussell 296)

In reply to Bain's wistful conjecture about future semanticists, Fussell wrily comments: "But what time seems to have shown our later selves is that perhaps there was less coherent meaning in the events of wartime than we had hoped" (296). Exactly so. Time should not be allowed to impose coherent meaning as though it inhered in the events themselves. Time creates an illusory coherence that does not substitute for or negate the impressionistic notations of those who suffered war firsthand.

War is experienced in scattered fragments. What is the participant to make of these small components of the scene that are united only by the fact of a single experiencing subject? What is to be made of the barrage of disruptive sound and the petal on the sleeping face? They do not make any sense except if they fit into some larger sense, some framework, best of all a myth, a war myth. The war myths of many cultures, including those of the Arab world, designate appropriate spaces for specific kinds of actions and appoint protagonists for particular preconfigured roles. When the fighting is done and it demands to be described, understood, and especially justified, then the war myth becomes the ultimate ordering principle.

But how is the myth evoked, and who invokes it? Whether the barrage of disruptive sound and the petal on the sleeping face are remembered depends on how the story is told, and who tells it. However, in most cultures' myths it is men who tell these stories, and they remember the components that add to the notion that war is an arena for the display of men's manliness and heroism. Thus, we see that details are not in themselves intrinsically important; they acquire long-term significance only if they find a context and a narrator to accommodate them. The ill-shaped components, e.g., the heroic women combatants, may tease for a while, may disturb apparently self-evident categorizations and classifications. However, if they are not given due heed within their own contexts and by multiple narrators, if they are not allowed to function outside the stranglehold of the mythic and too often male mold, they will soon be forgotten. I want these clumsy components, these heroic women combatants, to survive the manipulations of time.

The license to write the war experience at once defies the manipulations of time and destroys the neat and generally dichotomous categories that have shaped the Western war narrative since Homer and the Arab war story since the *Ayyam al-Arab*. It renders transparent the blatant falsifications inherent in other war narratives that continue to describe all war experience, however differentiated, in the same mythic terms. The old war story in the West, as in the Arab world, erases the experience by squeezing it into a bipolar mold. When critics like Fussell disdainfully dismiss as catharsis all war fiction unmediated by time, it seems to me that what they are actually dismissing is not so much the story as its impact: what they correctly perceive to be threatening signs of change in the story. So many loose ends, they may never be neatly tied. Such a situation is intolerable. In war, without closure, there is uncertain meaning. In war, without clear meaning, there is doubt about the war project. In war, where there is doubt there is a weakening of the will to fight. The spectre of the wimp—the dreaded alter ego to the male hero—looms large.

Hanley ascribes the reflexive male need for time and the dichotomous order it brings to a bellicose mentality that creates

> arbitrary categories that are presumed to be mutually exclusive and hostile (self/other, masculine/feminine, white/black, us/them), and of then insisting on the supremacy of one category over the other. . . . Since the assertion of the supremacy of one category over another requires, above all, an inflexible definition of membership, the bellicose mind is always resistant to any erosion of its "mystic boundaries." (7)

Whether the insistence on these mystic boundaries in itself denotes bellicosity is debatable, but what I shall argue is that these boundaries do play an important part in constructing, justifying, and enabling the easy and unchanging reiteration of war and its narration. It is not new that front and home front, combatant and civilian, friend and foe, defensive and offensive actions, victory and defeat[3] are not so easily distinguishable; not new at all that combatants are not always male, nor that noncombatants are not necessarily female or feminized. Yet, that is the frame that has shaped and contained most cultures' war stories. It was the way war was remembered until the late 20th century, until perhaps Vietnam and the postcolonial era.

What is new since the '60s is that the mystic boundaries that staked out a binary world have begun to be represented and discussed. This representation and these discussions have revealed that the mystic boundaries are at least in part responsible for the prosecution of war. What has changed since Vietnam and in the postcolonial era is that war is increasingly represented as spreading beyond its conventional boundaries. It is not a peaceful society but one that is at war that not only tolerates but encourages the growth of a military-industrial complex. In this postcolonial period, war metaphors abound, but I would suggest that by their very abundance they cease to be metaphors. As the sociolinguist George Lakoff tells us so starkly, "[m]etaphors can kill" (59–72). The inner city drug wars, in late April 1992 climaxing in the Rodney King riots in Los Angeles, and the failed wars on poverty are products of the militarization of postmodern society. In *Pure War,* Paul Virilio has written that *volens nolens* we are civilian soldiers waging hi-tech Pure War "which isn't acted out in representation, but in infinite preparation (which leads) toward a generalized non-development . . . of civilian societies" (56). How can we unsubstantiate such a grandiose claim? We cannot, but we can pursue it as a thesis to see whether or not Virilio etches the conditions of a world in which violence has increasingly become its own justification.

Postcolonial wars, of which the Vietnam War and the Gulf War are vivid examples, during their waging exploded binary oppositions, overflowed all categories. In Vietnam, the confusion between warrior and peasant, between South Vietnamese friend and Vietcong foe when both looked alike, and between masculinity and femininity became a commonplace of American filmic and literary representations. At times, even the boundary between the war and its representation was erased, so that performance could no longer be considered to be "not reality," but rather part of it. Indeed, during the filming of *Apocalypse Now,* Coppola and the Filipino army rotated military material according to need.

The merging of reality and performance that marked Vietnam can be seen in other postcolonial wars; in Soweto as in the West Bank, demonstrations and military reprisals merged with street theater performances (Slymovics 18–38). In the postcolonial period, war has been technologized to the extent that its representation has become implicated in its waging. As Simon During has written, "the fusion of theater and war, war as theater, is a product of modern communications technology" (37). Sophisticated media interact with and sometimes supplant superguns. Television viewers are becoming increasingly aware that the media closes the gap between the reality of war and its representation. Coverage of the Gulf War in the United States emblematized the conflation (Hoynes 305–26). Many have discussed the erasure of the boundary between the lens of the bomber pilots and that of the U.S. television viewers. Judith Butler writes that

> the visual record of this war is not a *reflection* on the war, but the enactment of this phantasmatic structure, indeed, part of the very means by which it is socially constituted and maintained as a war. The so-called "smart bomb" records its target as it moves in to destroy it—a bomb with a camera attached in front, a kind of optical phallus; it relays that film back to a command control and that film is reshown on television, effectively constituting the television screen and its viewer as the extended apparatus of the bomb itself. In this sense, by viewing we are bombing, identified with both bomber and bomb . . . and yet securely wedged in the couch of one's own living room. (75–76)

However, in the Gulf War the conflation of reality and representation in the media went beyond the collapse of the screen; it had above all something to do with the role of the media in the "100-Day War." A chronicle of the coverage of the war reveals that the media slipped constantly between reinforcing and undermining its differences from the reality lived in the Arabian desert. In its representative function, it seemed to maintain an independent perspective that allowed it to target and name what it willed: the line in the sand could be a metaphor for blurred boundaries between the two armies, just as it could conversely describe sharply demarcated zones. As participant, it lost this freedom to find itself constrained by its drive for power and influence. Between August 1990 and March 1991, it was not always clear that it was General Norman Schwartzkopf who was briefing the TV news anchor star Ted Koppel; it often seemed to be the reverse.

The liberty and sanction to narrate and represent directly the war experience captures these paradoxical moments. It does not attempt to resolve the paradox by eliminating inconvenient components; it allows contradictions to coexist. In so doing, it reveals that the disorganized, unarmed violence away from the epicenter of the theater of operations lies on a continuum with the "organized" whole that is called "war." The recognition of this continuum disables automatic adjudication about who has the right to write when about what. In contemporary civil wars like those in Lebanon, Northern Ireland, and Sri Lanka and increasingly in U.S. inner cities, it is less and less clear when it is war and when it is peace.[4] By the same token, it may be equally unclear when a writer is writing about "war" and when about "peace," especially when euphemisms like "the events," "the situation," "collateral damage," and "neutralizing assets" abound. Not only the war zone but the writers' guild collapses: the narration of postcolonial wars is no longer a male preserve. These war stories, although "men's domain," may also be interpreted as being about peace, "women's domain."

Before Vietnam, Lebanon, and the Cold War, women were not supposed to write of war. Often, as in Cassandra's case, they were not even to *speak* of war. Margaret Higonnet has shown how the European literary establishment rejected women's writings on the two world wars. Their pretext was that women could not experience the war firsthand and that they, being denied the experience, should not presume to write of it.[5] But was it true that the women had not experienced these wars? Of course not. However, because they had not been written, or had not written themselves, into the war, it was, with time, easy to conclude that women had not been there. In the interval, the wars had been re-membered, or, rather, crafted anew to fit their cultures' myths of how wars were thought to be fought. Ambiguities and inconsistencies were eliminated: men were warriors, women were watchers. Warriors talked about other warriors, women waited and listened.

* * *

The post-1948 wars in the Arab world demonstrate the transformation in the reality of war and its representation in the postcolonial era. This transformation is at once military and discursive. In what follows, I shall focus primarily on the literary impact of this change on women. There has not been a single way of representing their participation in combat, however defined; nor have there been uniform controls on their writings. During the Algerian Revolution, as well as in pre-1967 Israel, Arab women fought, but they fought as men, and women's writings were subject to men's control and therefore often also to internal censorship. Although the waging and writing of war were on the cusp of change, pressure to conform to conventional notions of war telling was too great to be withstood. This has not been so much the case in the post-'67 Israeli-occupied territories or in Lebanon, or even in Iraq.

The Algerian Revolution of 1954–62 provides a paradox: it set a precedent for women's visibility in national struggle, yet it has come to be regarded as also the source of their ills in the patriarchal postcolonial society to which it gave birth. Several reasons may be adduced for women's failure to exploit their opportunities during the Algerian Revolution. Firstly, the years of French colonial domination had been marked by attempts to coopt Algerian women through education and acculturation. Algeria of 1962 remained resistant to new values and concepts such as women's rights because they were linked with the hated, now departed colonial overlord. Hence, Algerian women did not have a feminist context within which to situate their struggle. This latter point is significant from both a military and a literary perspective. The women did what the men wanted them to do. Even when they were in charge of operations (Shaaban 182–219), they acted in place of men, never in ways that highlighted their otherness to the new role and the unprecedented nature of their visibility and behavior. Cross-dressing demanded conformity to the rules regulating the role. With such an attitude, they could change neither the role nor their consciousness. Thinking as men, they anticipated that participation and self-sacrifice would produce their own rewards. They did not realize that they had to fight to be recognized and to be remembered. They did not understand that they should not allow themselves to be caught up in the war of symbols that always follows the war of weapons. They allowed their return to the home, to the domain of women's activity, to epitomize the return of "peace." From then on, peace was conserved by eliminating ambiguity in the roles men and women played.

Algerian women did not recognize the importance of conserving the role ambiguity brought about by women acting in men's space, the advantages to be gained by confusing expectations of how men and women should behave. Unlike their sisters, students, and spiritual heirs from Northern Ireland[6] to Palestine, they did not realize that to change status quo they had to (1) emphasize their importance *as women* to Algerian success in the war; (2) continually affirm, particularly in writing, their presence and its importance so as not to be ignored or forcibly repressed; (3) articulate their experiences not as cross-dressing but as transformative; and (4) act in terms of the discourse they had thus created. Of course, many Algerian women wrote, but later. It was not enough to write later. They should have written at once. Since they did not, it was the men's books that flooded the market. Consequently, the story we now have of the women in the Algerian Revolution is one that tells *what happened to the women* and not *what the women did*. Even Djamila Boupacha's story is known primarily through the writing of Simone de Beauvoir and Gisele Halimi.

My comparative readings of Algerian women's and men's war literature indicate that, whereas the women themselves were not aware of their importance, the men were and they overreacted. Their writings reflect the post–World War I writings that Sandra Gilbert and Susan Gubar have analyzed in *No Man's Land: The Place of the Woman Writer in the 20th Century* (1988). Whereas the British women writers were scarcely aware of the significance of women's new visibility and particularly of their participation in the Great War, the men were wracked with anxiety. In Algeria, men like Muhammad Dib, Mouloud Feraoun, and Malek Haddad wrote on the one hand of Medusas and of monstrous daughters, and on the other hand of paralyzed and impotent intellectual men. Although women writers like Djamila Debeche and Assia Djebar gradually came to write about the war, they were less concerned with their just desserts than they were with the end of the war. The persistent problem for women of biculturalism (i.e., European-style education entailing certain expectations but marriage into non-European circumstances that made a mockery of such promises) was censored out of their fiction as men demanded total attention to the nationalist struggle. In *Les Enfants du Nouveau Monde* (1962), which was written and published in the last year of the war, Djebar did write of the new roles women were playing, but without any sense of moment. Even the dramatic first emergence out of the house and crossing of the city by the veiled Cherifa is presented as intimidating rather than as empowering. Her heroines seemed not to know that they might profit from their war experiences. Even in the one realm in which women fought as women, donating their bodies to the cause by alternately dressing as French women so that they might place bombs in the nouvelle ville and then reveiling so that they might hide the bombs they were moving around the medina, Djebar's assessment is negative: Touma is clearly a prostitute. The fact that, like women in the two world wars, the Algerian women had functioned effectively in roles traditionally assigned to men did nothing to change their self-image. They held on to the roles society had assigned to them. Neither they nor the context were redefined to accommodate a new reality. Women who for a period had done what men do went back to doing women's things. Status quo ante became everyone's overriding goal: to the men it represented a reaffirmation of control in the family; to the women it meant that the war was over and the foreigners had been expelled. The need for peace and self-governance after almost a century and a half of resistance and tutelage precluded the possibility of change. It was only considerably later that people began to understand the lessons of other 20th-century wars, particularly the Spanish Civil War—in other words, that political wars are often inseparable from social revolutions.[7] In the absence of a concerted attempt on the women's part to change their situation or even only to write of the war as transforming, Algerian men quickly imposed a neotraditional system that deprived the dreaded "new women" of any voice. Literary evidence supports recent sociopolitical contentions by women like Marie-Aimee Helie-Lucas that Algerian women were not so much forced back into oppression as they were blocked from pursuing opportunities they had not at the time recognized (104–14).

The transformation in the war narrative in the postcolonial period can be read in a single literature of the Arab world: Palestinian women's writings on two of their wars with the Israelis, the first in 1948 and the other the Intifada that broke out almost 40 years later. Many, especially political scientists, would contest my classification of the Intifada as a war except in the purely metaphoric sense.[8] However, I contend that it is. As I shall argue below, the Intifada may not confront equivalent forces, but it does line up a nation against the army of a nation-state. Above all, it functions within the parameters of military constructs.

Both men's and women's writings of the early post-1948 period out of Israel reflect great ambivalence about the Israelis as well as about their own status and future. There is little of the later anger that marks the post-'67 writings by Palestinians worldwide. The major concerns of both men and women writers from within Israel are survival with dignity and the establishment of a just if patriarchal society. There is no hint that radical changes must be contemplated so as better to confront new challenges. To the contrary, traditional values and roles, particularly for women, are enforced and often by women like Najwa Qawar Farah.

The year 1967 marks the beginning of a seismic shift. Wars in the Arab world, which until then had been treated as discrete events, usually in connection with a colonial power, came to be regarded as systemic. The Palestinians' plight became a pan-Arab cause, if not always in reality then certainly in rhetoric. With this came a change in expectations of Palestinian women's behavior and, coincidentally, of their writing. Five years after the end of the Algerian Revolution, Palestinians were invoking its lessons: the use of violence in the struggle for independence; the indispensability of women to national liberation; and the importance for women of remaining vigilant on all fronts so as to be able to withstand what the literary critic bell hooks has called "interlocking systems of domination" (175) that would force a repetition of Algerian women's experience.[9] Palestinian women writers, in concert with their Irish and South African counterparts, are claiming that not only are women as actors playing out new as well as traditional roles vital to the nationalist revolution but so is feminism as an ideology of radical social change.

The poetry, autobiographies, novels, and short stories of Fedwa Tuqan, Sahar Khalifa, and Halima Jauhar already in the late '60s and '70s draw the contours of the Intifada, which actually broke out in 1987. This popular uprising derived its name from the term the women had been using for 20 years to describe their women-specific ways of resisting Israeli aggression in Gaza and the West Bank. Their resistance drew upon strategies women have begun to practice *worldwide*. The mothers in South Africa and in Yugoslavia, the Women in Black in Israel, the Madres of the Plaza de Mayo all have recognized the power of the spectacle.[10] Women, particularly in the guise of "mothers," theatricalize confrontations and the struggle to control public space and attention. They are using the media against the guns.

This initiative and leadership by women *as women* in national struggle is one of the most visible aspects of the change in postcolonial warfare. In their struggle to control public space and attention, they refuse to play men's roles. As never before, women are occupying what were defined as male-specific arenas, but they do so as women, and, again, particularly as mothers. The woman whose resistance as a woman succeeds cannot be absorbed into a gender-neutral, or better, male movement. Out of a space presumed to be closed to her, she has asserted her right to launch action. Because the system is in crisis, normal policing procedures are on hold. Not only is there access to that space, but the fact of access changes that space into a hyperspace. It is no longer the front, that space that Cynthia Enloe tells us must always be redefined—relocated so as to remain that place where women are not. It has become the hyperspace of the home front, what Doris Lessing calls a "habit of mind, a structure of feeling, a cultural predisposition" (qtd. in Hanley 7), that ambiguous place that is neither home nor front because it has become both. And it houses Virilio's "civilian-soldiers," who are neither civilians nor soldiers because they have become both.

Palestinian women writers are aware of the advantages of mixing roles and genders in the hyperspace, and they describe and thus inscribe the process. Their stories of women going out into the streets and, under the ever watchful eye of the international television cameras, confronting soldiers with the vulnerable bodies of themselves and their children demonstrate how all the familiar binaries that structure the Israelis' expectations of and training for war are thrown into confusion. Soon after the men took it over in December 1987, the women-specific nature of the Intifada changed. The sporadic, individual happenings were controlled and strategized. The use of arms was encouraged, and young men wearing the national symbol of the *kuffiyeh,* or checkered scarf, tied about the head in a distinctive manner, became soldiers it was "legitimate" to shoot.

In her 1990 novel *Bab al-Saha,* Khalifa explores women's attitudes to the organizing and centralizing of the resistance and to the mobilizing of young men. Nuzha, the prostitute heroine, compels the men who enter her life to acknowledge that women's ways, often domestic ways, including unarmed, disorganized, fragmented struggle by women and children, were still the best way to achieve the kind of results they wanted. After seeing 20 men climb to their death as they try to get into an Israeli military headquarters, the prostitute offers an alternative access: through a trapdoor in her kitchen, to an underground passage, and then up into the heart of the headquarters.[11]

More than the Intifada, which blurred and challenged some of the binaries usual to war, yet had to acknowledge others, the Lebanese Civil War defied conventional categorizations. It confronted and undermined all the black and white distinctions that, once established, enable the tired repetition of the War Story, that reassuringly familiar skeleton we merely flesh out with new details. The Lebanese Civil War lent itself to multiple unorthodox narrations, especially by women (Cooke, *War's Other Voices*). It allowed the women to rewrite the violence so that, for example, passivity, endemic to many moments of war, could be written as activism. This discursive transformation can be read in women's evolving descriptions of waiting, that aspect of war that Fussell describes as so debilitating, probably because it is so feminizing (75–78). During the 7-year period that preceded the Israeli Invasion in June 1982, women like Emily Nasrallah wrote progressively of their staying in Lebanon and waiting as first "Doing Nothing," then as "Survival," and finally as "Resistance" (qtd. in Cooke, *War's Other Voices*). With time, they described this staying in Lebanon, which had originally been unthinking, as though it were a need, a response to a maternal instinct. Lebanon was a child in pain, it had to be protected. If mothers—not, of course, biological mothers, but rather what Sara Ruddick calls "maternal thinkers"—did not care for Lebanon, who would?

By the early 1980s, the women's writing became more assertive and self-consciously resistant. The tolerance of those who were leaving was fast disappearing. They were beginning to realize that whenever there was an opportunity to leave, it was generally the women who stayed and the men who departed. And when they stayed, the women remained vigilant against the war. As Evelyne Accad writes, whenever the demarcation line between the predominantly Christian East and the Muslim West Beirut closed, it was the women who organized or, like Andree Chedid, wrote about organizing protest marches. They believed, depite all odds, in a possible reunification and to this end they were prepared to sacrifice their lives (Accad 78–90). It was not that the men had no conscience and the women did, but rather that they had a different notion of responsibility. Whereas men, both writers and male protagonists in women's writings, pointed the finger of blame at others, particularly the fighters and every possible -ism, women constantly affirmed that responsibility is shared by all. Individual innocence, Ghada Samman insists, is not possible in a guilty society (14–15). The women's writings articulate their transformed consciousness. Whereas they had originally stayed out of selflessness, they were now staying to resist Lebanon's total destruction. Above all, they were staying to achieve for themselves a sense of self, as women and as Lebanese citizens.

Despite apparent differences in the nature of the Intifada and the Lebanese Civil War, their writings are comparable. What is shared is exemplified in a comparison between men's and women's writings. For the women writers, these are wars in which binary structures are recognized to be artificial and unhelpful in trying to understand and resolve their conflicts. In this destabilized context, Lebanese and Palestinian women are the ones to take the initiative in the struggle and to forge a new relationship between the individual and the collective. This relationship is premised on care for each other and on the hope for survival for oneself and by extension for the society as a whole. Lebanese and Palestinian men's writings, mirroring women's literary assessments of men's political actions, tend to trivialize the women's new strategies and the realities they produce. At the same time they continue to advocate the pursuit of traditional organized, armed conflict, however suicidal and unsuccessful it may have proved itself to be. Thus do they seek to rehabilitate the familiar binarisms. Wars in such a worldview seem to be necessary, the only solutions to apparently irresolvable conflicts.

The 8-year Iran-Iraq War would seem to be quite different, yet my reading of its literature suggests changes in war representation comparable to those that have taken place during other postcolonial wars waged in the Arab world. Like its successor, the Gulf

War, it was more a parody of conventional or, better, Total War. In 1980, Saddam Hussein launched what he thought would be a blitzkrieg. It was to be a show of strength, a bid for the leadership of the Arab world. In anticipation of an easy, resounding victory, in 1979 he was already lining up artists and artisans—whom he thus implicated in the military venture—to construct before the event its happy outcome. To boost the significance of the expected victory, Hussein dipped randomly into history's grab bag and, with the help of artists and writers, pastiched together a glossy facade that included New Babylons, Sharifian descents, and Qadisiyas.[12] The reality of the slaughter of little boys and old men in the mud was replaced by the reassurance of glorious monuments and victorious stories. Eight years later, exhausted and his army and arsenal depleted, Hussein declared a victory that allowed the fighting to stop.

Most of the Iran-Iraq war literature, like most of its cultural production, was state commissioned and published. Conferences and festivals were held to give a platform to this new literature. Only a few were able to overcome atomization and retain the sense of responsibility that many assumed all Iraqi writers and artists had perforce lost.[13] So closely did some artists collaborate with the government that their works came to shape reality. Victory and martyr monuments were constructed before any victory was in sight; millennial literary series celebrating the war were conceived before the war had even started. Image-making replaced creative reflection and production.[14] Could this be art, or was it pure propaganda? Can patronized but also terrorized writers question the validity of a patriotic war? How does one read such texts? One reads between the lines. Sometimes there is nothing there. Sometimes it turns out that there is *nothing on the line;* everything is in the "between."[15]

So, I have read between the lines of both women's and men's fiction on the Iran-Iraq War. Careful not to write of the front, women writers like Suhayla Salman, Aliya Talib, and Lutfiya al-Dulaymi were bravely critical of the war. They alluded, even though necessarily obliquely, to the ways in which the state had coopted not only people's minds but also their bodies, especially women's bodies. Women, who had achieved considerable gains in access to educational and professional opportunities, including military service, and even in some cases to equal pay, were told during the war they should turn their bodies over to the state and produce at least five children, preferably boys. Salman's strong women disdainfully reject Patriotic Motherhood. Yet, ironically, it *is* as mothers—not Patriotic, but rather Resisting Mothers—that they unmask a system that would turn their boys, the country's future, into dead heroes; they, like the Argentinian Madres and the Mothers of the Intifada, claim as each her own those non-kin men who are about to be wasted; they hold together a fragmenting society. Talib's stories again and again satirize notions of heroic masculinity and passive femininity in times of war that produce nothing but corpses. In 1988, the apparently pro-Baathist woman al-Dulaymi published *Seeds of Fire*. Appropriately enough for a woman writer, it refers only tangentially to the war and as though it were infinitely distant. This "home front novel" revolves around Layla, a graphic artist working for an advertising agency while her husband is away at the mines. As in Lebanese and Palestinian *Kuenstlerromane* on their wars, the role of the woman artist narrator is crucial. Through her creative production, Layla is liberated from the constraints of her body so that she may enter the heretofore forbidden zone of male exchange. Her presence in the agency is doubly disruptive: it is repeated that she is the only woman employee; her artwork is so accomplished and increasingly radical that it threatens to ruin the business. How? Her male director fears that if she emphasizes the aesthetic aspect of her work, consumers will focus on the creator of the message rather than on the message alone. Prospective consumers will think before buying. The parallels between these marketing strategies, and the production and dissemination of propaganda are striking. For when the people become aware that values they had thought to be essential are in fact packaged goods that they are supposed to consume spontaneously, they will begin to doubt the imperatives of martyrdom and patriotism. *Seeds of Fire* seems to suggest that during the war the woman artist may find at the very heart of a totalitarian system the key to its undoing.

Although some of the men write of women warriors,[16] the women do not. This is surprising in view of the fact that in 1976 women already had begun to enlist into popular militia forces and by 1982 their numbers had swollen to 40,000.[17] Why? I would suggest that this is the case because women soldiers, after all, are doing what the men are doing. These Iraqi women write of what the women are doing *as women*. They write on and through the war, yet also against it. They write their protest into a war they are supposed to support. Like the post-'48 Palestinian literature out of Israel, men and women seem to be subject to similar pressures. Yet, in Iraq it is primarily the women who have found ways to write against the war. For the men, who were more assured of an audience or, at least, of censorship, criticism was a more risky business.

* * *

My reading of Arab writers' fiction on their wars since 1948 suggests that attention to women, both as fighters and as writers, reveals a change in warfare and its representation over the past 40 years. During precolonial and colonial wars, women's participation in national conflict is presented as a copy of men's ways of fighting; they are femmes soldats. Temporary and expedient gender role reversals do not lead to narratives of role transformations or even ambiguities. In conventional war, women do not have the space to imagine another way to live or to fight. Like the Algerian women, they are temporarily transformed into something they know they do not wish to become. However, when writing out of postcolonial wars, many Arab women describe and extol women's agency as women in what used to be, but thus ceases to be, a male-only space. Their trespassing bodies break down the black and white distinctions that had shaped the war story and allow them to create countervisions of society and of war. In Lebanon, the women wrote of the need to reject the old norms of emigration and to stay, to adopt responsibility for the chaos, and to work for the survival of the self, of others, and of the country. Their message was stay and thus stop the war. Although in the wake of the war of 1967 the Palestinian women were agreed with the men on the need to resist the occupation, they did not agree on the means. They opposed the use of confrontational violence, which enabled the Israelis to fight as they had been trained to fight. They called for transformed social arrangements and gender relations and a valorization of women's ways of fighting so as to resist more effectively. The Iraqi women writers showed that their society's male-dominated values and the war they created were self-destructive. Since they could not with impunity criticize their leader, they directed themselves to their readers. Their writing creates citizens with a conscience who can see through the manipulation that mobilizes a whole nation to fight a foolish war.

In all of the Arab women's literature on postcolonial wars, images of motherhood have acquired centrality. The nurturing persona, who in the literature of the colonial period seemed bent on molding her daughter into her own oppressed shape, has multiplied so as to be able to play numerous roles. These mothers are both aggressive and pacific, patriotic and nationalist, desiring and destructive, martyr and prisoner. They may be all of these at once or at different times. Motherism as a multi-faceted strategy of resistance in postcolonial war and its literature is no longer a "mere" social fact; it has become a resisting act. As such, it is constantly reconstructed to suit its challenges. No boundary is so resilient that it cannot bend.

Postcolonial wars have transformed the relationship between women's participation in war and its narration: the change in women's experience has found a necessary corollary in the change in discourse. Women are inscribing their experiences in war into the war story. They are thus countering others' naming of women's experiences as having not been in war. The delicate balancing act between experience and its recording must be maintained so that action and its recording will remain in tension. The political mother only retains efficacy if she is *written* as politically effective. Yet, at the same time, she will only continue to have a literary voice if she can hold on to political agency. The postcolonial war writer realizes that her writing—the struggle to reclaim language in such a way that it will empower and no longer suppress her—is critical to her understanding of the role she may play in the war theater. Out of postcolonial war, women write to transform themselves, their relationships with others, and, by extension, the social context. Whereas Algerian women fought as men, Arab women after them have fought as women and often as mothers. Their participation cannot be forgotten or eliminated as women playing at men's roles, as cross-dressing, because it is written and will therefore be remembered as women fighting as women. These women writers have found a space in which to make their voices heard, and their heard voices are changing that space.

I would like to conclude with the words of Hanan Ashrawi, the spokesperson for the Palestinian delegation at the 1990s Middle East Peace Talks who expresses eloquently and forcefully the difference women make in war:

> And if we lose sight of the human substance then we lose sight of the basic essence of all our work. . . . Men always choose the politics of domination and destruction. . . . It is time to transcend the pain of the moment and to impose a woman's solution on the Palestinian-Israeli conflict, and the women's solution is based on equality, on non-discrimination, on the preservation of life and rights and on addressing the core issues of justice, freedom, with candor and with courage, not with weapons and power.

Notes

I would like to thank Evelyne Accad, Bruce Lawrence, Paul Vieille, and Jane Tompkins for reading earlier drafts of this article and for their helpful suggestions.

1. In the wake of the Gulf War, Cynthia Enloe writes that "contemporary warfare made the conceptual divide between combat and non-combat irrelevant" (107).

2. "Hemingway has written that some events are of such magnitude that 'if a writer has participated in them his obligation is to write them truly rather than assume the presumption of altering them with invention'" (Preface to Regler's *The Great Crusade* (1940), qtd. in Thomas 10). Ortega y Gasset, on the other hand, found "the reality of lived experience and aesthetic expression are incompatible in art" (qtd. in Thomas 20).

3. In this connection, it is worth noting that Saddam Hussein celebrated the anniversary of his victory in the Gulf War, saying, "We emerged triumphant from that war" (Hoagland).

4. In Yasmine Gooneratne's poem on the Sri Lankan Civil War, entitled "The Peace Game," she writes of children playing war and peace. She concludes: "We called the entertainment 'Peace'/or 'War'—I can't remember which . . ."

5. Higonnet, "Not So Quiet in No Woman's Land." See also Virginia Woolf's *Three Guineas*, in which she claims that women have not been considered capable of writing about war (9). See Bouthaina Shaaban 182–219.

6. Rita O'Hare, the head of the Sinn Fein Department of Women's Affairs, said at the Irish Women United Conference in 1981:

> Women in the Republican Movement have worked for, and welcomed, in recent years, the recognition by the Movement of the importance of building and developing a real policy on women's struggle and attempting to carry that out, just as it has realised the importance of developing the struggle in the labour movement, with-

out which socialism cannot be built. . . . In the aftermath of national liberation struggles around the world we have seen attempts made to force women who were active in those struggles alongside men back into subordinate roles in the new society. This danger cannot be overcome by standing on the sidelines. It can only be totally negated by the fullest possible involvement of determined women in the heart of that struggle. (22)

7. Thomas writes that this linkage is

a positive aspect which is lacking in the classical war novel. Man is not here a pawn of the possessing classes sent to fight a colonial war in the interests of capitalist exploitation, but a defender of rights by dint of collective political and syndical action. (13)

8. Paul Vieille, in a reaction to this essay, wrote in a letter to me that the Intifada is "not war in the real meaning of the term, i.e., the confrontation of armies. It is rather a new form of opposition to a national domination, a non-military resistance to oppression by another. It is only war in the metaphoric sense."

9. In her 1980 novel *Abbad al-shams*, Sahar Khalifa writes:

What happened to the Algerian women after independence? Women returned to the rule of the harem and to covering their heads. They struggled, carried arms and were tortured in French prisons—Jamila, Aisha and Aishas. Then what? They went out into the light and the men left them in the dark. It was as though freedom was restricted to men alone. What about us? Where is our freedom and how can we get to it? They shall not deceive us! (119)

10. Michael Rogin says that spectacles,

in the postmodern view, define the historical rupture between industrial and post-industrial society—the one based on durable goods production, the other on information and service exchange. With the dissolution of individual subjectivities and differentiated autonomous spheres, not only does the connection between an object and its use become arbitrary . . . but skilled attention to display also deflects notice from the object to its hyperreal, reproducible representation. The society of the spectacle provides illusory unification and meaning, Guy Debord argues, distracting attention from producers and from classes in conflict. Simulacric games have entirely replaced the real, in Jean Baudrillard's formulation, and offer not even a counterfeit representation of anything outside themselves. (106)

11. When I interviewed Sahar Khalifa in Nablus in June of 1991, I asked her about the domestic symbolism evident in this her most recent novel. Her reaction was first confusion and then amusement. She said that she had not chosen the kitchen site self-consciously, but now she was glad that she had.

12. Qadisiya is the name of the first battle that the Arab Muslims won against non-Arabs, in fact Iranians, in 637 C.E.

13. At the modern Arabic literature conference held at the University of Nijmegen (Holland) in May 1992, Sabry Hafez attacked me for choosing to take Iraqi war literature seriously. Everybody, he assured me, knew that what these women and men wrote was rubbish. Of what possible value could such propaganda be? Samir al-Khalil seems to support such an attitude. He has attacked all artists who stayed in Iraq and continued to create:

> The peculiarity of the Iraqi regime therefore is to have involved
> enormous numbers of people directly in its crimes over twenty years,
> while making the rest of the population at the very least complicit
> in their commission. Yet, everyone inside the country, including the
> opposition outside, denies all responsibility for what they know has
> been going on. (*The Monument* 129)

14. "Substituting symbols for substance, these staged events (Grenada, Libya, etc.) constitute the politics of postmodernism, so long as one remembers that symbols produced for consumption at home and abroad have all too much substance for the victims of those symbols, the participant-observers on the ground" (Rogin 116).

15. Lev Losev describes the same phenomenon in Russian literature. He analyzes what he refers to as "slavish" language, which is "a systemic alteration of the text occasioned by the introduction of hints and circumlocutions" (6). For over 100 years, Russians have themselves been using the term "Aesopian" to describe such techniques. He argues that it emerges in response to state-imposed censorship and chronicles over two centuries of writing that had to find ways to express itself in spite of wary censors.

16. Salah al-Ansari writes of Tiswahun, who took up her husband's rifle when he was killed. Carrying her baby daughter on her back she forayed into the battlefield and killed many (39).

17. Samir al-Khalil, *Republic of Fear* 92.

Works Cited

Accad, Evelyne. *Sexuality and War: Literary Masks of the Middle East.* New York: New York UP, 1989.

al-Ansari, Salah. *Alphabet of War and Love.* Baghdad: Si al-Thaqasa wa al-Harb, 1988.

Ashrawi, Hanan. "Address to the 25th Anniverary Conference of the National Organization of Women." January 1992. *Episcopal Life* March 1992: 1.

Badron, Margot, and Miriam Cooke, eds. *Opening the Gates: A Century of Arab Feminist Writing.* Bloomington: Indiana UP, 1990.

Bain, Donald. "War Poet." 1944. Fussell 296.

Butler, Judith. "The Imperialist Subject." *Journal of Urban and Cultural Studies* 2.1 (1991): 73–78.

Cooke, Miriam. *War's Other Voices: Women Writers on the Lebanese Civil War.* New York: Cambridge UP, 1988.

Cooke, Miriam, and Angela Woollacott, eds. *Gendering War Talk.* Princeton: Princeton UP, 1993.

de Beauvoir, Simone, and Gisele Halimi. *Djamila Boupacha.* Paris: Gallimard, 1962.

Djebar, Assia. *Les Enfants du Nouveau Monde.* Algiers: René Julliard, 1962.

al-Dulaymi, Lutfiya. *Seeds of Fire.* Baghdad: Si al-Thaqasa wa al-Harb, 1988.

During, Simon. "Postmodernism or Post-colonialism Today." *Textual Practice* 1.1 (1987): 32–47.

Enloe, Cynthia. "The Gendered Gulf." *Collateral Damage: The "New World Order" at Home and Abroad.* Ed. Cynthia Peters. Boston: South End P, 1992. 107.

Fussell, Paul. *Wartime: Understanding and Behavior in the Second World War.* Oxford: Oxford UP, 1989.

Gilbert, Sandra, and Susan Gubar. *No Man's Land: The Place of the Woman Writer in the 20th Century.* New Haven: Yale UP, 1988.

Gooneratne, Yasmine. "The Peace Game." *Blood into Ink: Twentieth-Century Middle Eastern and South Asian Women Write War.* Ed. Miriam Cooke and Roshni Rustomji-Kearns. Boulder: Westview, 1994.

Halimi, Gisele. *Djamila Boupacha.* Trans. Peter Green. London: New English Library, 1963.

al-Hamid Hammudi, Basim Abd. *Al-naqid wa qissat al-harb. Dirasa tahliliya* [*The Critic and the War Story*]. Baghdad: Si al-Thaqasa wa al-Harb, 1986.

Hanley, Lynne. *Writing War: Fiction, Gender and Memory.* Amherst: U of Massachusetts P, 1991.

Helie-Lucas, Marie-Aimee. "Women, Nationalism, and Religion in the Algerian Struggle." Badron and Cooke 104–14.

Higonnet, Margaret. "Not So Quiet in No Woman's Land." Cooke and Woollacott 205–66.

Hoagland, Jim. "Unfinished Business Muddies Impact." *Denver Post* 12 Jan. 1992: 18A.

hooks, bell. *Talking Back: Thinking Feminist, Thinking Black.* Boston: South End P, 1989.

Hoynes, William. "War as Video Game: Media, Activism, and the Gulf War." Peters 305–26.

Khalifa, Sahar. *Abbad al-shams.* Beirut: Daval-Adab, 1980.

———. *Bab al-Saha.* Beirut: Daval-Adab, 1990.

al-Khalil, Samir. *The Monument: Art, Vulgarity, and Responsibility in Iraq.* Berkeley: U of California P, 1991.

———. *Republic of Fear: The Politics of Modern Iraq.* Berkeley: U of California P, 1989.

Lakoff, George. "Metaphor and War: The Metaphor System Used to Justify War in the Gulf." *Journal of Urban and Cultural Studies* 2.1 (1991): 59–72.

Losev, Lev. *On the Beneficence of Censorship: Aesopian Language in Modern Russian Literature.* Trans. Jane Bobkol. Munich: Verlag Otto Sagner in Kommission, 1984.

O'Hare, Rita. "Irish Women United Conference in 1981." *Iris: The Republican Magazine* 7 Nov. 1983: 22.

Rogin, Michael. "'Make My Day!' Spectacle as Amnesia in Imperial Politics." *Representations* 29 (1990): 99–111.

Ruddick, Sara. *Maternal Thinking: Toward a Politics of Peace.* Boston: Beacon P, 1989.

Samman, Ghada. *Beirut Nightmares.* Beirut: Kawabis Bayrut, 1980.

Shaaban, Bouthaina. *Both Right and Left Handed: Arab Women Talk About Their Lives.* London: Women's P, 1988.

Slymovics, Susan. "'To Put One's Fingers in the Bleeding Wound': Palestinian Theater under Israeli Censorship." *Drama Review* 35.2 (1991): 18–38.

Talib, Aliya. *Greening.* Baghdad: Si al-Thaqasa wa al-Harb, 1988.

Thomas, Gareth. *The Novel of the Spanish Civil War: 1936–1975.* New York: Cambridge UP, 1990.

Vieille, Paul. Letter to the author. 20 June 1992.

Virilio, Paul. *Pure War.* New York: Semiotext, 1983.

Woolf, Virginia. *Three Guineas.* New York: Harcourt, 1966.

Queer Visibility in Commodity Culture

Rosemary Hennessy

For a lesbian and gay political project that has had to combat the heteronormative tyranny of the empirical in order to claim a public existence at all, how visibility is conceptualized matters. Like "queer," "visibility" is a struggle term in gay and lesbian circles now—for some simply a matter of display, for others the effect of discourses or of complex social conditions. In the essay that follows I will try to show that for those of us caught up in the circuits of late capitalist consumption, the visibility of sexual identity is often a matter of commodification, a process that invariably depends on the lives and labor of invisible others.[1]

This argument needs to be prefaced, however, with several acknowledgements and qualifications. First of all, the increasing cultural representation of homosexual concerns and the recent queering of sex-gender identities undoubtedly have had important positive effects. Cultural visibility can prepare the ground for gay civil rights protection; affirmative images of lesbians and gays in the mainstream media, like the growing legitimation of lesbian and gay studies in the academy, can be empowering for those of us who have lived most of our lives with no validation at all from

© 1995 by *Cultural Critique*. Winter 1994–95. 0882-4371/95/$5.00.

the dominant culture. These changes in lesbian and gay visibility
are in great measure the effect of the relentless organizing efforts
of lesbians and gay men. In the past decade alone groups like The
National Gay and Lesbian Task Force, The Human Rights Campaign Fund, GLADD, and ACT-UP have fought ardently against
the cultural abjection and civic eradication of homosexuals. Like
other gay and lesbian academics now who are able to teach and
write more safely about our history, I am deeply indebted to those
who have risked their lives and careers on the front lines to make
gay and lesbian studies a viable and legitimate intellectual concern.
Without their efforts my work would not be possible.

But the new degree of homosexual visibility in the United
States and the very existence of a queer counterdiscourse also need
to be considered critically in relation to capital's insidious and relentless expansion. Not only is much recent gay visibility aimed at
producing new and potentially lucrative markets, but as in most
marketing strategies, money, not liberation, is the bottom line.[2] In
her analysis of the commodification of lesbians, Danae Clark has
observed that the intensified marketing of lesbian images is less
indicative of a growing acceptance of homosexuality than of capitalism's appropriation of gay "styles" for mainstream audiences.
Visibility in commodity culture is in this sense a limited victory for
gays who are welcome to be visible as consumer subjects but not as
social subjects. The increasing circulation of gay and lesbian images in consumer culture has the effect of consolidating an imaginary, class-specific gay subjectivity for both straight and gay audiences. This process is not limited to the spheres of knowledge
promoted by popular culture and retail advertising but also infil-
trates the production of subjectivities in academic and activist
work.

Because so much of lesbian and gay studies and queer theory
has all but ignored the historical relationship between (homo)sexu-
ality and capitalism, however, one of the dangers of an analysis
that sets out to address the connection between the processes of
commodification and the formation of lesbian and gay identities is
that it risks being misread. Drawing attention to the operations of
commodity capitalism on lesbian, gay, and queer knowledges can
be misconstrued to mean—*as I certainly do not*—that the material
processes of commodification are only economic, and that they are

all determining and impossible to oppose. As I understand it, the materiality of social life consists of an ensemble of human practices whose complex interdeterminate relations to one another vary historically. These practices include economic divisions of labor and wealth, political arrangements of state and nation, and ideological organizations of meaning-making and value. Although capitalism is a mode of production characterized by the economic practice of extracting surplus value through commodity exchange, the processes of commodification pervade all social structures. In certain social formations under late capitalism, information has become so much the structure in dominance that language, discourse, or cultural practice is often taken to be the only arena of social life. The challenge for social theory now is to queer-y the reigning Foucauldian materialism that reduces the social to culture or discourse and to refute misreadings of postmodern historical materialism as advocating a return to economic determinism. To examine the historical relations between homosexuality and commodification as they operate at all levels of capitalist societies does not mean dismissing the materiality of discourse and the ways culture constructs subjectivities, reproduces power relations, and foments resistance. Quite the contrary. Postmodern historical materialist critiques of sexuality are postmodern to the extent that they participate in postmodernity's historical and critical remapping of social relations, but at the same time they maintain that sexuality is a material practice that shapes and is shaped by social totalities like capitalism, patriarchy, and imperialism as they manifest differently across social formations and within specific historical conjunctures. As social practice, sexuality includes lesbian, gay, and queer resistance movements that have built social and political networks, often by way of capitalist commercial venues. That academic gay studies and queer theory have not very rigorously inquired into the relations between sexuality and capitalism is indicative of the retreat from historical materialism in social and cultural theory in the past decade. But I think it also suggests the particular class interests that have increasingly come to define lesbian and gay studies.

Although I have been using the words "queer" and "lesbian and gay" as if they were interchangeable, these are in fact contentious terms, signifying identity and political struggle from very different starting points. The now more traditional phrase "lesbian and gay" assumes a polarized division between hetero- and homo-sexuality and signals discrete and asymmetrically gendered identi-ties. The more fluid and ambiguous term "queer" has recently be-gun to displace "lesbian and gay" in several areas of urban industrialized culture—under the signature of "queer theory" in the realm of cultural studies; in avant-garde, gay, and lesbian sub-cultures; and in new forms of radical sexual political activism. Lending a new elasticity to the categories "lesbian" and "gay," "queer" embraces a proliferation of sexualities (bisexual, transves-tite, pre- and post-op transsexual, to name a few) and the com-pounding of outcast positions along racial, ethnic, and class, as well as sexual lines—none of which is acknowledged by the neat binary division between hetero- and homosexual. In other words, "queer" not only troubles the gender asymmetry implied by the phrase "lesbian and gay," but potentially includes "deviants" and "perverts" who may traverse or confuse hetero-homo divisions and exceed or complicate conventional delineations of sexual identity and normative sexual practice. "Queer" often professes to define a critical standpoint that makes visible how heteronormative at-tempts to fix sexual identities tend to fail often because they are overdetermined by other issues and conflicts—race or national identity, for example. To the extent that "queer" tends to advance a subjectivity that is primarily sexual, it can threaten to erase the intersections of sexuality with class as well as the gender and racial histories that still situate queer men and women differently. In this respect "queer" is, as Judith Butler indicates, a "site of collective contestation" (*Bodies* 228) that is only partially adequate to the col-lectivity it historically represents.

While in this essay I may string together the terms "lesbian and gay" and "queer," then, this is not in order to conflate them but to indicate that both expressions are being used to name ho-mosexual identities now, even if in contesting ways. To the extent that my analysis focuses primarily on "queer" issues, this is because they are increasingly shaping postmodern reconfigurations of gay and lesbian cultural study and politics. Even though many formu-lations of queer theory and identity are to my mind limited, it does not follow that the viability of "queer" as a sign of collective history and action is to be dismissed. Instead, I would argue for a renarration of queer critique as inquiry into the ensemble of social processes—systems of exploitation and regimes of state and cultural power—through which sexualities are produced. I agree with Judith Butler that the two dimensions of queering—the historical inquiry into the formation of homosexualities it signifies, and the deformative and misappropriative power the term enjoys—are both constitutive (*Bodies*). But I would add that these dimensions of queer praxis need to be marshalled as forces for collective and transformative social intervention.

Queer Theory and/as Politics

Most well known in political circles from the activities of Queer Nation, "queer" has recently begun to circulate more widely in public and academic writings, the sign of an unsettling critical confrontation with heteronormativity, a distinctly postmodern rescripting of identity, politics, and cultural critique. Although queer academic theory and queer street politics have their discrete features and histories, both participate in the general transformation of identities occurring in Western democracies now as new conceptions of cultural representation are being tested against the political and economic arrangements of a "New World Order"—postcolonial, post–Cold War, post-industrial. The emergence of queer counterdiscourses has been enabled by postmodern reconfigurations of subjectivity as more flexible and ambivalent and by shifting political pressures within the gay community. Among them are the new forms of political alliance between gay men and lesbians yielded by activist responses to the spectacle and devastation of AIDS and to a lesser extent by challenges to gay politics from radical race movements in the seventies and eighties. In troubling the traditional gay versus straight classification, "queer" draws upon postmodern critiques of identity as stable, coherent, and embodied. Queer knowledges upset traditional identity politics by foregrounding the ways contested issues of sexuality involve concerns that, as Michael Warner puts it, are not captured by the languages designed to name them (xv). By targeting heteronormativity rather than heterosexuality, queer theory and activism also acknowledge that heterosexuality is an institution that organizes

more than just the sexual: it is socially pervasive, underlying myriad taken-for-granted norms that shape what can be seen, said, and
valued. Adopting the term that has been used to cast out and exclude sexual deviants is a gesture of rebellion against the pressure
to be invisible or apologetically different. It is an "in your face"
rejection of the "proper" response to heteronormativity from a
stance that purports to be both antiassimilationist and antiseparat-
ist. Like lesbian feminism and the gay liberation movement, the
queer critique of heteronormativity is intensely and aggressively
concerned with issues of visibility. Chants like "We're here, We're
Queer, Get Used To It" and actions like Queers Bash Back, Queer
Nights Out, Queer Kiss-Ins, and Mall Zaps are aimed at making
visible those identities that the ubiquitous heteronormative culture
would erase. Politically, the aim of queer visibility actions is not to
include queers in the cultural dominant but to continually pressure and disclose the heteronormative.

Although their often distinct institutional positions situate
queer theorists and activists differently in relation to the professional managerial class and the regimes of power-knowledge they
help organize, ideologically these contrasts are less neat than is
often acknowledged. Both queer activists and theorists employ
some of the same counterdiscourses to expand and complicate the
parameters of sexuality; both set out to challenge empiricist notions of identity as grounded in an embodied or empirical visibility; and both recast identity as a version of performance: as drag,
masquerade, or signifying play. Across the promotion of more per-
meable and fluid identities in both queer theory and activism, however, visibility is still fetishized to the extent that it conceals the
social relations new urban gay and queer identities depend on.
The watchwords of queer praxis in both arenas are "make trouble
and have fun" (Berube and Escoffier 15). But often trouble-
making takes the form of a cultural politics that relies on concepts
of the social, of resistance, and of pleasure that keep invisible the
violent social relations new urban identities depend on.

In order to examine some of these concepts and their consequences I want to look more closely at academic and activist knowledges, beginning with three academic theorists whose writings are
shaping the new queer theory and whose reputations now rest on
their work in this area: Judith Butler, Diana Fuss, and Teresa de

Lauretis. All three articulate a version of cultural studies with loose affiliations to post-structuralism. All three offer critiques of heteronormativity that, to paraphrase de Lauretis, are interested in altering the standard of vision, the frame of reference of visibility, of what can be seen and known ("Film" 224). And all three are concerned to varying degrees with the invisibility of lesbians in culture.

Butler's book *Gender Trouble* (1990) offers one of the most incisive and widely read critiques of heterosexuality. Against what she calls "the metaphysics of substance" or empiricist and humanist conceptions of the subject, Butler launches a rearticulation of gender identity aimed at making visible the ways in which the fiction of a coherent person depends on a heterosexual matrix. How we see sex and gender is for Butler a function of discourses that set the limits to our ways of seeing. From Butler's postmodern vantage point, the seeming internal coherence of the person is not natural but rather the consequence of certain regulatory practices that "govern culturally intelligible notions of identity" (16–17). Identity, then, is not a matter of a person's experience, self-expression, or visible features but of "socially instituted and maintained norms of intelligibility" (17). Intelligible genders are those that inaugurate and maintain "relations of coherence and continuity among sex, gender, sexual practice and desire" (17). In this sense, gender intelligibility depends on certain presuppositions that the dominant knowledges safeguard or keep invisible. Chief among them is the heterosexual "matrix of intelligibility" that produces "discrete and asymmetrical oppositions between 'masculine' and 'feminine,' where these are understood to be expressive attributes of 'male' and 'female'" (17). All sexual practices in which gender does not follow from sex and desire does not follow from either sex or gender thereby become either invisible or perverse (17).

Despite the efforts to safeguard these presuppositions, the fiction of a coherent identity is inevitably vulnerable to exposure as a representation, and it is the deliberate enactment of this fiction as a fiction, and not some utopian sexuality outside or free from heterosexual constructs, that for Butler serves as the site of resistance to heterosexuality. She argues that if sex is released from its naturalized meanings it can make gender trouble—subverting and displacing reified notions of gender that support heterosexual power. This process can only occur *within* the terms set by the culture, however, through parodic repetitions like drag that expose the heterosexual matrix as a fabrication and sex as "a performatively enacted signification" (33). Drag for Butler is not merely a matter of clothing or cross-dressing. It is a discursive practice that discloses the fabrication of identity through parodic repetitions of the heterosexual gender system. As parody, drag belies the myth of a stable self preexisting cultural codes or signifying systems. Against the dominant reading of drag as a failed imitation of the "real thing," Butler posits it as a subversive act. By turning a supposed "bad copy" of heterosexuality (butch and femme, for example) against a way of thinking that posits heterosexuality as the "real thing," drag exposes this pseudo-original as itself a "copy" or representation. It follows for Butler that lesbian or gay identity is inevitably drag, a performance that plays up the indeterminacy of identity and for this reason can be seized upon for political resistance.[3]

According to Butler, then, visibility is not a matter of detecting or displaying empirical bodies but of knowledges—discourses, significations, modes of intelligibility—by which identity is constituted. In this sense, her work is clearly a postmodern critique of identity, identity politics, and positivist notions of the visible. Her analysis of sexuality and gender undoubtedly has a strong social dimension: she speaks to and out of feminism and understands the processes that construct sexuality and gender as political. For Butler heterosexuality is a regime of power and discipline that affects people's lives. But her reconceptualization of the experiential and embodied self as only a *discursive* construct is a strategy that safeguards some presuppositions of its own.

One of them is that the social is equivalent to the cultural. Throughout her work, Butler's approach to the problem of identity begins with the premise that identity is only a matter of representation, of the discourses by which subjects come to be established. This notion of the discursively constructed subject is heavily indebted to Foucault, and it is Foucault's problematic concept of materialism and of discursive practices that troubles Butler's analysis as well. While Foucault understands the materiality of the social to be comprised of both discursive and nondiscursive practices, he never explains the material connection between them. Furthermore, most of his attention is invariably devoted to discursive practices.[4] This social logic of noncorrespondence appears in Butler's analysis, too, and is most explicit in her explanation of materialism in *Bodies That Matter* (1993). In her own words, this new book is a "poststructuralist rewriting of discursive performativity as it operates in the materialization of sex" (12). This post-structuralist reading of materiality begins with the premise that matter is never simply given but always materialized. But what constitutes this materializing is one domain of social production only—the regulatory practices, norms, and discourses that constitute ideology (10). Butler's version of materiality is directed against notions of the body and of sex common among constructionists who still maintain them to be in some ways "matter" in the sense of a constitutive "outside" that exceeds the boundaries of discourse. But by explaining materiality so exclusively in terms of discursive practices, Butler effectively conflates the materiality of the social into culture. While she frequently refers to heterosexuality as an institution or a norm, she never explains the material differences or relations between institutions and normative discourses. Are they one and the same? Do institutions like the family, the military, or schools organize and rely on more than discourses: aspects of life like labor and wealth, or social resources like health and health care, the distribution of food and shelter? All of these aspects of social life are, of course, discursively mediated and regulated, but at the same time their materiality is not simply discursive.

I am not disputing that the insidious dictates of heterosexuality operate through the discourses of culture, but surely they organize and help shape other features of social life as well. While political and economic practices are always made intelligible and shaped by our ways of making sense of them, reducing materiality to discourse alone has the effect of obscuring much of social life. The ways of making sense of sexuality that are dispersed through institutions like the military, churches, or the media also depend on and condition divisions of labor and are affected by the operations of particular state and national formations. The proposal to lift the ban on gays in the U.S. military, for instance, threatens to disclose the fiction of heterosexual coherence. But the discourses of identity and sexual citizenship that organize this proposal have only become possible under certain historical conditions, among them changes in the place of the United States in global politics after the Cold War and in the sexual division of labor that has enabled a more flexible patriarchal gender ideology in multinational capitalist economies.

Given Butler's reduction of the social to discourses, it is not surprising that she understands history in very local, limited terms, a feature of her work that is in keeping with its post-structuralist roots. For example, at one point she admits that gender parody in itself is not subversive, rather its meaning depends on "a context and reception in which subversive confusions can be fostered" (*Gender* 139). She quickly passes over the problem of historical "context" (it appears in one of her frequent series of rhetorical questions). But it is, I think, a crucial issue for queer politics now. What does it mean to say that what can be seen as parodic and what gender parody makes visible depend on a context in which subversive confusions can be fostered? What exactly is meant by "context" here?

As Butler uses it, context would seem to be a crucial feature of the meaning-making process: its contingent foundation serves as a backdrop of sorts linking one discursive practice—drag, for example—to others; through these links, presumably, meaning is produced. But considering historical context is quite different from historicizing. Historicizing does not establish connections only in this local scene of reception—between one discursive practice and another—nor does it leave unaddressed the relationship between the discursive and the nondiscursive. Historicizing starts by acknowledging that the continuation of social life depends on its (re)production in various spheres. As a mode of reading, it traces connections between and among these spheres at several levels of analysis—connecting particular conjunctural arrangements in a social formation to more far-reaching ones. To historicize the meaning of drag among the urban middle class in the United States at the turn of the 21st century would be to link it as a discursive practice to the social relations that make it possible and in so doing situate practices specific to a particular social formation in the United States within the larger frame of late capitalism's geopolitics and multinational economy. Butler's presupposed concept of the social displaces analysis of social totalities like capitalism and patriarchy, however, in favor of an exclusive emphasis on the specific and the local (a la Foucault). In so doing, she confines history to a very limited frame whose unspoken "context" has a very specific address: the new bourgeois professional class.

This historical address is most evident in her earlier conceptions of drag as subversive political practice. For Butler, drag challenges the notion of identity implicit in "coming out," the act of making visible one's homosexuality. In her essay "Imitation and Gender Insubordination," she argues that coming out is a process one can never completely achieve. No homosexual is ever entirely "out" because identity, always undermined by the disruptive operations of the unconscious and of signification, can never be fully disclosed. This means that any avowal of the "fact" of one's homosexual (or heterosexual) identity is itself a fiction. Performative activities like drag play up the precarious fabrication of a coherent and internal sexual identity by putting on display the made-up (in)congruity of sex, gender, and desire. In her essay "Performative Acts and Gender Constitution," Butler acknowledges these social limitations on signification: "one is compelled to live in a world in which genders constitute univocal signifiers, in which gender is stabilized, polarized, rendered discrete and intractable" and where performing one's gender wrong initiates a set of punishments (279). But here as elsewhere the critical force of Butler's commentary denaturalizes reified versions of sexuality by addressing them as discursively constructed rather than considering why they are historically secured as they are. Even though Butler concedes that the subversiveness of gender parody depends on the historical context in which it is received, most of her earlier analysis assumes that *anyone* might participate in exposing the fiction of sexual identity.

But of course, they cannot. One reason is that, unfortunately, societies are still organized so that meaning is taken to be anchored in referents or signifieds; "lesbian" and "gay" are often read as referring to authentic identities, either benign or malevolent perversions of a naturalized norm. To date, the indeterminate meanings Butler assigns these words are not shared by all. Gay bashings, at times with murderous outcomes, indicate that the insistence of the signified in the symbolic order continues to organize social life, as does the military's latest "don't ask, don't tell" policy. And in both cases the disclosure of the identity "homosexual" has definite consequences for people's lives. A book like Leslie Feinberg's *Stone Butch Blues* or a film like Jennie Livingston's *Paris Is Burning*, both of which document the ways "gender parody" often blurs into "passing," each demonstrates the powerful hold on lesbian and gay imaginations of the notion that sex should align with gender. For many lesbians and gays who have not had the social resources or mobility to insulate themselves from heteronormativity's insistence that sex equals gender, drag has been not so much playful subversion as a painful yearning for authenticity, occasionally with brutally violent results.

In *Bodies That Matter,* Butler addresses some of the ways Livingston's documentary of the Harlem balls in *Paris Is Burning* tests her own earlier arguments on performative subversion and the contextual boundaries of drag. As Butler reads their representation in *Paris Is Burning,* drag balls are highly qualified social practices that can both denaturalize and re-idealize gender norms. Furthermore, the murder of Venus Xtravaganza by one of her clients (for whom the discovery that Venus had male genitals is perhaps not at all a playful subversion of gender identity) dramatizes the limits of gender parody. In other words, as she puts it, "there is passing and then there is passing" (130). Unlike Willie Ninja, who "makes it" as a gay man into the mainstream of celebrity glamour, Venus is ultimately treated the way women of color are treated. Butler's reading of the film acknowledges the insistence of the signified in the symbolic order—Venus dies, she tells us, because the possibilities for resignifying sex and race that the drag balls represent are eradicated by the symbolic. Her death "testifies to a tragic misreading of the social map of power" (131) and suggests that the resignification of the symbolic order along with the phantasmic idealizations that drag enacts do have their refusals and their consequences.

There are moments in this book when Butler hints that the social map of power, while discursive, also includes more than the symbolic order—for example, when she refers to the situation of the numbers of poor black women that the balls' idealizations deny, or when she indicates that the balls' phantasmic excess constitutes the site of women "not only as marketable goods within an erotic economy of exchange, but as goods which, as it were, are also privi-

leged consumers with access to wealth and social privilege and protection" (132). But for the most part, here, too, the materiality of
social life is ultimately and insistently confined to the ideological.
While she makes use of concepts like "ideology" and "hegemony"
here to conceptually relate discourse, subjectivity, and power, the
systemic connections among ideology, state, and labor in the historical materialist theories of Althusser and Gramsci are dropped
out. The result is that important links among social contradictions
that materially effect people's lives—uneven and complex though
they may be—remain unexplained. I am thinking here especially
of connections between the continual effort (and failure) of the heterosexual imaginary to police identities and the racialized gendered division of labor Butler alludes to earlier.

To sum up, my reading of Butler's work suggests several
points about the materiality of sexuality that are politically important to queer theory and politics. First of all, if the materiality
of social life is taken to be an ensemble of economic, political, and
ideological production, we can still acknowledge that the coherent
sex-gender identities heterosexuality secures may be fabrications
always in need of repair, but their fragility can be seen not as the
property of some restlessness in language itself but as the effect of
social struggle. Second, the meanings that are taken to be "real"
are so because they help secure a certain social order, an order that
is naturalized as the way things are or should be and that "illegiti-
mate" meanings to some degree threaten. Because it is the social
order—the distribution of wealth, resources, and power—that is
at stake in the struggle over meanings, a politics that contests the
prevailing constructions of sexual identity and that aims to disrupt
the regimes they support will need to address more than discourse. Third, the naturalized version of sexual identity that currently dominates in the United States as well as the oppositional
versions that contest it are conditioned by more than just their local contexts of reception. Any specific situation is made possible
and affected by dimensions of social life that exceed it. A social
practice like drag, then, needs to be analyzed at several levels: in
terms of the conjunctural situation (whether you are looking at
what drag means when walking a ball in Harlem or turning a trick
in the Village, performing in a Hasty Pudding revue at Harvard
or hoping to pass in Pocatello); in terms of its place in the social

formation (whether this local scene occurs in an urban or rural area, in the United States, Germany, Nicaragua, or India, at the turn of the 20th or of the 21st century); and in terms of the global relations that this situation is tied to—how even the option of drag as a flexible sexual identity depends on the availability not only of certain discourses of sexuality, aesthetics, style, and glamour, but also of a circuit of commodity production, exchange, and consumption specific to industrialized economies. Recognizing that signs are sites of social struggle, then, ultimately leads us to inquire into the social conditions that enable and perhaps even foster the slipping and sliding of signification. Is the subversiveness of a self-consciously performative identity like drag at risk if we inquire into certain of the other social relations—the relations of labor, for instance—that help enable it? What is the consequence of a theory that does not allow this kind of question?

I want to suggest that one consequence is the risk of promoting an up-dated, postmodern, reinscription of the bourgeois subject's fetishized identity. Alienation of any aspect of human life from the network of social relations that make it possible constitutes the very basis of fetishization. By limiting her conception of the social to the discursive, Butler unhinges identity from the other material relations that shape it. Her performative identity recasts bourgeois humanist individuality as a more fluid and indeterminate series of subversive bodily acts, but this postmodern subject is severed from the collective historical processes and struggles through which identities are produced and circulate. Moreover, in confining her analysis of the inflection of sexuality by racial, national, or class difference to specific historical contexts, she forecloses the possibility of marshalling collectivities for social transformation across differences in historical positioning.

This postmodern fetishizing of sexual identity also characterizes the recent essays of Fuss and de Lauretis. While their projects are distinct and differently nuanced, they share an ideological affiliation in that the subjects their work constructs are in many ways much the same. Unlike Butler, both Fuss and de Lauretis reference commodity culture in the cultural forms their essays target—advertising and film—and, significantly, de Lauretis occasionally explicitly mentions the commodity. For some readers, Fuss's emphatic psychoanalytic approach and de Lauretis's more insistently political feminist analysis might seem to distinguish their theoretical frameworks both from Butler's and from one another's. But it is precisely these differences that I want to question.

In "Fashion and the Homospectatorial Look," Fuss is concerned with relations of looking that structure fashion photography, in particular the tension between the ideological project to invite viewers to identify with properly heterosexual positions and the surface structure of the fashion photo, which presents eroticized images of the female body for consumption by a female audience (713). Her essay sets out to decode this tension, which Fuss formulates in terms of the "restless operations of identification" (716). Drawing primarily on psychoanalytic theories of subjectivity (Freud, Lacan, Kristeva), Fuss explains this restlessness of identity as an effect of the subject's entry into the symbolic and its subjugation to the law of the father, a law that mitigates against return to an always irretrievable presymbolic unity. Fuss argues that by persistently representing the female body "in pieces" (showing only a woman's legs, hands, arms, face . . .), fashion photography reminds the woman spectator of her fetishization. But unlike Marx, who takes fetishization to be the concealment of a positive network of social relations, Fuss understands fetishization as Freud does, that is, as a lack (castration). For Freud fetishization is the effect of a failed resolution to the oedipal romance whereby the child disavows his knowledge that the mother does not have a penis by substituting other body parts (a leg, a hand, a foot) for it. Through their fixation on women's body parts, Fuss argues, fashion photos dramatize the role woman plays in the disavowal of the mother's castration, at the same time the fragmented body serves as substitute for the missing maternal phallus (720). Fashion fetishism is in this sense an effort to compensate for the "divisions and separations upon which subjectivity is based" (721). At the same time, it also points to some of the mechanisms of primary identification, in particular the "fundamental female homosexuality in the daughter's preoedipal identification with the mother" (721). The fascination of fashion photography with repeated close-ups of a woman's face, Fuss argues, entails the ambivalent disavowal—denial and recognition—of the source of pain and pleasure invoked by the potential restitution of this lost object for an always imperfectly oedipalized woman.

The Freudian concept of the fetish Fuss appropriates might be read as itself a symptom of capitalism's fetishizing of social relations in that it condenses into the nuclear family circle and onto a psychically charged object—the phallus—the more extensive network of historical and social relations the bourgeois family and the father's position within it entail.[5] Fuss fetishizes identity in the sense that she imagines it only in terms of atomized parts of social life—a class-specific formation of the family and the processes of signification in the sphere of cultural representation. Her concepts of vision and the look participate in this economy of fetishization in that visibility is divorced from the *social* relations that make it possible and understood to be only a matter of *cultural* construction: "If subjects look differently," she asserts, "it is only the enculturating mechanisms of the look that instantiate and regulate these differences in the first place" (736–37).

Like Butler's theory, her analysis is not aimed at claiming lesbian or gay identity as a resistant state of being in its own right, but instead sets out to queer-y the dominant sexual symbolic order by exposing the ways it is continually disrupted by the homospectatorial gaze. Heterosexuality is not an original or pure identity; its coherence is only secured by at once calling attention to and disavowing its "abject, interiorized, and ghostly other, homosexuality" (732). For her, too, identity is postmodern in its incoherence and social in its constructedness, but because it is consistently framed in terms of the individual psyche and its history, the subject for Fuss is ultimately an updated version of the bourgeois individual. This individual, moreover, constitutes the historical frame for the images of fashion photography that "tell us as much about the subject's current history as they do about her already shadowy prehistory, perhaps even more" (734). The "perhaps even more" is significant here because it is this individualized "prehistory," a story of lost origins and mother-daughter bonds, that Fuss emphasizes. Indeed it constitutes the basis for the homospectatorial look. Although she insists that the lesbian looks coded by fashion photography "radically de-essentialize conventional notions of identity" (736), contradictorily, an essentially gendered and embodied spectatorial encounter between infant and mother anchors the "history" that constitutes the fashion text's foundational reference point. If history is localized in Butler's queer theory, then, it is even more narrowly circumscribed in Fuss's reading of fashion ads, where it is reduced to an individual's presocial relationship to the mythic mother's face (722).

Locating the basis for identity in a space/time outside history—in memories of an archaic choric union between mother and child—has the effect of masquerading bourgeois individualism's universal subject—with all of the political baggage it carries—in postmodern drag. Like Butler, Fuss admits history makes a difference to meaning: "more work needs to be done on how spectators from different gendered, racial, ethnic, economic, national and historical backgrounds might appropriate or resist these images" (736). But the recognition of sexuality's differential historical context so late in her essay echoes the familiar liberal gesture. Premised on a notion of history as "background," this assertion thematizes difference by encapsulating the subject in individualized cultural slots, while the social struggles over difference that foment the "restless operations of identity" remain safely out of view.

Teresa de Lauretis's essay "Film and the Visible," originally presented at the conference *How Do I Look?: Queer Film and Video* (1991), shares many of the features of Butler's and Fuss's analyses. While she, too, draws upon psychoanalysis as well as a loosely Foucauldian analytic, her work is, I think, generally taken to be more "social" in its approach, and she will at times situate it as such against a more textual analysis. Her purported objective in this essay is indeed "not to do a textual analysis" but to "put into discourse" the terms of an autonomous form of lesbian sexuality and desire in relation to film (224). While there are films about lesbians that may offer positive images, she argues, they do not necessarily produce new ways of seeing or new inscriptions of the lesbian subject (224). De Lauretis presents Sheila McLaughlin's *She Must Be Seeing Things* as an exemplary alternative because it offers spectators a new position for looking—the place of a woman who desires another woman. While the effort to articulate the dynamics of a specifically lesbian sexuality links de Lauretis's work with Fuss's essay, unlike Fuss, she renounces formulations of lesbian sexuality founded in the mother-child dyad. At the same time, for de Lauretis lesbian sexuality is neither contingent with heterosexual female sexuality nor independent of the oedipal fantasy structure.

However, the presuppositions on which these two assertions rest belie her antitextualist stance and link her "new subjectivity" with other fetishized queer identities in the post-structuralist strand of cultural studies.

De Lauretis reads McLaughlin's film as a tale of two women who are lovers and image makers. One (Jo) literally makes movies, and the other (Agatha) does so more figuratively in the fantasies she fabricates about her lover. The film demonstrates the ways a pervasive heterosexuality structures the relations of looking for both women; at the same time, the two women's butch-femme role playing flaunts its (in)congruence with heterosexual positions by marking these roles *as* performances. De Lauretis contends that this role playing is always at one remove from the heterosexual paradigm, and it is the space of this "remove" that constitutes for her the "excess" of the lesbian subject position. As in Butler's similar argument about performative identities, however, lesbian excess is fundamentally and exclusively a matter of cultural representation. This partial frame of reference for the social is compounded by de Lauretis's reading of Jo's film-within-the-film as a lesbian revision of the psychoanalytic oedipal drama. Although she reads the interpolated film as a skewed rewriting of the primal scene from the perspective of a woman desiring another woman, de Lauretis's endorsement of this origin story has the effect of equating generic lesbian identity with a very specific bourgeois construction, founded in highly individualized notions of fantasy, eroticism, scopophilia, and romance.

That the narrow limits of her conception of the subject are ultimately the effect of the historical position from which she is reading becomes clear in the audience discussion of her essay included in this collection. The first question from the audience addresses a gap in de Lauretis's text—one might even call it an "excess"—that is, her erasure of the film's treatment of racial difference. Her response to this question reveals the fascination with form that underlies de Lauretis's way of reading. Although she may seem more "social" in her orientation, like Fuss and Butler, she too fetishizes meaning by cutting it off from the social and historical forces that make texts intelligible. In defense of her omission of any discussion of race, de Lauretis argues that she has "concluded that the film *intentionally focuses on other aspects of their*

relationship" [emphasis added] ("Film" 268). Despite her initial dis-
claimers to the contrary, meaning for de Lauretis here seems to be
firmly rooted in the text. Indeed throughout the essay she defines
the "new position of seeing" McLaughlin's film offers the viewer
by reference to the various textual devices that comprise it—the
film's reframing of the oedipal scenario, its structuring of the spectator's look, its title, and its campy use of masquerade, cross-
dressing, and Hollywood spectacle. The audience's insistent return
to the problem of racial difference can be read as resistance both
to this formalist approach to visibility and to the generic lesbian
subject it offers.

     While de Lauretis insists that race "is not represented as an
issue in this film" ("Film" 268), clearly for her audience this is not
the case. Their questions suggest the need for another way of understanding meaning, not as textual but as historical—the effect
of the ways of knowing that spectators/readers bring to a text, ways
of making sense that are enabled and conditioned by their different social positions. For some viewers this film may not deal with
Freud or Oedipus, show Agatha sharing a common fantasy with
Jo, or any number of the things de Lauretis sees in it, but it may
deal with a black Latina who is also a lesbian and a lawyer in love
with a white woman. The "visibility" of these issues is not a matter
of what is empirically "there" or of what the film intends, but of
the frames of knowing that make certain meanings "seeable."
From this vantage point, a text's very limited "dealing" or "not
dealing" with a particular social category can be used to make
available another possible telling of its tale, one that might begin
to inquire into the historical limits of any particular construction
of social reality.[6] At the very least, the problem of Agatha as a Bra-
zilian Latina pressures de Lauretis's closing assertion that *She Must
Be Seeing Things* "locates itself historically and politically in the
North American lesbian community" (263).

     In another essay, "Sexual Indifference and Lesbian Repre-
sentation,"[7] de Lauretis acknowledges that lesbian identity is affected by the operation of "interlocking systems of gender, sexual,
racial, class and other, more local categories of social stratification"
(148). However, the conception of the social hinted at here and the
notion of community it entails are somewhat different from those
offered above. For in this essay de Lauretis uses Audre Lorde's

image of the "house of difference" ("our place was the very house
of difference rather than the security of any one particular difference") to define a social life that is not pluralistic and a community
that is not confined to North America, but (in de Lauretis's words)
"at once global and local—global in its inclusive and macro-
political strategies, and local in its specific, micro-political practices" (148). If taken seriously, the social and historical frame de
Lauretis alludes to briefly here would radically recast the fetishized
conception of identity that leads her to suggest that in order to
address the issue of race we would need to "see a film made by or
about lesbians of color" (269). But even in her allusion to a more
systemic mode of reading the connection between sexuality and
divisions of labor remains entirely invisible, an excess whose traces
are hinted only in passing references to the commodity. What
would it mean to understand the formation of queer identities in
a social logic that did not suppress this other story?

While queer theorists generally have not elaborated the answer, two of de Lauretis's brief remarks on commodification provide glimpses of this unexplored way of seeing. One of them appears in a fleeting comment on Jill Dolan's contention that "desire
is not necessarily a fixed, male-owned commodity, but can be ex-
changed, with a much different meaning, between women," an assertion de Lauretis reads as either "the ultimate camp representation" or "rather disturbing. For unfortunately—or fortunately, as
the case may be—commodity exchange does have the same meaning between women as between men by definition, that is, by
Marx's definition of the structure of capital" ("Indifference" 152).
The other appears in her argument that the critique of heterosexuality in films like *The Kiss of the Spider Woman* and *The Color Purple*
is "suppressed and rendered invisible by the film's compliance with
the apparatus of commercial cinema and its institutional drive to,
precisely, commodity exchange" ("Indifference" 153). Both of
these remarks suggest an order of (in)visibility that queer theory's
critique of heterosexuality does not explore. What is the connection between the ways commodity exchange renders certain social
relations (in)visible and the ways of looking that structure heteronormativity or even queer theory? Do fetishized versions of identity in queer theory comply with the institutional drive to commodity exchange in the academy?

Queer Nationalism: The Avant-Garde Goes SHOPping

If academic queer theory for the most part ignores the relationship between sexuality and commodification, groups like Queer Nation do not. Founded in New York City in 1990 by a small group of activists frustrated by ACT-UP's exclusive focus on AIDS, Queer Nation has grown into a loosely organized collection of local chapters stretching from coast to coast.[8] The list of affinity groups comprising Queer Nation is too long and too variable to list here; included among them are the Suburban Homosexual Outreach Program (SHOP), Queers Undertaking Exquisite and Symbolic Transformation (QUEST), and United Colors, which focuses on the experiences of Queers of color.[9] Queer Nation is less committed to ACT-UP's strategies of direct action through civil disobedience than to creating awareness and increasing queer visibility. Often representing their tactics as explicitly postmodern, Queer Nation shares many of the presuppositions of queer theory: deconstructing the homo vs. hetero binary in favor of a more indeterminate sexual identity; targeting a pervasive heteronormativity by miming it with a campy inflection; and employing a performative politics that associates identity less with interiority than with the public spectacle of consumer culture.

The signifier "nation" signals a commitment to disrupting the often invisible links between nationhood and public sexual discourse as well as transforming the public spaces in which a (hetero)-sexualized national imaginary is constructed in people's everyday lives—in shopping malls, bars, advertising, and the media. In seizing the public space as a "zone of political pedagogy," Queer Nation, like ACT-UP, advances some useful ways of thinking about pedagogy as a public political practice.[10] My concern here, however, is with how their antiassimilationist politics understands and makes use of the commodity as part of a campaign for gay visibility.

For Queer Nation, visibility is a crucial requirement if gays are to have a safe public existence. To this end, they reterritorialize various public spaces through an assortment of strategies like the policing of neighborhoods by Pink Panthers dressed in "Bash Back" T-shirts or Queer Nights Out and Kiss-Ins where groups of gay couples invade straight bars or other public spaces and scandalously make out (Berlant and Freeman 160–63). In its most "postmodern moments," Queer Nation uses the hyperspaces of commodity consumption as sites for political intervention. Queer Nation is not interested in marketing positive images of gays and lesbians so much as inhabiting and subverting consumer pleasure in commodities in order to "reveal to the consumer desires he/she didn't know he/she had" (Berlant and Freeman 164). Tactics like producing Queer Bart Simpson T-shirts or rewriting the trademarks of corporations that appropriate gay street styles (changing the "p" in GAP ads to "y") are meant to demonstrate "that the commodity is a central means by which individuals tap into the collective experience of public desire" and to disrupt the heterosexual presupposition on which that desire rests (Berlant and Freeman 164). To this end, the Queer Shopping Network of New York and the Suburban Homosexual Outreach Program of San Francisco (SHOP) stage mall visibility actions. By parading into suburban shopping spaces dressed in full gay regalia, holding hands or handing out flyers, they insert gay spectacle into the centers of straight consumption. Lauren Berlant and Elizabeth Freeman argue that the queer mall spectacle addresses "the consumer's own 'perverse' desire to experience a different body and offers *itself* as the most stylish of the many attitudes on sale at the mall" (164).

If in postmodern consumer culture the commodity is a central means by which desire is organized, how are Queer Nation's visibility actions disrupting this process? I want to suggest that, while Queer Nation's tactics attend to the commodity, the framework in which the commodity is understood is similar to the informing framework of much queer theory. It is, in short, a cultural one in which the commodity is reduced to an ideological icon. Like queer theory, Queer Nation tends to focus so exclusively on the construction of meanings, on forging an oppositional practice that "disrupts the *semiotic* boundaries between gay and straight" (Berlant and Freeman 168; emphasis added), that social change is reduced to the arena of cultural representation. Condensed into a cultural signifier, the commodity remains securely fetishized. Infusing consumer space with a gay sensibility may queer-y commodities, but "making queer good by making goods queer" (Berlant and Freeman 168) is hardly antiassimilationist politics! If the aim of mall visibility actions is to make the pleasures of consumption available to gays too and to commodify queer identity as "the most stylish of the many attitudes on sale at the mall," then inclusion seems to be precisely the point. Disclosing the invisible heterosexual meanings invested in commodities, I am suggesting, is a very limited strategy of resistance, one that ultimately nourishes the commodity's gravitation toward the new, the exotic, the spectacular.

As in queer theory, many of the activities of Queer Nation take visibility at face value and in so doing short-circuit the historicity of visibility concealed in the logic of the commodity. In *Capital*, Marx demonstrates that this sort of "oversight" is very much a part of the commodity's secret and its magic: "A commodity appears at first sight an extremely obvious, trivial thing. But its analysis brings out that it is a very strange thing, abounding in metaphysical subtleties and theological niceties" (163). Marx's "analysis" of the commodity explains this "first sight" as a fiction, not in the sense that it is false or merely a copy of a copy but in the sense that it confuses the seeable with the visible. The visible for Marx is not an empirical but a historical effect. Indeed, it might be said that much of Marx's critique of the commodity redefines the nature of vision by establishing the connection between visibility and history.[11] Marx demonstrates that the value of a commodity is material, not in the sense of its being made of physical matter but in the sense that it is socially produced through human labor and the extraction of surplus value in exchange. Although the value of commodities is materially embodied in them, it is not visible in the objects themselves as a physical property. The illusion that value resides in objects rather than in the social relations between individuals and objects Marx calls commodity fetishism. When the commodity is fetishized, the labor that has gone into its production is rendered invisible. Commodity fetishism entails the misrecognition of a structural effect as an immediate property of one of its elements, as if this property belonged to it outside of its relation to other elements (Žižek 24). This fetishizing is enhanced and encouraged under late capitalism, when the spheres of commodity production and consumption are so often widely separated.

Any argument for the continued pertinence of Marx's theory of the commodity risks being misread as a reductive "return" to orthodox marxism. While a more extensive engagement with contemporary rewritings of Marxian commodity theory, Baudrillard especially, is necessary to forestall such a misreading, it is beyond the scope of this essay. Certainly Marx was not theorizing commodity fetishism from the vantage point of late capitalism's flexible production and burgeoning information technologies and their effects on identities and cultures. Nonetheless, because his reading of the commodity invites us to begin by seeing consciousness, state, and political economy as interlinked historical and material forces by which social life is made and remade, it is to my mind a more politically useful critical framework for understanding and combatting the commodification of identities than a political economy of the sign. When the commodity is dealt with merely as a matter of signification, meaning, or identities, only one of the elements of its production—the process of image-making it relies on—is made visible. The exploitation of human labor on which the commodity's appearance as an object depends remains out of sight. Changing the Bart Simpson logo on a T-shirt to "Queer Bart" may disrupt normative conceptions of sexuality that infuse the circulation of commodities in consumer culture, but it offers a very limited view of the social relations commodities rely on, and to this extent it reinforces their fetishization.

Queer-y-ing the Avant-Garde

Some of the problems in queer theory and politics I address above are reminiscent of the contradictions that have punctuated the history of the avant-garde in the West over the past hundred years. It is a history worth examining because the modes of reading in cultural studies and queer intellectual activity now are in the process of repeating it. The genealogy of the concept of the avant-garde in radical political thought dates from the 1790s when it signalled the progressive romantic notion of art as an instrument for social revolution (Calinescu). Early 20th-century avant-garde movements, provoked by the enormous social upheavals of the First World War and the Revolution of 1917, promoted a critical rejection of bourgeois culture. Like the aesthetes at the turn of the 20th century, the avant-garde reacted to the increasing fragmentation of social life in industrialized society. But while aestheticism responded to the commercialization of art and its separation from life by substituting reflexive exploration of its own processes of creation for social relevance, the avant-garde attempted to reintegrate art into meaningful human activity by leading it back to social praxis (Burger). As Raymond Williams has pointed out, there were innumerable variations on avant-garde complaints against the bourgeoisie—often articulating quite anthithetical political positions—depending on the social and political structures of the countries in which these movements were active (54). Despite these variations, like queer theory and activism, avant-garde movements—among them Dada, Surrealism, Italian Futurism, the German Bauhaus, and Russian Constructionism—attacked the philosophical and political assumptions presupposed in the reigning bourgeois realist conceptions of representation and visibility. Like Queer Nation, Dada was a broad and disparate movement, crossing national boundaries as well as the ideological divisions between art, politics, and daily life. It, too, found expression in a variety of media: poetry, performance, painting, the cinema, and montage. Attacking the cultural, political, and moral values on which the dominant social order relied, it set out to "shock the bourgeoisie" (Plant 40–41). The Surrealists, many of whom had participated in the Dadaist movement in France, rejected Dada's shock tactics and its purely negative approach, and aimed instead to try to make use of Freud's theory of the unconscious in order to unleash the pleasures trapped in experience and unfulfilled by a social system dependent on rationality and the accumulation of capital (Plant 49). Convinced that the union of art and life, of the individual and the world, was "possible only with the end of capitalism and the dawn of a new ludic age," nonetheless, like other avant-garde movements, their experiments were pursued mainly in the cultural domain (Plant 52).

The Situationist International movement that surfaced in France in the late fifties and lasted through 1972 is an interesting example of a political project that attempted to reclaim the revolutionary potential of the avant-garde and supersede the limitations of its cultural politics. The Situationists acknowledged the historical importance of their avant-garde antecedents' efforts as an effective means of struggle against the bourgeoisie, but were also critical of their failure to develop that spirit of revolt into a coherent cri-

tique. Consequently, they set out to transcend the distinction between revolutionary politics and cultural criticism once and for all,
and in some respects went further than their predecessors in doing
so (Plant 55–56).[12] Several of their strategies for disrupting the
spectacular organization of everyday life in commodity culture
share much in common with those of queer activism.

The tactic of *detournement,* for instance, is one—that is, the
rearrangement of a preexisting text like an advertisement to form
a new and critical ensemble. The Situationist critique of consumer
society, political agitation in commodity culture, and efforts to
form an international collective had both a revolutionary and a
ludic dimension. Sorting out the contradictions in their vision and
accounting for the failures in their attempt to revamp the avant-
garde might be a useful project for queer intellectuals to pursue
and learn from.

Historically, the dissolution of the more revolutionary aspira-
tions and activities of the early avant-garde movements cannot be
separated from political forces like Stalinism and Nazism that were
responsible for the suppression of their potential oppositional
force by the mid-20th century. But their critical edge was also
blunted by their own participation in the increasing commodification of social life by retreating to cultural experimentation as their
principal political forum. That the term "avant-garde" now con-
notes primarily, even exclusively, artistic innovation is in this regard symptomatic. Seen from this vantage point, the distinction
between the direction the avant-garde finally pursued and aestheticism seems less dramatic—as does the distinction in contemporary
theory between post-structuralism's fixation on representation and
more recent formulations of social postmodernism. Many of the
aesthetic features of the avant-garde reverberate in this more
worldly "social postmodernism": a tendency toward formalist
modes of reading, a focus on performance and aesthetic experimentation, an idealist retreat to mythic/psychic spirituality, and
the disparity between a professed agenda for broad social change
and a practice focused exclusively on cultural politics. One way
to begin to understand this gravitation toward cultural politics
in the history of the avant-garde is to consider it in relation to
the more general aestheticization of everyday life in consumer
capitalism.

At the same time that oppositional intellectuals struggle against the separation of art from daily life, capitalism's need for expanding markets has in its own way promoted the integration of art and life—but in accordance with the requirements of commodity exchange. The aestheticization of daily life is one consequence of this process. By "the aestheticization of daily life," I mean the intensified integration of cultural and commodity production under late capitalism by way of the rapid flow of images and signs that saturate myriad everyday activities, continuously working and reworking desires by inviting them to take the forms dictated by the commodity market. Advertising epitomizes this process and is its primary promoter. Along with computer technology, advertising permeates the fabric of daily life with an infinity of visual spectacles, codes, signs, and information bits. In so doing it has helped erase the boundary between the real and the image, an insertion of artifice into the heart of reality that Baudrillard has coined "simulation."

One effect of the aestheticization of daily life in industrial capitalism is that the social relations cultural production depends on are even further mystified. The aestheticization of everyday life encourages the pursuit of new tastes and sensations as pleasures in themselves while concealing or backgrounding the labor that has gone into making them possible. In keeping with the aesthetic emphasis on cultural forms, "style" becomes an increasingly crucial marker of social value and identity. While the term has a more restricted sociological meaning in reference to specific status groups, "lifestyle" as a way of making sense of social relations crystallized in the 1980s in the United States as new forms of middle-class professionalism became the focal point for heightened involvement in consumption and the promotion of cosmopolitanism (Clarke 67–68).[13] The concept of identity as "lifestyle" serves to manipulate a system of equivalences that structures the connection between the economic functions of the new middle class and their cultural formation (Clarke 68). The economic remaking of the middle class depends on the rising significance of the sphere of circulation and consumption and the invisible though persistent extraction of surplus value through exploited human labor. Although their cultural formation is increasingly flexible, "middle-class identities" continue to be organized by gender and racial hierarchies as well as by a residual individualism. "Lifestyle" obscures these social hierarchies by promoting individuality and self-expression but also a more porous conception of the self as a "fashioned" identity. Advertising, especially, champions a highly coded self-consciousness of the stylized construction of almost every aspect of one's everyday life: one's body, clothes, speech, leisure activities, eating, drinking, and sexual preferences. All are regarded as indicators of individuality and style, and all can be acquired with a few purchases (Featherstone and Goldman). Reconfiguring identities in terms of "lifestyles" serves in some ways, then, as a linchpin between the coherent individual and a more porous postmodern one. "Lifestyle" consumer culture promotes a way of thinking about identity as malleable because open to more and more consumer choices rather than shaped by moral codes or rules. In this way, "lifestyle" identities can seem to endorse the breakup of old hierarchies in favor of the rights of individuals to enjoy new pleasures without moral censure. While the coherent individual has not been displaced, increasingly new urban lifestyles promise a decentering of identity by way of consumer practices which announce that styles of life that can be purchased in clothes, leisure activities, household items, and bodily dispositions can all dissolve fixed status groups. Concern with the stylization of life suggests that practices of consumption are not merely a matter of economic exchange but also affect the formation of sensibilities and tastes that in turn support more flexible subjectivities. At the same time, the capacity for hyperconsumption promoted by appeals to lifestyle as well as the constituent features of various "lifestyles" are class specific. For example, in the eighties in the United States, the class-boundedness of stylization became evident in the polarization of the mass market into "upscale" and "downscale," as middle-class consumers scrambled to shore up symbolic capital through stylized marks of distinction: shopping at Bloomingdales or Neiman Marcus, as opposed to K-Mart; buying imported or chic brand name foods (Becks or Corona, rather than Miller and Budweiser) or appliances (Kitchen Aid or Braun, vs. Sears' Kenmore (Ehrenreich 228).

Aestheticization in consumer culture is supported by philosophies of the subject in postmodern theory that, for all of their "social" dimensions, nonetheless pose art—not social change—as the goal of a new ethics. In one of his last interviews, for instance, Michel Foucault protests,

> But couldn't everyone's life become a work of art? Why should the lamp or the house be an object, but not our life? . . . From the idea that the self is not given to us, I think that there is only one practical consequence: we have to create ourselves as a work of art ("Ethics" 236–37).

The aestheticized technology of the self here, and in Foucault's later writings generally, is taken straight from Nietzsche's exhortation to "give style to one's character—a great and rare art!" (290).[14] Queer theory and activism's conception of identities as performative significations anchored in individual psychic histories is not very far from this notion of identity as self-fashioning. For here, too, visibility is theatrical, a spectacle that shows up the always precarious stylization of identity. Foucault's equation of lamp, house, and life as "created" objects elides the different social relations that go into their making by securing them in individual creation. But the answer to why everyone's life couldn't become a work of art could take us somewhere else, to another story, one that makes visible the contradictory social relations the aestheticization of social life conceals. For even as the regime of simulation invites us to conflate style and life, some people's lives are not very artful or stylish, circumscribed as they are by limited access to social resources. How might the woman earning $50 a week for 60 hours of work operating a sewing machine in a sweat shop in the South Bronx or the exhausted migrant worker in the San Joaquin Valley harvesting tomatoes for 12 hours a day at $2 an hour make their lives an art? How artful was the life of Venus Xtravaganza, forced to support herself as a prostitute until she was murdered? Unless "art" is so reunderstood as to be disconnected from individual creation or choice and linked to a strategy for changing the conditions that allow so many to suffer an exploited existence, making one's life an art is an intelligible possibility only for the leisured class and their new yuppie heirs. When queer theory reconfigures gender identity as a "style of the flesh" (*Gender* 139), to use Judith Butler's phrasing, or as "the most stylish of the many attitudes on sale in the mall" (Berlant and Freeman 167), it is taking part in the postmodern aestheticization of daily life.

In the Life(style): Postmodern (Homo)sexual Subjects

It is not accidental that homosexuals have been most conspicuous in the primary domains of the spectacle: fashion and entertainment. In 1993 no fewer than five national straight news and fashion magazines carried positive cover stories on lesbians and gays. One of the most notable among them was the cover of *New York Magazine*'s May 1993 issue, which featured a dashingly seductive close-up of k. d. lang dressed in drag next to the words "Lesbian Chic: The Bold, Brave World of Gay Women." Every imaginable facet of gay and lesbian life—drag, transsexuality, gay teens, gay parents—has been featured on daytime talk shows. *The New York Times'* recently inaugurated "Styles of the Times" section now includes along with the engagement and marriage announcements regular features on gay and lesbian issues, here explicitly figured as one of many life "styles." The drag queens Ru Paul and Lady Bunny have both been profiled there, and in 1993 the front page of the section carried full-page stories on the Harlem balls and gay youth.

Gays and lesbians have been more visible than ever in arts and entertainment, despite the industry's still deeply entrenched investment in heteronormativity. Tony Kushner's "joyously, unapologetically, fabulously gay" play, *Angels in America,* won the Pulitzer Prize in 1993 and was nominated for nine Tony Awards. The list of commercial film and video productions on gay subjects grows monthly and includes such notables as Neil Jordan's transvestite love story, *The Crying Game;* Sally Potter's film version of Virginia Woolf's transsexual, *Orlando;* Jonathan Demme's AIDS courtroom drama, *Philadelphia;* Barbara Streisand's film production of Larry Kramer's *The Normal Heart;* and HBO's adaptation of Randy Shilts's AIDS exposé, *And the Band Played On.* While the movie industry still fears a subject it wouldn't touch 5 years ago, it goes where the money is, and so far in the nineties "gay" is becoming a warmer if not a hot commodity.

    Nowhere is gay more in vogue than in fashion, where homo-
erotic imagery is the epitome of postmodern chic. Magazines
firmly situated in the middle-class mainstream like *Details, Esquire,
GQ,* or *Mademoiselle* have all recently carried stories addressing
some aspect of gay life and/as fashion, and it is here that gay and
lesbian visibility blurs readily into a queer gender-bending aesthetic. The June 1993 issue of *Details,* for example, featured a story
on couples that included one gay and one lesbian couple; another
story offered a gay man's perspective on lifting the ban on gays in
the military (including a graphic account of his one-night-stand
with a marine who is "not gay") and a favorable review by gay
novelist David Leavitt of Michelangelo Signorile's book *Queer in
America.* The first volume of *Esquire*'s new fashion magazine, *Esquire Gentleman,* carried a feature on "The Gay Factor in Fashion"
that declared "Just about everyone dresses a little gay these
days. . . . It is now a marketing given that gay sensibility sells to
both gay and straight" (Martin 140). *Esquire*'s regular June 1993
issue included a review of Potter's *Orlando* as well as a short story
by Lynn Darling entitled "Single White Male Seeks Clue."
    Darling's story is a symptomatic example of the incorporation
of a queer aesthetic into the gender structure of postmodern patriarchy. "It's not easy to be the scion of a dying WASP culture," the
cover blurb announces, "when women have more confidence, gay
men have more style, and everyone seems to have the right to be
angry with you." This is a tale of young urban professional man-
hood in crisis, a crisis managed through nostalgic detours into the
"now vanished set of certainties" preserved in the world of boxing.
As the story draws to a close, John Talbot, the single white male of
the title, and his girlfriend look out of their hotel room and find
in their view a gay couple "dry-humping" on a penthouse roof
right below them. "Talbot was tempted to say something snide, but
he checked himself. In fact, it was really sweet, he decided, and
in his happiness he saw them suddenly as fellow travellers in the
community of desire" (Darling 104). Talbot's inclusion of gays in
the diverse community of "fellow travellers" offers an interesting
rearticulation of Cold War moral and political discourses that once
made all homosexuals out to be communists. Here, gays are included in an elastic community of pleasure seekers and a tenta-
tively more pliant heterosexual sex-gender system.

As Talbot's story suggests, the once-rigid links between sex, gender, and sexual desire that the invisible heterosexual matrix so firmly secured in bourgeois culture have become more flexible as the gendered divisions of labor among the middle class in industrialized countries have shifted. While these more accommodating gender codes are not pervasive, they have begun to take hold among the young urban middle class particularly. There are hints, for instance, that wearing a skirt, a fashion choice once absolutely taboo for men because it signified femaleness and femininity, is now more allowed because the gender system's heteronormative regime is loosening. The designers Betsy Johnson, Matsuda, Donna Karan, and Jean Paul Gaultier all have featured skirts on men in their spring and fall shows for the last few years. Some rock stars (among them Axl Rose of *Guns N Roses*) have worn skirts on stage. But skirts for men are also infiltrating more mundane culture. The fashion pages of my conservative local newspaper features sarongs for men, and my 15-year-old daughter, Kate, reports that at the 2-week co-ed camp she attended in the summer of 1993 at least one of the male counsellors wore a mid-calf khaki skirt almost every day.

As middle-class women have been drawn into the professional work force to occupy positions once reserved for men, many of them are now literally "wearing the pants" in the family, often as single heads of household, many of them lesbians and/or mothers. The "new man," like Talbot, has managed the crisis of "not having a clue" where he fits anymore by relinquishing many of the former markers of machismo: he expects women of his class to work outside the home and professes to support their professional ambitions, he "helps out" with the housework and the kids, boasts one or two gay friends, may occasionally wear pink, and perhaps even sports an earring. Men of Talbot's class might also read magazines like *GQ* or *Esquire,* where the notion of the "gender fuck" that queer activists and theorists have presented as subversive cultural critique circulates as radical chic—in essays like David Kamp's piece "The Straight Queer" detailing the appropriation of gay codes by hip heteros or in spoofs like "Viva Straight Camp" that parody ultra straight gender codes by showing up their constructedness (Powers).

Much like queer theory, the appropriation of gay cultural

codes in the cosmopolitan revamping of gender displays the arbitrariness of bourgeois patriarchy's gender system and helps to reconfigure it in a more postmodern mode, where the links between gender and sexuality are looser, where homosexuals are welcome, even constituting the vanguard, and where the appropriation of their parody of authentic sex and gender identities is quite compatible with the aestheticization of everyday life into postmodern lifestyles. In itself, of course, this limited assimilation of gays into mainstream middle-class culture does not disrupt postmodern patriarchy and its intersection with capitalism; indeed, it is in some ways quite integral to it.

Because patriarchy has become a buzzword in some post-modern/queer circles, I should explain what I mean by it here. I understand patriarchy to be a concept that explains the systematic gendered organization of all areas of social life—economic, political, and ideological—such that more social resources, power, and value accrue to men as a group at the expense of women as a group. In this sense, patriarchy is social, not merely cultural, and the privilege it accords some at the expense of others affects more than the making of meaning. Many post-structuralist critiques rightly target "the notion that the oppression of women has some singular form discernible in the universal or hegemonic structure of patriarchy or masculine domination" and remind us that any sort of monolithic theory of *the* patriarchy fails to account for the workings of gender oppression in the concrete cultural contexts in which it exists (Butler, *Gender* 3). But often they also reduce patriarchy to contingent cultural forms or dismiss it as a viable concept altogether. Like capitalism, patriarchy is a politically urgent concept because it allows us to analyze and explain social hierarchies by which gender, sexuality, and their racial articulations are organized. Patriarchy is a variable and historical social totality in that its particular forms for organizing social relations like work, citizenship, reproduction, ownership, pleasure, or identity have had a persistent effect on heterogendered[15] structures in dominance at the same time these structures vary and are the sites of social struggle.

Some patriarchal formations entail kinship alliances ruled by fathers, although in industrialized countries this form of patriarchy has been unevenly and gradually displaced as the ruling paradigm by bourgeois patriarchy. In bourgeois patriarchy, kinship alliances are subordinate to a social organization split between public wage economy and unpaid domestic production, both regulated by the ideology of possessive individualism. In advanced capitalist countries, public or postmodern patriarchy has recently begun to emerge as the prevailing form. It is characterized by the hyperdevelopment of consumption and the joint wage earner family, the relative transfer of power from husbands to professionals in the welfare state, the rise of single-mother headed and other alternative households, and sexualized consumerism (Ferguson 110). While any one patriarchal formation may dominate, it often co-exists with other contesting or residual forms. Policy debates like the current controversy over lifting the ban on gays in the U.S. military as well as cultural narratives of various sorts (films like *A Few Good Men*, *Jungle Fever*, or *The Firm*, for instance) can be read as articulations of the struggle between bourgeois patriarchal formations and their accompanying moral ideologies and postmodern patriarchy's newer forms of family, gender, sexuality, and work.

Finally, patriarchy is differential. This means that while all women as a group are positioned the same (as subordinate or other) in relation to men, they are positioned differently in relation to each other and at times in relation to men in subaltern groups. Some women have access to resources—a professional job, an urban condo, a cleaning lady, a vacation home, a fancy car—that are only possible because of the work of other women and men who do not have these resources. Because patriarchy functions in concert with a racial system of white supremacy, disproportionate numbers of people of color, men and women alike, have historically occupied these exploited, underresourced social positions. That more women than men fill the ranks of the impoverished speaks loudly to the ways class exploitation is reinforced by patriarchal structures. Similarly, some men have more patriarchal power than others, sometimes power over and at the expense of other men. This difference means that not all men benefit the same from patriarchy. Because the division of labor in general is racialized at the same time race is not necessarily congruent with class, the cultural capital people of color might gain on entry into any class can be canceled out or undermined by the operations of racism. Consequently, the white gay psychiatrist or lawyer is not in the same patriarchal position as his white straight colleagues nor is he in the same patriarchal position as a black gay man of the same class. Some women, lesbians among them, can claim patriarchal power over other women and men by virtue of their institutional privilege. For instance, women, lesbians included, in administrative or managerial positions can make use of their institutional positions to wield power over men and other women who work for them or are affected by the policies they draft.

But even women who benefit from patriarchy in some areas of their lives are disadvantaged in a society that systematically accords men power over women. The pervasiveness of rape and wife battering across classes and races and the general invisibility of lesbians in the culture demonstrate the systematic persistence of patriarchy despite the claims of a postmodern cosmopolitanism that gender hierarchies no longer operate or are readily subverted.

In positing male and female as distinct and opposite sexes that are naturally attracted to one another, heterosexuality is integral to patriarchy. Woman's position as subordinate other, as (sexual) property, and as exploited laborer depends on a heterosexual matrix in which woman is taken to be man's opposite; his control over social resources, his clear thinking, strength, and sexual prowess depend on her being less able, less rational, and never virile. As a pervasive institution within other institutions (state, education, church, media), heterosexuality helps guarantee patriarchal regulation of women's bodies, labor, and desires. Queer critiques of heterosexuality have often not acknowledged—in fact, they often disavow—the relationship between heterosexuality and patriarchy. But the struggles of lesbians in groups like Queer Nation and other gay political organizations are testimony that gender hierarchies persist between men and women even when both are fighting against heterosexuality as a regime of power (Maggenti).

The gender flexibility of postmodern patriarchy is pernicious because it casts the illusion that patriarchy has disappeared. But behind this facade corporate interests are delighting in the discovery of new markets. Among the most promising are gays and lesbians in the new professional/managerial class. Among them are "lifestyle lesbians" like the Bay area vice president of a lesbian-owned business group who announced, "Here I am, this funny,

warm person that you like and I happen to be a lesbian. I am bourgeois. I have a house in the suburbs. I drive a Saab" (Stewart 56).
Given the increased "visibility" of this sort of gay consumer, "tolerance of gays makes sense" (Tobias). Increasingly marketers of
mainstream products from books to beer are aiming ads specifically at gay men and lesbians; *Fortune* magazine contends "it's a
wonderful market niche, the only question is how to reach it"
(Stewart). Reaching it has so far involved manufacturing the image
of a certain class-specific lesbian and gay consumer population.
"Visibility is what it is all about," says David Ehrlich, of Overlooked
Opinions (Gluckman and Reed 16). These stereotypes of wealthy
free-spending gay consumers play well with advertisers and are
useful to corporations because they make the gay market seem potentially lucrative; they cultivate a narrow but widely accepted
definition of gay identity as a marketing tool and help to integrate
gay people as gay people into a new marketing niche (Gluckman
and Reed 17, 18). But if gay visibility is a good business prospect,
as some companies argue, the question gay critics need to ask is
"for whom?" Who profits from these new markets?

Out of Sight, Out of Mind

Commodification structures much more than the exchange
of goods on the market; it affects even as it depends on the knowledges that mediate what and how we see. The commodification of
gay styles and identities in the corporate and academic market-
places is integrally related to the formation of a postmodern gay/
queer subjectivity, ambivalently gender coded and in some instances flagrantly repudiating traditional, hetero and homo bourgeois culture. Nonetheless, as I have been arguing, to a great extent the construction of a new "homosexual/queer spectacle"
perpetuates a class-specific perspective that keeps invisible the capitalist divisions of labor that organize sexuality and in particular
lesbian, gay, queer lives. In so doing queer spectacles often participate in a long history of class-regulated visibility.[16] Beginning
around the mid-19th century, the bourgeoisie mediated their experience of the working class through spatial as well as cultural/
ideological arrangements. The erection of physical barriers—sub-

way and rail construction and the siting of retail and residential districts—structured the physical arrangement of the city so as to foreclose the trauma of seeing the laboring classes (Kester 73). This physical regulation of class visibility was also compounded by the consolidation of a characteristically "bourgeois" mode of perception through an array of knowledges, the philosophic and aesthetic chief among them. The notion of an autonomous aesthetic perception, first developed by 18th-century philosophers (Kant, Hume, Shaftsbury), whereby perceived objects are abstracted from the social context of their creation, provided the foundation for a way of seeing that has dominated modern culture and aesthetics through the late 20th century (Kester 74). This mode of perception reinforces and is indeed historically necessary to commodity exchange and comes to function as a "phenomenological matrix" through which the bourgeoisie confront an array of daily experiences through modes of seeing that erase the differently valued divisions of labor that organize visibility (Kester 75). In late 20th-century "post-industrial" societies like the United States, the (in)visibility of class divisions continues to be spatially regulated by urban planning, but it is also reinforced by changes in first world relations of production as industry has been increasingly consigned to sites in "developing countries" outside the United States. Capital has not been significantly dispersed or democratized in "first world" economies as a result, simply transferred to more profitable sectors (the so-called "tertiary" or service sectors, banking, finance, pension funds, etc.) (Evans 43). The escalating domination of the ideological—the proliferation of information technologies, media images, codes—in post-industrial cultures has helped to reconfigure bourgeois modes of perception in first world populations, producing subjects who are more differentiated and less likely to experience capitalism collectively through production relations and more likely to experience it through relations of consumption. As a result, the neat subject-object split of Kantian aesthetics has been troubled and to some degree displaced, even as the invisibility of social relations of labor in corporate and intellectual commodity spectacles persists.

Gay-friendly corporations like Levi-Strauss, for example, reinforce the gender-flexible subjects their advertising campaigns promote through gay window dressing strategies by way of public

relations programs that boast of their progressive corporate policies for lesbians and gays. Levi's gives health insurance benefits
to unmarried domestic partners of their employees, has created a
supportive environment for employees who test HIV⁺, and has a
Lesbian and Gay Employees Association. Members of this association prepared a video for the company to use in its diversity training in which they, their parents, and their managers openly discuss
their relationships (Stewart 50). But Levi's workers in the sweatshops of Saipan who live in cramped and crowded barracks and
earn as little as $2.15 an hour remain largely invisible. Although
Levi's ended its contracts last year with the island's largest clothes
maker after an investigation by the company found evidence of
unsatisfactory treatment of workers in his factories, they still continue to make shirts at five plants there (Shenon). Meanwhile, back
in the United States, Levi's closed its San Antonio plant in 1990,
laying off 1,150 workers, 92% of them Latino and 86% of them
women, and moved its operations to the Caribbean, where it can
pay laborers $3.80 a day, roughly half the average hourly wage
of the San Antonio workforce (Martinez 22). Displaying the
gay-friendly policies of "progressive" U.S. corporations often deflects attention from the exploitative international division of labor
they depend on in the interests of the company's bottom line—
profits.[17]

The formation of a gay/queer imaginary in both corporate
and academic circles also rests on the suppression of class analysis.
There have been all too few books that treat the ways gay history
and culture has been stratified along class lines.[18] With several notable exceptions, studies of the relationship between homosexuality and capitalism are remarkably sparse, and extended analyses
of lesbian and gay poverty are almost nonexistent.[19] To ask the
more pointed question of how the achievement of lesbian and gay
visibility by some rests on the invisible labor of others is to expose
the unspeakable underside of queer critique.

The consolidation of the professional middle class during the
1980s brought with it an array of social contradictions. The re-
cruitment of more and more women into the workforce bolstered
the legitimation of both the professional "New Woman" and of academic feminism. The increasing, albeit uneven and complicated,
investiture of lesbians and gays into new forms of sexual citizenship and the relative growth of academic lesbian and gay studies

accompanied and in some ways were enabled by these changes. But these were also decades when the chasm between the very rich and the very poor widened and poverty became more than ever feminized. As the 1990s began, a total of 33 million people in the United States—more than 13.5% of the population—were officially living in poverty. While estimates of the numbers of people who are homosexual are notoriously unreliable (ranging from the 1993 Batelle Human Research Center's 1.1% to the 1948 Kinsey Report's 10%), assuming that somewhere between 1% and 10% of the population are homosexual, it would be fair to say that there are between 1.65 and 3.3 million impoverished lesbians and gay men in the United States today.[20]

Most lesbians are leading less glamorous lives than their chic commodity images suggest, and poor lesbians of color are the most invisible and worst off. While the wage gap between women and men has supposedly narrowed in the eighties—in 1990, women earned 72% of what men did—much of this change is due to a drop in men's earnings, while the incomes of women have stayed the same (U.S. Bureau of the Census 1991). Furthermore, the bulk of necessary work at home, by some estimates 70%, is still left up to women. In other words, women as a group do more than half of all the work in this country and make less than half of what men do (Abelda et al. 52). Of all poor people over 18, 63% are women, with 53% of poor families headed by women (Maciones 282). While there is no reliable data available on the numbers of poor who are lesbian or gay, the racialized and gendered division of labor suggests that there are more lesbians than gay men living in poverty and proportionately more of them are people of color.[21]

Redressing gay invisibility by promoting images of a seamlessly middle-class gay consumer or by inviting us to see queer identities only in terms of style, textuality, or performative play helps produce imaginary gay/queer subjects that keep invisible the divisions of wealth and labor that these images and knowledges depend on. These commodified perspectives blot from view lesbians, gays, queers who are manual workers, sex workers, unemployed, and imprisoned. About a quarter to a half million homosexual and bisexual youths are thrown out of their homes and subjected to prostitution and violence in the streets (Galst). Severing queer and homo sexuality from the operations of class keeps these lives from view, forecloses consideration of the ways sexual

identities are complicated by the priorities imposed by impover-
ishment, and keeps a queer political agenda from working collectively to address the needs of many whose historical situation is
defined in terms of counter-dominant sexual practices. That so
little work has been done in the academy, even within lesbian and
gay studies, to address these populations and the invisible social
relations that maintain their marginality and exploitation speaks
loudly to the ways a class-specific "bourgeois (homosexual/queer)
imaginary" structures our knowledge of sexual identity, pleasure,
and emancipation.

Critique-al Visibility

Critique is a political practice and a mode of reading that establishes the intimate links between the visible and the historical by
taking as its starting point a systemic understanding of the social. A
radical critique of sexuality understands that the visibility of any
particular construction of sexuality or sexual identity is historical
in that it is shaped by an ensemble of social arrangements. As a
way of seeing sexuality, critique insists on making connections between the emergence of a discourse or identity in industrialized
social formations and the international division of labor, between
sexy commodity images and labor, the spectacle and the sweat-
shop, style and class. This sort of critique-al intervention into heterosexuality, therefore, does not see sexuality as just the effect of
cultural or discursive practice, merely the product of ideology or
institutions, but as a regulatory apparatus that spans the organization of social life in the modern world and that works in concert
with other social totalities—capitalism, patriarchy, colonialism.
    As a political practice, critique acknowledges the importance
of "reading" to political activism. Understood broadly as all of
those ways of making sense that enable one to be conscious, to
be literate in the culture's codes and so to be capable of acting
meaningfully in the world, reading is an activity essential to social
life. Although they often go unacknowledged, modes of reading
are necessary to political activism. Paying attention to how we read
and considering its implications and consequences is a key component of any oppositional political work. To ignore this crucial di-

mension of social struggle is to risk reproducing the very conditions we seek to change. The ways of making sense available in any historical time will tend to support the prevailing social order, but they are also contested. A critical politics joins in and foments this contest not just to reframe how we interpret the world but in order to change it. It is radical in the sense that it does not settle just for a change in the style or form of commodities but demands a change in the invisible social relations that make them possible.

I have tried to show that this way of reading is not just a matter of widening the scope of what we see, but of starting from a different place in how we see. Understanding social life to be "at once global and local" requires that we analyze what presents itself on first sight as obvious in order to show its connection to social structures that often exploit and oppress. While local situations (the commodification of pleasure in suburban malls, for instance) are necessary and important places to disrupt heteronormativity, they do not exist on their own, and we read them as such only at a cost. I am suggesting that a radical sexual politics that is going to be, in Butler's words, "effectively disruptive, truly troubling" needs a way of explaining how the sexual identities we can see are systemically organized. We need a way of understanding visibility that acknowledges both the local situations in which sexuality is made intelligible as well as the ties that bind knowledge and power to commodity production, consumption, and exchange.

The critical way of reading I am proposing in this essay is indeed queer. If it is not very well received now in the academy or in activist circles—and it is not—that may be because in challenging the postmodern fetishizing of social life into discourse, culture, or local contexts, critique puts into crisis the investments of middle-class academics and professionals, queers among us, in the current social order. For this reason it is undoubtedly a risk. Perhaps it is also our best provisional answer to the question, "What is to be done?"

Notes

1. For sharing her many resources and ideas and for her strong readings of various drafts of this essay, I want to thank Chrys Ingraham. I am also indebted to the students in graduate courses I taught in 1993 on the topics of Lesbian and

Gay Theory and Critique of Commodity Culture at the State University of New York at Albany. Their work inspired and challenged me, and offered a critical forum for developing many of the arguments I present here.

2. For an astute analysis of the commodification of gay and lesbian culture, see Gluckman and Reed.

3. In *Bodies That Matter* (1993), Butler qualifies her earlier position by asserting that drag may not always be unproblematically subversive. Nonetheless, due to the theatrical gender trouble that drag incites, it remains for her a commendable practice, perhaps the only viable form of political resistance to heterosexuality's regulatory power.

4. For a more detailed critique of Foucault's concept of discursive practice, see Hennessy, 37–46.

5. While the concept of the fetish has been taken up in some recent work in cultural theory (a few of the many recent examples include Adams, Apter, Findlay, and Mercer), the relationship between Freud's theory of the fetish and Marx's theory of commodity fetishism has not been very rigorously addressed from a materialist perspective. Most analyses tend to draw upon one theoretical framework or the other, with the Freudian version receiving most attention. Žižek's work on ideology, for example, makes use of Lacanian analysis and post-structuralist reconceptualizations of the social (vis-à-vis Laclau and Mouffe) to elaborate and extend the post-marxist return to idealism in cultural theory; his endorsement of the Freudian concept of the fetish as "lack" ignores the possibility that the very notion of castration might be read as the effect of a positive network of (patriarchal) social relations.

6. For a much fuller elaboration of this distinction between the see-able and the visible and its bearing on the reception of film, see Zavarzadeh.

7. I have chosen this essay of de Lauretis's for its attention to issues of visibility but also because of its institutional impact which is indicated by its publishing history. Originally appearing in *Theatre Journal* (1988), it has since been reprinted in *Performing Feminisms* (Case, 1990) and most recently in *The Lesbian and Gay Studies Reader* (Abelove et al., 1993). The page numbers I am using are from Abelove.

8. For summary analyses of Queer Nation's history, see Baker et al; Berlant and Freeman; Berube and Escoffier; Bull; Chee; Duggan; Signorile, 88, 317–18; and Smyth. For more critical assessments, see Fernandez, Maggenti, Mitchell and Olafimihan, and Smith. Since 1992, Queer Nation, like ACT-UP, has been riven by internal strife over whether its focus and political actions should also address issues of racism and sexism; as a result, several chapters have been dissolved or fragmented.

9. For more extended lists of affinity groups, see Berlant and Freeman, 152n3, and Berube and Escoffier, 16.

10. For a more detailed analysis of the concept of nationhood in Queer Nation, see Berlant and Freeman.

11. Ann Cvetkovich's chapter on *Capital* in her study of Victorian sensationalism offers an incisive reading of the relationship between visibility and the commodity.

12. On the SI, see Knabb, Marcus, and Plant.

13. On the former connotations of lifestyle, see Bourdieu, Sobel, and Rojek. On the latter, see Ehrenreich, Featherstone.

14. See Callinicos, 62–91, 168–71, on the connection between post-structuralism and aestheticism, particularly in Foucault. See also Hennessy, 55–59, on the relationship between the aesthetic and the ethical in Foucault.

15. For an elaboration of the concept of "heterogender" and its effects on the disciplining of knowledge, see Ingraham.
16. Grant Kester's fine essay on the imaginary space of post-industrial culture prompted my analysis of the class dimensions of visibility here; the phrase "Out of Sight, Out of Mind" is in part a reference to his title.
17. I am grateful to Catherine Sustana for pointing out to me the following detail: Levi's is owned by Robert Haas, the great-great grand nephew of the company's founder; when Haas staged a successful leveraged buyout to take the company private in 1985, profits rose by a staggering 31% (Sustana).
18. Among the books that address the class dimension of lesbian and gay history and culture are Bunch, Faderman, Kennedy and Davis, Moraga, and Nestle. Essays include D'Emilio, Franzen, and Weston and Rofel.
19. On the relationship between (homo)sexuality and capitalism, see Altman, D'Emilio, and Evans. Most of the little work on gay poverty has, not accidentally, focused on lesbians and has circulated mostly in alternative/activist presses. Notable examples include Egerton, Helmbold, and Lavine.
20. The accuracy of the federally funded Batelle Institute's findings has been questioned for a number of reasons: the study was aimed at addressing behavior related to AIDS, not homosexuality per se; the survey was based on self-reports from men; the interviewers were exclusively women who were not trained in sex research; and the questions about sex with men had a 30% nonresponse rate.
21. About 30% of the poor in the U.S. are black (U.S. Bureau of the Census, 1991).

Works Cited

Abelda, Randy, Elaine McCrate, Edwin Melendez, June Lapidus, and the Center for Popular Economics. *Mink Coats Don't Trickle Down: The Economic Attack on Women and People of Color.* Boston: South End P, 1988.
Abelove, Henry, Michèle Aina Barale, and David M. Halperin, eds. *The Lesbian and Gay Studies Reader.* New York: Routledge, 1993.
Adams, Parveen. "Of Female Bondage." *Between Feminism and Psychoanalysis.* Ed. Teresa Brennan. London: Routledge, 1989. 247–65.
Altman, Dennis. *The Homosexualization of America.* Boston: Beacon, 1982.
Apter, Emily. *Feminizing the Fetish: Psychoanalysis and Narrative Obsession in Turn-of-the-Century France.* Ithaca: Cornell UP, 1991.
Baker, James N., Anthony Duignan-Cabrera, Mark Miller, and Michael Mason. "What Is Queer Nation?" *Newsweek* 12 Aug. 1991: 24+.
Berlant, Lauren, and Elizabeth Freeman. "Queer Nationality." *boundary 2* 19.1 (1992): 149–80.
Berube, Allan, and Jeffrey Escoffier. "Queer Nation." *Out/Look* 11 (1991): 12–14.
Bourdieu, Pierre. *Distinction: A Social Critique of the Judgement of Taste.* Trans. R. Nice. London: Routledge, 1984.
Bull, Chris. "Queer Nation Goes on Hiatus in San Francisco." *Advocate* 14 Jan. 1992: 24.
Bunch, Charlotte. *Passionate Politics.* New York: St. Martins, 1987.
Burger, Peter. *Theory of the Avant-Garde.* Trans. Michael Shaw. Minneapolis: U Minnesota P, 1984.

Butler, Judith. *Bodies That Matter: On The Discursive Limits of "Sex."* New York: Routledge, 1993.

———. *Gender Trouble: Feminism and the Subversion of Identity.* New York: Routledge, 1990.

———. "Imitation and Gender Insubordination." *Inside/Out: Lesbian Theories, Gay Theories.* Ed. Diana Fuss. New York: Routledge, 1991.

———. "Performative Acts and Gender Constitution: An Essay in Phenomenology and Feminist Theory." Case 270–82.

Calinescu, Matei. *Five Faces of Modernity: Modernism, Avant-Garde, Decadence, Kitsch, Postmodernism.* Durham: Duke UP, 1987.

Callinicos, Alex. *Against Postmodernism: A Marxist Critique.* New York: St. Martins, 1989.

Case, Sue-Ellen, ed. *Performing Feminisms: Feminist Critical Theory and Theatre.* Baltimore/London: Johns Hopkins UP, 1990.

Chee, Alexander S. "Queer Nationalism." *Out/Look* Winter 1991: 15–19.

Clark, Danae. "Commodity Lesbianism." *Camera Obscura* 25–26 (1991): 181–201.

Clarke, John. *Old Times, New Enemies: Essays on Cultural Studies and America.* London: Harper, 1991.

Cvetkovich, Ann. *Mixed Feelings: Feminism, Mass Culture, and Victorian Sensationalism.* New Brunswick: Rutgers UP, 1992.

Darling, Lynn. "Single White Male Seeks Clue." *Esquire* June 1993: 97–104.

de Lauretis, Teresa. "Sexual Indifference and Lesbian Representation." Abelove et al. 141–58.

———. "Film and the Visible." *How Do I Look? Queer Film and Video.* Ed. Bad Object Choices. Seattle: Bay P, 1991. 223–76.

D'Emilio, John. *Sexual Politics, Sexual Communities: The Making of a Homosexual Minority in the United States.* Chicago: U Chicago P, 1983.

———. "Capitalism and Gay Identity." *Powers of Desire: The Politics of Sexuality.* Ed. Ann Snitow, Christine Stansell, and Sharon Thompson. New York: Monthly Review P, 1983.

Duggan, Lisa. "Making It Perfectly Queer." *Socialist Review* 22.1 (1992): 11–31.

Egerton, Jayne. "Out But Not Down: Lesbians' Experience of Housing." *Feminist Review* 36 (1990): 75–88.

Ehrenreich, Barbara. *Fear of Falling: The Inner Life of the Middle Class.* New York: Harper, 1989.

Evans, David T. *Sexual Citizenship: The Material Construction of Sexualities.* London: Routledge, 1993.

Faderman, Lillian. *Odd Girls and Twilight Lovers: A History of Lesbian Life in Twentieth Century America.* New York: Penguin, 1991.

Featherstone, Mike. *Consumer Culture and Postmodernism.* London: Sage, 1991.

Feinberg, Leslie. *Stone Butch Blues.* Ithaca: Firebrand, 1993.

Ferguson, Ann. *Blood at the Root: Motherhood, Sexuality, and Male Dominance.* London: Pandora, 1989.

Fernandez, Charles. "Undocumented Aliens in the Queer Nation." *Out/Look* Spring 1991: 20–23.

Findlay, Heather. "Freud's 'Fetishism' and the Lesbian Dildo Debates." *Feminist Studies* 18.3 (1992): 563–79.

Foucault, Michel. *An Introduction.* Vol. 1 of *The History of Sexuality.* 4 vols. Trans. Robert Hurley. New York: Vintage, 1980.

———. "On the Genealogy of Ethics: An Overview of Work in Progress." *Michel*

Foucault: Beyond Structuralism and Hermeneutics. Ed. Herbert Dreyfus and Paul Rabinow. U Chicago P, 1983. 229–59.

Franzen, Trisha. "Differences and Identities: Feminism and the Albuquerque Lesbian Community." *Signs* 18.4 (1993): 891–906.

Fuss, Diana. "Fashion and the Homospectatorial Look." *Critical Inquiry* 18.4 (1992): 713–37.

Galst, Liz. "Throwaway Kids." *Advocate* 29 Dec. 1992: 54.

Gluckman, Amy, and Betsy Reed. "The Gay Marketing Moment." *Dollars and Sense* Nov.–Dec. 1993: 16–35.

Goldman, Robert. *Reading Ads Socially.* New York: Routledge, 1992.

Helmbold, Lois Rita. "Shopping Bag Lesbians." *Common Lives/Lesbian Lives* 5 (1982): 69–71.

Hennessy, Rosemary. *Materialist Feminism and the Politics of Discourse.* New York: Routledge, 1993.

hooks, bell. "Is Paris Burning?" *Black Looks: Race and Representation.* Boston: South End P, 1992. 145–55.

Ingraham, Chrys. "The Heterosexual Imaginary: Feminist Sociology and Theories of Gender." *Sociological Theory* 12 (July 1994): 203–219.

Kamp, David. "The Straight Queer." *GQ* July 1993: 94–99.

Kennedy, Elizabeth Lapovsky, and Madeline D. Davis. *Boots of Leather, Slippers of Gold: The History of a Lesbian Community.* New York: Routledge, 1993.

Kester, Grant H. "Out of Sight Is Out of Mind: The Imaginary Spaces of Postindustrial Culture." *Social Text* 35 (1993): 72–92.

Knabb, Ken, ed. *Situationist International Anthology.* Berkeley: Bureau of Public Secrets, 1981.

Lavine, Rebecca. "The Lesbian and Gay Prisoner Project: A Vital Connection." *Gay Community News* 19.26 (1992): 5.

Maciones, John J. *Sociology.* Englewood Cliffs: Prentice, 1993.

Maggenti, Maria. "Women as Queer Nationals." *Out/Look* 11 (1991): 20–23.

Marcus, Greil. *Lipstick Traces: A Secret History of the Twentieth Century.* Cambridge: Harvard UP, 1989.

Martin, Richard. "The Gay Factor in Fashion." *Esquire Gentleman* 13 July 1993: 135+.

Martinez, Elizabeth. "'Levi's, Button Your Fly—Your Greed Is Showing.'" *Z Magazine* Jan. 1993: 22–27.

Marx, Karl. *Capital.* Vol 1. Trans. Ben Fowkes. New York: Random, 1977. 3 vols.

Mercer, Kobena. "Skin Head Sex Thing." *How Do I Look? Queer Film and Video.* Ed. Bad Object Choices. Seattle: Bay P, 1989. 169–222.

Mitchell, Hugh, and Kayode Olafimihan. "Living." *Living Marxism* Nov. 1992: 38–39.

Moraga, Cherríe. *Loving in the War Years.* Boston: South End P, 1983.

Nestle, Joan. *A Restricted Country.* Ithaca: Firebrand, 1987.

Nietzsche, Friedrich. *The Gay Science.* New York: Penguin, 1974.

Plant, Sadie. *The Most Radical Gesture: The Situationist International in a Postmodern Age.* London: Routledge, 1992.

Powers, Ann. "Queer in the Streets, Passing in the Sheets." *Village Voice* 29 June 1993: 24+.

Rojek, Chris. *Capitalism and Leisure Theory.* London: Tavistock, 1985.

Shenon, Philip. "Saipan Sweatshops Are No American Dream." *New York Times* 18 July 1993: 1+.

Signorile, Michelangelo. *Queer in America: Sex, the Media, and the Closets of Power.* New York: Random, 1993.

Smith, Barbara. "Where's the Revolution?" *Nation* 5 July 1993: 12–16.

Smyth, Cherry. *Queer Notions.* London: Scarlet P, 1992.

Sobel, E. *Lifestyle.* New York: Academic, 1982.

Stewart, Thomas. "Gay in Corporate America." *Fortune* 16 Dec. 1991: 42+.

Sustana, Catherine. "The Production of the Corporate Subject." Conference on Literary/Critical Cultural Studies. University at Albany, SUNY, Dec. 1993.

Tobias, Andrew. "Three Dollar Bills." *Time* 23 Mar. 1992.

Warner, Michael. Introduction. *Fear of a Queer Planet.* Minneapolis: U Minnesota P, 1993.

Weston, Kathleen, and Lisa Rofel. "Sexuality, Class, and Conflict in a Lesbian Workplace." *Signs* 9.4 (1984): 623–46.

Williams, Raymond. *The Politics of Modernism.* London: Verso, 1989.

Zavarzadeh, Mas'ud. *Seeing Films Politically.* Albany: State U of New York P, 1991.

Žižek, Slavoj. *The Sublime Object of Ideology.* London: Verso, 1989.

Documenting Barbarism: Yourcenar's Male Fantasies, Theweleit's Coup

Michael Rothberg

> Fantasy is on the side of reality.
>
> —Slavoj Žižek

I

In a famous phrase from his "Theses on the Philosophy of History," Walter Benjamin asserted that "there is no document of culture which is not at the same time a document of barbarism" (256; translation modified). True enough. But in considering Marguerite Yourcenar's *Coup de Grace* (written, like Benjamin's theses, at the very end of the 1930s) and Klaus Theweleit's *Male Fantasies*, I want to ask if the reverse is true: Is every document of barbarism also a document of culture?[1]

I am not arguing that this novel and this historical work are themselves necessarily barbaric, but I do want to draw attention to the risks involved in the task of documenting barbarism. Theweleit's literary historical project takes seriously the fictions and fanta-

© 1995 by *Cultural Critique*. Winter 1994–95. 0882-4371/95/$5.00.

sies of the men of the *Freikorps*—proto-Nazi bands of German soldiers for whom World War I never really ended—in order to
demonstrate in frightening detail how barbaric desire resides "on
the side of reality." Yourcenar's novel recounts the sordid adven-
tures of one fictional *Freikorps* soldier during the unrest following
the end of the First World War and the Russian Revolution. Yourcenar provides the kind of subjective "document" that Theweleit
demands that we comprehend in order to understand and combat
the reality of fascism as it lives on beyond the inter-war period of
its germination.

    Yet after a generation or more of post-structuralism we know
that no documentation (just as no documentary) can document
any historical or psychological situation innocently. Such questions
are immediately mediated, which is to say, ideological. To document barbarism is to risk the purity of one's own position as the
speaking subject of "culture." My initial question thus becomes:
What are the politics of documenting fascism? And—given the
specificity of the texts at issue here—what are the *sexual* politics
of fascism and its critique?[2] I will explore these questions by
reading Yourcenar's and Theweleit's texts together and historically situating them in their sites of production in order to
glimpse the politics of their representation (or lack of representation) of politics.

II

    In reading *Coup de Grace* with *Male Fantasies* we must immedi-
ately move beyond the certainties that traditional criticism has
posed vis-à-vis historical understanding. Over the last two decades
various post-structuralist critics have complicated the notion of situating a text historically by simultaneously engaging "the historicity of texts and the textuality of history" (Montrose 20). Critics may
no longer conceive of history as a linear narrative of discrete texts
and periods, but rather as what Louis Montrose calls "a dynamic,
unstable, and reciprocal relationship between the discursive and
material domains" (23). Furthermore, instead of delineating texts
from the historical contexts in which they arise and in which they
are read, "the post-structuralist orientation to history . . . necessi-

tates efforts to historicize the present as well as the past, and to historicize the dialectic between them" (20, 24).

Such "new historical" innovations have reinvigorated the study of literature, opening up multiple paths out of the stale formalist certainties of the pre- and new-critical past. Yet, at the same time, we have witnessed the development of a new *doxa:* the belief that "so many cultural codes converge and interact [within a text] that ideological coherence and stability are scarcely possible" (Montrose 22). Since there *does* seem to be a "coherence and stability" to this particular belief in today's theoretical marketplace, we are probably justified in asking how this unity could be possible and what it might mean.

In fact, given the definition of ideology which Montrose claims to be working with, it would be "scarcely possible" for ideology *not* to create "coherence and stability" out of the contradictions of the text. In Althusser's famous definition, cited by Montrose, ideology "represents the imaginary relationship of individuals to their real conditions of existence" (Althusser 162). As a representation of an imaginary relationship, ideology reproduces a coherence and stability which are, on the one hand, false, but, on the other hand, a lived "reality" (which, in a Lacanian discourse such as Althusser's, must be differentiated from the Real, which eludes mimesis). Even if the subject, who constitutes and is constituted by ideology, is a "term inaccurately used to describe what is actually a series of the conglomeration of positions . . . into which a person is called momentarily by the discourses and the world that he/she inhabits" (Paul Smith, qtd. in Montrose 31n), this inaccuracy is also a lived experience, not simply an illusion which the theorist or critic can wish away in an act of demystification. Furthermore, the replacement of the notion of the subject by that of subject-positions in fact does little to displace the metaphysics of individualism since it merely takes the logic of coherence to a different, "sub-atomic" level. Some tendencies within Lacanian theory have been more radical in developing a notion of the subject as precisely that lack (of coherence) which Montrose would like to understand as making the notion of the subject obsolete (Žižek 174–75).

The subject, ideology, and history may all be in some way "impossible" or incoherent, but, ironically, this lack of order structures the social whole, providing its contingent coherence. Post-

structuralist history, as summarized by Montrose, dissolves the tension between the universal and the particular, highlighting multiplicity at the price of recognizing the *totality-effect* that it supports
and that makes domination and resistance possible. The very "iter-
ability" of the text, cited by Derrida (326) as that which makes the
notion of context impossible, actually constitutes history. Thus, for
example, the (re)publication of Yourcenar's novel in translation
bears the traces of a new historical moment and contributes to the
constitution of this context. The fact that it takes on unforeseen
meanings (that it is an unstable multiplicity) does not detract from,
but establishes, its efficacy in producing a context-specific totality-
effect that, as we will see, aims to secure a certain ideological position. The historical methodology which I am laying out here seeks
to politicize citation, to "gras[p] the constellation which [our] own
era has formed with a definite earlier one," and "to brush history
against the grain," thus wresting the past away from its necessarily
constant reappropriation by the status quo (Benjamin 263, 257).

In the context of a project which seeks to investigate the sexual politics of representation, we cannot simply rely on psychoanalytic, marxist, and post-structuralist theories, but must acknowledge the ways in which feminist-inflected (and, more recently,
queer-inflected) critique has brushed traditional and even radical
history "against the grain." Feminist historians such as Joan Kelly-
Gadol have put into question the overarching diachronic narrative
of progress which anchors much historical thinking and which has
been written through the exclusion of women's experience. Jane
Marcus, in considering the specific conjuncture relevant to this essay, has cited "the necessity to free women's history from the yoke
of male periodization" ("Asylums" 140) and has demonstrated how
various women writers "allow the reader to escape from the standard historical confines of wartime and peacetime" (Afterword
254) that have structured not just literary, but nearly all attempts
to periodize the 20th century.

My reading of *Coup de Grace* and *Male Fantasies* is indebted to
this "escape" from a restrictive tradition which feminism has enabled. We have here two books that are thoroughly saturated in
war, but that illuminate what we usually call the "inter-war" period,
those years between the two world wars. They propose, in their
different ways, a state of permanent aggression that constitutes

both the social and the individual within the ever-widening Western sphere of influence. Both Yourcenar's novel and Theweleit's
historical documentation suggest, through a particular depiction
of warrior/fascist subjectivity, a psychological universality, and this,
in Theweleit's case, despite a postmodern theoretical apparatus.

In order to rise from this important, but abstract, universality,
to a more concrete level (following Marx's methodological sugges-
tion in the *Grundrisse*, 38), we can rehistoricize the two texts, seeking in them an open-ended dialectic appropriate to the multiple
moments in which they "take place." This will allow us to regain a
concept of periodization adequate to the nonidentical trajectories
of the international, gender, and sexual politics at work here. I
have conceived of this project in the early years of what I would
call a neo-nationalist era. Since 1989 and the collapse of the Soviet
bloc, unification on the level of economics (i.e., global capitalism)
has coexisted with the proliferation of local political and ethnic
differences (i.e., nationalisms).[3] As I write, the newspapers bring
reports of atrocities in what used to be Yugoslavia which hauntingly recall not only the civil wars of the time "between the wars,"
but also the Nazi genocide. My study, which proposes to look back
at the immediate aftermath of World War I in Europe through the
lens of a work of fiction, arises out of contemporary concerns about
this "return of the repressed," and out of questions about the historical genealogy of those contemporary concerns.

The era that both *Coup de Grace* and *Male Fantasies* "document" mirrors our own, serving as an imaginary double through
and against which we might attempt to define ourselves. The recently concluded First World War had done more to unsettle European politics than to grant closure to the struggles of its various
nations and ethnic groups. Arno Mayer has described this moment
following the Versailles Peace Conference as "reflect[ing] the intersection of the ending of a gigantic military conflict with the opening of a universal international civil war" (vii). The two works I
am considering here take us inside the experience of this terrible
historical moment. The landscape that Yourcenar's (anti)hero,
Erick von Lhomond, and Theweleit's *Freikorps* occupy seems to
consist solely of roving bands of soldiers torturing, killing, and
slogging their way through mud and snow. But, as historian Claudia Koonz suggests about Weimar Germany, we must consider this

time with "a retrospective double vision that encompasses both the prospect of emancipation and progress . . . and the etiology of a disreputable and insignificant movement which spread, unde-tected, through the body politic and was diagnosed only after it could not be halted" (21). I will argue that, for all their perspicacity, the stories that both Yourcenar and Theweleit construct retroac-tively about their subjects show us predominantly the latter side of this dialectic between emancipation and terror. While this surpris-ing "univocality" might derive from the polemical nature of these texts within their original, intended contexts, by shifting the ter-rain and exploring the linguistic and spatiotemporal "translations" of these texts, we begin to grasp their politics at a deeper level.

III

Klaus Theweleit's two-volume study of the novels and mem-oirs of the fascist and proto-Nazi *Freikorps* soldiers was originally published in Germany in 1977, but only translated into English in 1987 and 1989. In its original context, Theweleit's work chal-lenged German citizens' pre-1960 refusal to accept responsiblity for their role in the recent Nazi past, and it grew out of a move-ment of students obsessed with their parents' guilt and with the psychology of fascism and authoritarianism. *Male Fantasies* also re-sponded to what Theweleit understood as a shortcoming in the dominant marxist models of fascism provided by the Frankfurt School: an inability to acknowledge the reality of fascist fantasy and to understand the attraction of fascist violence (see Anson Rabin-bach and Jessica Benjamin's foreword to Vol. II, xii). Although *Male Fantasies* was written with the belief that the authoritarian structures of contemporary German society carried with them the possibility of fascist renewal, there was no explicit Nazi mobiliza-tion during the era in which Theweleit wrote.

Male Fantasies appeared in English, however, on the cusp of the neo-nationalist era, during a rebirth of fascist street violence and amid a series of "scandals" which caused cultural workers to confront the politically suspect pasts of some of their intellectual forbears. In 1987, Victor Farias published *Heidegger and Nazism* in France (it was translated into English 2 years later), causing a furor among latter-day Heideggerians and deconstructionists with his claims that the German philosopher was significantly more implicated in fascism than had previously been popularly believed. Also in 1987, scholars discovered that Yale literary critic Paul de Man had written a number of articles for a collaborationist newspaper in Nazi-occupied Belgium during World War II.[4] My concern here is neither to defend nor to indict Heidegger, de Man, or the philosophies with which they are associated, but rather to outline the conjuncture in which Theweleit's study of fascist subjectivity was introduced into American discourse. The Heidegger and de Man cases not only testify to a "crisis in witnessing" brought about by the experience of fascism and genocide, as Shoshana Felman has argued about de Man (120–64), but are also witnesses to a crisis of nationalism which irrupted on the world stage shortly after their unearthing in the late 1980s. Theweleit's work (and its translation into English at the same moment as the Heidegger and de Man cases attained public attention) also anticipated the political upheavals of national and ethnic violence with which we continue to struggle vainly.

While crises in ethnic and national identity obviously constitute part of Theweleit's landscape, upheaval in the realms of gender and sexual identities have also invigorated his intellectual project. Thus, we ought to situate Theweleit's endeavor in specifically feminist contexts. Although not explicitly acknowledged in the text, Theweleit wrote *Male Fantasies* during a decade of intensive feminist activism in West Germany. Starting with the founding of the Action Council for Women's Liberation in 1968 and the first national women's conference (of the new movement) in March 1971, and continuing through the establishment of women's centers and battered women's shelters during the rest of the decade, the issues of violence, gender, and sexuality addressed by Theweleit were brought into public discourse and consciousness by the Autonomous Women's Movement. From the mid-1970s, theoretical work from France also began to influence German feminists, along with the theoretical stylistics of Irigaray's and Cixous's *écriture feminine*, which Theweleit's "flowing" style often seems to be approximating.[5] In Alice Kaplan's words, "the authority he substitutes for the fascist one is female" (160).[6] Given this context, it is not surprising that Theweleit would be welcomed by many feminists upon his text's translation into English. Both volumes of his work, for instance, were prefaced with essays by prominent feminists (Barbara Ehrenreich, for the first volume, and Jessica Benjamin, with Anson Rabinbach, for the second). At the same moment, the issue of "men in feminism" was also coming to attention in the English-speaking world, and Theweleit's text, I will argue, illustrates some of the benefits and many of the pitfalls of that troubled "subject-position."[7]

We can best arrive at an understanding of Theweleit's problematic relationship to feminism if we first understand his explicit debts to a certain version of psychoanalysis. His approach to the subjectivity of the soldier males derives not from Freud or Lacan, but from Deleuze and Guattari's heterodox *Anti-Oedipus,* published in the early 1970s. According to Deleuze and Guattari, the Oedipal structure is not a human universal, as Freud and some anthropologists have attempted to demonstrate, but rather a determinate social relation enforced from above (Theweleit I: 210). In the anti-Oedipal model, the concept of unlimited desire displaces Oedipus as the universal upon which the theorists found their model. The anti-Oedipal model privileges neither the father nor the phallus (II: 175), but rather the subject's relation to its own desiring-production.

Theweleit understands drives within the body to produce revolutionary streams of desire. The soldier represses not the specific desires themselves, but the fact that he produces them: "he subjects the unconscious itself . . . to repression" (II: 6). This repression effects a "progressive displacement of libido . . . from inside the body . . . to the periphery of the body" (II: 216), according to Margaret Mahler's research on psychotic children (another model upon which Theweleit draws). The communists, workers, women, and Jews who haunt the soldier male threaten the boundaries of his body because they embody the liberation of the very desiring-production which he has repressed (II: 7). Julia Kristeva's writings on the "abject" emphasize this same anxiety over the boundaries of the body which she also finds in both "borderline" psychotic patients and in fascist writing, such as that of Céline.

But if we can always rely on Kristeva to find *"jouissance"* in the experience of limits, Theweleit's warrior is in fact an ascetic subject, and what he produces is not bliss, but death (I: 216). The

Freikorps sees itself engaging in "a battle against everything that constitutes enjoyment and pleasure" (II: 7). Theweleit understands anti-Semitism as deriving not primarily from anticapitalist sentiments about Jews as exploiters, but "instead [from] a coupling of 'Jewishness' with a 'contagious' desire for a better life" (8–9). Given the micro-politics of his theory of fascism, Theweleit probably would not want to admit it, yet this unveiling of asceticism does not differ enormously from Adorno's analysis of anti-Semitism.[8] Adorno implicitly links anti-Semitism to the workings of the capitalist Culture Industry by explaining both phenomena as (in Fredric Jameson's words) "negative embodiments of the deeper *ressentiment* generated by class society itself" toward the "promise of social and personal happiness," which both Jews and art represent (Jameson 154). The most significant difference is that Adorno's analysis explains asceticism as a social fact, while for Theweleit it derives from psychological structures.

According to this psychoanalytic model, the very tenuousness of the soldier male's ego, the fact that he is "not yet fully born" (II: 213), requires him to establish "maintenance mechanisms" as a prop to identity. The soldier male's ego comes not from identification with the father, as in the Oedipal model, but, rather, through punishment. The fascist "must acquire an enveloping 'ego' from the outside," but his only experience of the outside comes through acts of violence, first perpetrated against himself, and later against others. As Theweleit paraphrases Freud, "Where pain is, there 'I' shall be" (II: 164). In military drills and beatings, the soldier's body submits to "the pain principle," which reorganizes his fragmented drives and organs into a bodily whole bounded by skin which is quite literally becoming thick beneath the blows of the whip (II: 150, 144). Such a process of ego constitution guarantees that, in the face of the ostensibly liberated and threatening other, this subject will only be able to ensure "his own survival, his self-preservation and self-regeneration" through "the act of killing" or other expressions of violence.

In Theweleit's account, the threatening other is almost always female, and fascism in fact derives from the relations between the sexes established by a transhistorical patriarchy. His methodology seeks to "trace a straight line from the witch to the seductive Jewish woman" (I: 79). Fascism represents, then, not a break with traditional gender relations, but an extreme example of the norm, "the tip of the patriarchal iceberg" (I: 171). When killing women, or fantasizing about killing them, the soldier male also expresses hatred of his own self as patriarchy has formed it. He must "dam up" the feminized, interior drives of his body: "When a fascist male went into combat against erotic, 'flowing,' nonsubjugated women, he was also fighting his own unconscious, his own desiring-production" (I: 434). The soldier's permanent state of war against communists, women, and Jews tenuously props up his ego, just as the permanent war economy enables the survival of capitalism, although at the cost of deferring the liberation of desire.

Since the ego of the fascist is not a given, but an external imposition, it best fixes itself in external structures, such as the army or youth organization. In Germany these institutions in part derived significance from historical circumstances. With the nationalist hysteria of the beginning of World War I (also documented by Modris Eksteins, 55–64), "the soldierly core of the army . . . became nation, and leader of the people" (II: 81). With the mortifying defeat of 1918, and the truly external imposition of Weimar democracy (see Koonz, chapter 2), "the key to [the nation's] rebirth was the arming of the *Freikorps* against the Republic" (II: 81). The true Nation, a roving band of assassins, saw itself as shaping the People out of an amorphous mass, all in the name of the Fuhrer. But at the same time, "the army, high culture, race, nation, Germany—all of these appear to function as a second, tightly armored body enveloping [the soldier male's] own body armor" (II: 84). For Theweleit, the social and the psychological mutually constitute each other, although, in the last instance, the process starts with the attempt to establish the borders of the body.

Taking off from Deleuze and Guattari, Theweleit derives two basic social structures which he defines as fascist and revolutionary, respectively: the molar mass and the molecular masses (II: 3, 75). According to Theweleit, Deleuze and Guattari define the molecular as a fluid, always changing multiplicity, while the molar mass channels the flow of desiring production into rigid organizational structures overlooked by a Fuhrer or leader. These two structures probably coexist under "normal" circumstances; for

> the soldier male, however, the two appear strictly antitheti-
> cal. . . . [H]is bodily interior (the molecular ordering of the un-

conscious) is incarcerated by an incarcerating body armor (the molar arrangement of domination), and the two are irreconcilably opposed, one subject to the other. (II: 75)

In fact, Deleuze and Guattari's elaboration of the molar/molecular model is considerably more subtle than Theweleit's appropriation. They claim, for example that "every politics is simultaneously a *macropolitics* and a *micropolitics*," and that fascism, in particular, "is inseparable from a proliferation of molecular focuses in interaction, which skip from point to point, *before* beginning to resonate together in the National Socialist State" (*A Thousand Plateaus* 213–14).[9]

Despite such theoretical simplifications, Theweleit's critique of the Left's attempts to understand fascism, which follows from this distinction between the molar and the molecular, puts forward valuable, if not always original, theses. According to his argument, the old Left inevitably reproduced the same "molar" organizational structures as did the fascists, therefore blocking and channeling the potentially revolutionary flows of desire. By calling the language of the fascists "irrational, insane, lacking in substance," leftists missed the point of such discourse: that "what the texts [of the soldier males] have most clearly demonstrated is a refusal by fascism to relinquish desire—desire in the form of the demand that 'blood must flow,' desire in its most profound distortion" (II: 188–89). The refusal to relinquish desire (also the source of Lacan's ethics) does not constitute fascism—to the contrary, the source of fascism's violence comes from the coexistence of overflowing desire with structures of containment which reterritorialize its revolutionary power by repressing the subject's own production and projecting it onto the Other. If the Left cannot learn "that there might be pleasure in liberation, pleasure in new connections, pleasure in the unleasing of new streams" (189), fascism will continue to grip the masses.

Because it recognizes the powers of desire, fascism interpellates the People in the name of desire and then channels this force into hatred and nation-building. The truly revolutionary subject—the schizo—in the truly revolutionary molecular mass will never cede its desire and will never have desire reterritorialized by social constraint. Because of the contradictions of fascism (its ultimate reterritorialization of the desire it unleashes), it produces a psychotic and paranoid subject. This "persecuted persecutor" can to-day be found among supporters of white supremacy in the United States, among anti-Semites in European countries without Jews, and perhaps in the U.S. men's movement, with its stress on the "iron"/"wild" man.

IV

The psychotic subject which Theweleit derives from the writings of *Freikorps* soldiers and other proto-Nazis finds a remarkable expression in Yourcenar's *Coup de Grace*. Her depiction of Erick von Lhomond foreshadows many of the theoretical precepts which Theweleit develops in coming to terms with fascism forty years later. Von Lhomond represents an almost pure example of the warrior-male as it developed during the epoch of the *Freikorps* soldier. The narrator who frames Erick's story describes him as "one of those men who were too young to have done more than brush with danger, but who were transformed into soldiers of fortune by Europe's post-war disorders, and by their incapacity for satisfaction or resignation, either one" (4). Although a soldier of fortune ought in principle to be less "ideological" than the nationalist groups of *Male Fantasies,* in fact Erick signs on only with reactionary causes: fighting the Bolsheviks in the Russian Civil War and siding with Franco in Spain.

As with the soldier males, Erick can only give form to the social and psychological "disorders" of his era by joining with the repressive state apparatus as it wages, in one or another of its forms, permanent war against "the enemy." Erick describes his first military experience—the defeat of 1918—as a losing battle with bodily and political boundaries:

> the time came when I had to slip over the border to report for military training. . . . I took my first drill under sergeants weakened from dysentery and hunger. . . . Some of my drill-mates were agreeable enough, and were already launched upon the wild freedom of the postwar era to come. Two months more and I should have been used to stop the gap which the Allied artillery had made in our ranks, and should

at this very moment, perhaps, be peacefully amalgamated to French soil. (15)

Although Erick preserves his own life, the defeat confronts him with "a totally empty future" (16). Erick's military training follows from a desire, a movement across a border, which should be reterritorialized by his "first drill" [*mon entraînement* (144)]. However, since the sergeants cannot control the boundaries of their own bodies, they have dysentery [*les maux de ventre*], they cannot tame "the wild freedom" [*le grand chahut* (145)] which will therefore reign during the years of Weimar emancipation. Since Erick has not been used to "stop the gap" [*remplir une brèche* (145)], and the gap has not been stopped, his first experience with the military does not fully accomplish his disciplining and subjection. Even though he appears to laud his drillmates' freedom, he cannot acknowledge the desiring production within his body—the way it wants to "slip over the border" [*faufiler à travers la frontière* (144)]—rather, he winds up feeling "hollow" and "empty."

Only in the Russian Civil War does Erick find his place and develop what Theweleit calls a "body-armor" which is full, but contained: "The fullest ten months of my life were passed in a command in that godforsaken district where even the names . . . meant nothing" (7–8). Erick's position in the army comforts him by inserting him in a rigid hierarchical machine; although he commands, he is in turn commanded: "Once swept into the Baltic imbroglio I tried only to be a useful wheel in the whole machine, and to play as rarely as possible the role of crushed finger" (10) [*d'y jouer le plus souvent le rôle de la roue de métal, et le moins possible celui du doigt écrasé* (140)]. This odd, bodily metaphor follows close on the heels of a description of torture, which, although projected onto the "Mongol traditions" of "the Reds" [*les bourreaux rousses* (139)], divulges what is at stake in Erick's self-construction. (Theweleit includes images of Soviets "orientalized" by Nazi propaganda; cf. II: 270.) Coyly taking pleasure in his description of the "Chinese Hand" [*le supplice de la main chinoise* (139)], Erick recounts that the unfortunate "victim was slapped with the skin of his own hand stripped from him while he was alive" (8–9). He reminds us that such stories "harden the auditor that much more" [*durcir chez l'auditeur quelques fibres de plus* (139)], clearly revealing the connections between torture, the military machine, the armored soldier, and the experience of the body's boundaries (see also the discussion of the Medusa's head below).

If Erick takes a certain "idle excitement" in the telling of such details and in his soldiering experiences generally, these would seem to be the only pleasures in his life. Like the *Freikorps* adherents, Erick ascetically denies his own desiring-production, instead projecting it onto the female other and hinting at, but ultimately repressing, a homosexual subplot. Beneath the triangular, if not strictly Oedipal structure which Erick applies to the characters' relations, we sense that the flow of desire between Erick, Sophie, and Conrad is polymorphous and fluid. In order to take himself out of the flow of sexual drives the narrator uses two strategies: he attempts to turn all interpersonal relations into family ones, and he repeatedly insists on his own utter lack of desire in the face of the other's overflowing want.

When Erick brings his command back to Kratovitsy for the first time, he is greeted by Sophie:

> in the first excitement of our return she had kissed me warmly [*à pleines lèvres*], and I could not help thinking, with a shade of melancholy, that that was my first kiss from a young girl, and that I had never had a sister [*et que mon père ne m'avait pas donné de soeur*]. So of course, in so far as was possible, I made a sister of Sophie [*j'adoptai Sophie* (152)]. (24)

The surprising insincerity of the "of course" [*bien entendu*] gives it away; faced with the unfamiliarity of desire evoked by Sophie's passionate kiss, Erick can do nothing but transcode his emotion to an ostensibly safe arena, the family. [He also refers to her boyishness, asserting that she could be "a brother to her brother" (30).] In a moment of particularly twisted logic, he attempts to explain Sophie's alleged desire by way of the family:

> I seemed just made to fulfill the aspirations of an immature girl confined, up to that time, to the company of a few dull brutes of no consequence and the most seductive of brothers; nor had Nature seemed to endow her with the slightest inclination towards incest. But perhaps even incest figured here,

for memory's magic transformed me, in her eyes, into an elder
brother (33).

The breathtaking contradictions of this passage (equally present in
the French, of which this is a fairly literal rendition) demonstrate
that Erick will go to any length to avoid what would appear the
most obvious explanations of desire. Perhaps desire is not normal-
izable in *Coup de Grace;* just beneath the surface it flows indiscrim-
inately without respect for social categories such as gender or
kinship, but overtly it must be totally denied. Like Theweleit's soldiers, Erick "familializes" the erotic and eroticizes the family (I:
152).

Erick also goes out of his way to emphasize the fraternal nature of his (eroticized) relationship with that "most seductive of
brothers," Conrad. Not only did they leave "identical footprints on
the sand" (12) during their youthful frolics, but their "physical
make-up" was similar right down to the requisite "shade of blue
in [their] eyes" (14).[10] Naturally, "the country folk took [them] for
brothers, a simple solution for those who have no conception of
ardent friendship" (14); although the precise name of this ardent
friendship remains unspoken, Erick is pleased at the familial alibi
provided by their homologous physiques. Such insinuations add
erotic resonance to Erick's assertion that although "there was no
lack of girls" during their youth, he "treated all such fancies [*en-
gouements*] with scorn" (13).

Male homoeroticism, according to Theweleit, served certain
purposes among the Nazis: it was "simultaneously prohibited and
commanded," punished and held as a reward for initiation into
the power elite (II: 339). Before the purge of the openly homosexual SA commander, Ernst Rohm, in 1934, a male homosexual tendency existed within Nazism and can be seen in the writings of
Hans Bluher, author of *The Role of Eroticism in Male Society* (II: 138)
(Vol. I refers to Bluher as Ernst). Since Conrad drops out of focus
almost entirely after the first few pages of the novel, we could read
Erick's relationship with Conrad as mimicking the tendential repression of homosexuality during the course of German fascism's
rise and fall. But, regardless of the historical parallel in Nazi Germany (the full examination of which would take us beyond the
scope of this essay), *Coup de Grace* bears out Craig Owens's more

general assertion that a common "legal and medical apparatus" produces both homophobia and misogyny (219).[11]

The novel suggests that this commonality finds its most obvious expression in anti-sex ideology. In turning away from homoeroticism, Erick certainly does not turn toward heterosexuality. Like the rest of the soldier males, he experiences either a "lack of inclination" or "disgust" and "aversion" (54) vis-à-vis sexuality. Almost the only sympathy evinced by Erick for Sophie comes when he senses a "lack of inclination" on her side:

> Here before me was a Sonia indignant [*une enfant outragée* (154)—another familial metaphor] at the slightest suspicion of desire, and everything in me which differentiates me from mere women-chasers, for whom any girl is a windfall, could not but approve her despair. (27)

Immediately afterward he learns of her rape by a Lithuanian sergeant:

> now that she was sullied, her experience bordered on my own [*souillée, son expérience avoisinait la mienne*], and the episode of the sergeant made a queer parallel [*équilibrait bizarrement* (155)] with my unique and revolting visit to a brothel in Brussels. (28)

In Erick's "queer" logic, the "parallel" equates not the prostitute's experience, but Erick's voluntary visit with Sophie's involuntary violation. In an attempt to repress his own "queer parallel" with Conrad through a trip to the brothel, Erick also belittles female sexual exploitation and represses female sexual agency.[12]

As the novel progresses and the idealistic homosocial world recedes behind the more realistic homosocial world of war, Erick's misogyny overflows across the page. To describe the horrors of Sophie and other women, Erick draws on classical images of threatening women, also found in *Freikorps* discourse (cf. II: 4–6). Sophie's hair in curlers "made her look like Medusa, serpent-crowned" [*une Méduse coiffé de serpents* (173)], and the "humble cafe singer" he picks up in Riga ends up clinging to him "with the tenacity of an octopus" [*une tenacité de poulpe* (175)] (52, 55). In the former case, the simple evocation of femininity (the curlers) threatens, and in the latter, the equation of femininity with insatiable

desire provokes a similar dread. Later, the one time Erick kisses
Sophie on the lips, he finds that his "ecstasy changed into horror"
almost immediately, and he remembers a starfish [*cette étoile de mer*]
that his mother had forced into his hand, "almost provoking con-
vulsions in [him]" (76–77).[13] If these confrontations with the ten-
tacles of the feminine evoke something beyond "hatred or terror"
in Erick, they also form the basis of his self-conception. As Freud
describes it, "the sight of the Medusa's head makes the spectator
stiff with terror," but this bodily erection ultimately offers him
"consolation," for it reminds him that he, at least, has a penis (273).
The fascist subject similarly uses the revolting female to remind
him of his hard, military body. But both Freud and the soldier
males may, according to Theweleit, be producing a similar repression in their confrontation with the Medusa's head. What Theweleit finds significant in this symbol is not the woman's castration,
emphasized by Freud as the antinomy of male "stiffness," but *her
ability to castrate:* "It is in no sense, as Freud thinks, the castrated
genitals of the mother that she displays as a deterrent; it is the
symbol . . . of man's fear of her uncastrated, horrifying sexual po-
tency" (I: 201). In Theweleit's view, then, the hardness of the male
body is always much more tenuous than either Freud or the soldiers would want to admit; hence the need to expel Sophie from
the scene.[14]

Indeed, only when Sophie has left Kratovitsy can Erick regain
the imaginary fusion of his early days of male homosociality: "Our
ever diminishing group was returning to the great traditions of
austerity and manly courage [*courage viril*]; Kratovitsy was becoming again what it had been in times supposedly gone by, an outpost
of the Teutonic Order, a frontier fortress of the Livonian Brothers
of the Sword [*un poste de l'Ordre Teutonique, une citadelle avancée de
Chevaliers Porte-Glaives* (226)]." This "ideal of happiness" reminds
him of his childhood (123–24). The casting out of the "Red
woman," the Communist sympathizer, turns the men's bodies into
a fortress, an outpost, a borderline experience of ascetic and racial
purity. In what Theweleit calls the "troop-machine," "new body-
totalities are formed," as the parts of individual soldiers re-fuse
into "other totality formations between men, such as the 'nation'"
(II: 154–55). Since the re-establishment of the Teutonic nation is
constructed on the absence and demonization of Sophie, *Coup de*

Grace confirms in this specific instance Theweleit's overly general (and thus problematic) assertion that "racism must be seen as patriarchal domination in its most intense form" (II: 77).

But the absent woman, since they have projected her from out of the flood of their own desiring production, continually threatens to expose the frailty of these soldiers "clad in armor" [*à l'intérieure d'une armure* (227)]. Only the tenuous totality of the troop-machine protects them from being "lionized by women" [*livrées . . . aux femmes*] and

> subject to certain insidious dissolution, like the loathsome decay of iris . . . [which] die miserably in their own sticky secretion [*la gluante agonie*], in marked contrast to the slow, heroic drying of the rose [*le dessèchement héroïques des roses* (227)]. (125)

But, since the troop-machine "*is* the front," a permanent war-machine, it must continually transgress and reterritorialize its borders (II: 155). The attempt to keep his mechanized body dry leads the fascist to wade in blood, the "sticky secretion" of the enemy; only by killing, by actually moving through corpses which serve as so many Medusa's heads, can the fascist confirm the "hardness" and dryness [*dessèchement*] of his own body.

In the end, Erick's hatred of women, of communism, of everything which threatens property and his proper body, must culminate in a slaughter. Erick rediscovers Sophie "in the middle of flooded land" [*en plein terrain inondé* (234)], where several soldiers had already drowned (136). For the soldier males, communism and the sexuality of women both seem "to be a kind of ocean that surges onward in waves, inundating and engulfing" (I: 229). It is ironic, then, and perhaps ultimately troubling to Erick's narrative strategy, that his murder of Sophie turns his own past into pure flow, cut off from solid ground: "The disappearance of Conrad's sister would at least liquidate [*liquiderait*] my youth for good, and would cut the last bridge between that country and me" (147, translation modified; see French version, 243). Sophie, a reminder of his own internal drives, creates "a kind of sickening fury in the pit of [his] stomach that made [him] say 'all the better' for her death" (146). But before he actually kills her, Erick literally defaces her: "The first shot did no more than tear open the face" (150). As de Man has provocatively argued, one of the primary structures of language may concern the trope of prosopoeia, a "giving face" to subjects that also "de-faces" them by subjecting them to the impersonal machine of language ("Autobiography" 930). de Man discusses de-facement as an attribute of autobiography, and indeed de-facement figures importantly in the ways de Man's own life has come to be understood; here, however, the narrator, Erick, de-faces the narrative's object, Sophie. Thus, the narrative shifts the uncertainty at the heart of its own enunciation (its own potential de-facement) onto the scapegoated woman, who now becomes a repository for fears not only about femininity and communism, but about the slippage of language itself. The author's interest in shifting responsibility for contradictions in the text will become clear in the discussion of the preface.

But language, in any post-Lacanian context, immediately entails questions of desire. It becomes clear that in killing Sophie, Erick is killing more than just "woman." As he approaches her with his gun, he "clung to the thought that [he] had wanted to put an end to Conrad [*j'avais désiré achever Conrad* (245)], and that this was the same thing" (150). In killing Conrad and Sophie simultaneously, he kills desiring-production itself, the whole tangled web of drives which unconsciously saturates all of the social relations represented in the novel.

But Erick cannot simply kill desire once; it demands constant vigilance; hence, his own retelling of the story—"the interminable confession which he was making, in reality, to no one but himself" (5). Instead of coming to consciousness of his polymorphous drives, he attempts to fix them through one final projection onto Sophie: "One is always trapped, somehow, in dealing with women" (151). For Erick, however, being trapped is the condition of his paranoid subjectivity; the real "disorder" lies in the repression of the entire unconscious. This repression amounts, in Theweleit's terms, to the fascist mode of production, an "antiproduction" whose goal is "the transformation of life into death" (I: 216).

V

The above reading derives from an application of the theoretical apparatus provided by Theweleit to the text of Yourcenar's novel. *Coup de Grace* lends itself to such a reading, given Erick's resemblance to the *Freikorps* warriors. Since Yourcenar initially published the novel in France in 1939, just before the beginning of World War II and just before she left Europe for the United States, it would have been hard for contemporary readers not to understand it as a novelistic indictment of fascism. But if we consider the prefatory material the author appends to her U.S. editions of the novel, an entirely different reading emerges. Although the gloss which Yourcenar gives to her novel in and after 1957 initially appears diametrically opposed to Theweleit's critique of fascism, I will show that they actually share certain precepts.

In 1957, Yourcenar published the novel in English, translating it "in Collaboration" with her companion, Grace Frick (to cite the title page). At this time, she affixes a curious foreword to the story, which, in a later edition, expands into an even more curious preface dated 1962.[15] The preface attempts to forestall any reading which does not accept Erick as the "clear sighted" "hero" of the novel. She claims that the narrative depicts not a sadist, as "a naive reader might make . . . of Erick," but rather "a human being . . . looking squarely upon his own life." In claiming to depict what Derrida would call a subject self-consciously present to himself, Yourcenar attempts to solidify her own authority to dictate the terms of her text at a moment in literary history when the author is, if not dead, at least withering away.

But the stakes are not strictly literary, as Yourcenar's own language reveals. Her preface demands "strict collaboration from the reader" [*la collaboration du lecteur* (130)]; we must not "mistake [Erick] for a professional anti-Semite" [*un antisemite professionel* (131)]. The reader must collaborate in wiping out the traces of fascist collaboration. But, just as Marcus argues in considering the relation of de Man's late writings to his early journalism, such theoretical anti-historicism needs to be "instantly historicized" ("Asylums" 132). Yourcenar's plea for a vigilant forgetting, for the power that comes with ignorance, occurs just around the moment when the "Holocaust" first comes into public consciousness (but not with that specific name until later in the 1960s); that is, when the "professional anti-Semites" have regained their amateur status, which they will secretly cherish until the late 1980s when they will once again "go professional."

The year 1957 is also when, in France, Céline publishes *D'un château l'autre*, his novelistic attempt to produce collaborationist-readers who will help erase his guilt. In a manner similar to Yourcenar, Céline both rewrites the past and, in a radio interview from that same year, claims that his work has only aesthetic, and not political, significance: he is merely "a stylist."[16] If Yourcenar's novel can so easily be read as a critique of fascism, why, outside of personal predilection, would Yourcenar want to use the same strategy as Céline, whose anti-Semitism could never be "mistaken" by even a "naive" reader? As Marks argues in an extremely perceptive consideration of the relations between the preface and the novel, Yourcenar "naturalizes" anti-Semitism and links it to the sadistic and sexist acts which the text details (212, 217). Marks also places the novel in the context of Céline's 1937 anti-Semitic pamphlet, *Bagatelles pour un massacre*, claiming that "it is impossible . . . not to implicate the author" of *Coup de Grace* in anti-Semitism (212).[17]

While I am in complete agreement with Marks, I would also claim that Yourcenar's collaborationist strategy has another agenda, particular to the postwar era. The late 1950s and early 1960s in Yourcenar's adopted home, the United States, were a time of fierce ideological containment characterized in part by the polarity of the Cold War and by claims that, in fact, we had reached "the end of ideology."[18] Consonant with the antipolitical politics of the time, Yourcenar stresses that in telling Erick's story she has "tried to show that particular intimacy or affinity that is stronger than either conflicts of political allegiances or physical passions" [*la passion charnelle* (133)]. She explicitly represses desiring-production, which, for Theweleit, would include precisely what this formulation precludes—passion and politics. Instead of reading politics or passion into the novel, we should look to its value as a "psychological" or "human . . . document" [*un document humain* (134)]. Thus, according to this author-ity, "*Coup de Grace* does not aim at exalting or discrediting any one group or class, any country or party" (French version, 134).

But why not discredit fascism? The answer, again, slips out of the otherwise rigidly controlled language. In the 1957 cloth edition, Yourcenar phrases her apologia this way: "In the present state of the world, and in view of the conflicting attitudes of our day, the author wishes to stress the fact that this account is not

intended to defend or descredit any particular group or party."
Underneath this seemingly balanced sentence lurks the problem.
If we were to discredit Erick and fascism, we would have to accept
Sophie and, thus, communism as the only textually available heroines of the anti-fascist struggle. Given "the present state of the
world" and "the conflicting attitudes" of Cold War politics, given
rabid anti-communism in other words, such an option becomes
untenable for Yourcenar. In the two decades after its initial publication, *Coup de Grace* took on new meanings its author could not
control. Her depoliticizing reassertion of authority amounts to a
reterritorialization of what once had been a potentially liberating
text.

As is almost always the case, appeals to "human" meaning
tend to exclude women. Ironically, this happens in *Coup de Grace*
at the very moment when a woman enters the text: in the establishment of a pact between the female author and reader. In her
preface, Yourcenar repeats what Ingeborg Majer O'Sickey has
found to be Erick's relation to Sophie. Both author and "hero"
"retrieve [themselves] from exile," and establish their authority,
by "ingesting" Sophie (382). Yourcenar manages this by first
portraying Sophie only through Erick's narrative, and then,
more seriously, by portraying this portrait as the product of a
"clear-sighted" narrator, not the sadist we sophisticated readers
know him to be.

VI

If Yourcenar opposes human psychology to politics, and in
doing so exiles women from the social realm, Theweleit unifies
psychology and politics, claiming that desiring-production and
material production are one (I: 323). But, despite his obvious intentions, Theweleit also banishes women and, ultimately, the social
itself from his study. Although he succeeds so well in conveying
the intimate thoughts of his subjects, Theweleit fares less well in
establishing the context of their literary output. Theweleit's very
considerable contribution to the understanding of fascism—that it
is a form of reality production, that we must "feel" its utopian
pull—ends by limiting his discussion. Just as Yourcenar does in

Coup de Grace, Theweleit constantly evokes women, but he never takes them seriously as anything but effects of male fantasies.

If, as he claims, "a specific male-female (patriarchal) relation might belong at the center of our examination of fascism," not much can be gained by understanding these relations as simply expressing the "sexuality of the oppressor and the oppressed" (I: 227, 221). Women have no place in Theweleit's history (which he attempts to extend to all of Western history), except as either victims or possessors of some vague, emancipatory "nature." The "male-female" relation, which Theweleit promises to unpack, turns out to be simply a "male-male" relationship in which women are "malleable" and passive. In this, he proves himself no different than most historians, who "have not defined women's support for Nazi Germany as a historical problem" (Koonz 4), and have thus reinforced the appearance of the lack of female agency throughout history. Despite the misogyny of the *Freikorps* and later the Nazis, women supported them out of "conviction, opportunism, and active choice. Far from being helpless or even innocent, women made possible a murderous state in the name of concerns they defined as motherly" (Koonz 4–5). In showing that the soldier males were not insane or irrational, Theweleit leaves us with the impression that any woman who supported them would have to be.

What *Male Fantasies* lacks is not a consideration of the "reality" of women's agency, where reality would be opposed to the fantasies of the soldier males, but rather an analysis of the discursive context in which the soldiers enunciated their desires—in other words, to understand fascism and patriarchy, we need to end the segregation of texts by gender. Women did produce texts during this period, and a real counterdiscourse would consider these female fantasies alongside more traditional, male documents. The few places where Theweleit promises to reveal "the actual behavior of those women" (I: 138) whom the soldiers depict end in yet more male fantasies. Take, for example, the "Aside on Proletarian Reality, Proletarian Woman and Man of the Left" (I: 138–71). Although Theweleit cites one or two primary sources by women, practically the only ones in either volume, he ends up using these pages to discredit marxism by revealing that proletarian men and communist theorists were almost as misogynistic as the *Freikorps* troops. Similarly, after asserting that the oppressive male ego could not evolve "without the (admittedly enforced) cooperation of women themselves" (I: 301), Theweleit launches a 150-page history of the world that is unorthodox in everything except its refusal to acknowledge women as political agents or subjects of their own desires.

Although Theweleit wields a politicized psychoanalysis like his subjects wield a bayonet, his analysis falls more on the side of the psyche than the political. He understands the fascists' permanent state of war as "a function of the body of these men" (I: 192) and as "the ultimate form of male sexuality at odds with itself" (II: 84). Since his view of social formations—any social formations—derives from his study of the patriarchal male body, he reproduces the *Freikorps* dystopia of a society without women. Like Yourcenar, he "ingests" possible female subjectivites in order to "armor" his own theoretical construction of men as the sole social agents. He cannot conceive that, despite, or rather because of, patriarchy, both men and women actively construct society, although not to their equal satisfaction.[19] He cannot see, therefore, that to take society apart will entail not an asocial explosion of desiring-production, but a dismantling from within received identities and positions.

Although I would not in any way claim that Theweleit, like Yourcenar, collaborates with fascism and patriarchy, his figurations of women are idealistic—"Female chauvinism is a contradiction in terms" (II: 87)—and his only solutions remain utopian: "The pathway to a nonfascist life is marked out a little further by every act of lovemaking in which the participants touch neither as images nor as bearers of *names* defined by the social" (II: 104). This may simply sound like the early 1970s love-in, which it is. But such an equation between fascism and the symbolic and social orders suggests a problematic notion of sexuality and a dangerous paucity of political options. The idea that "participants" could confront each other without bearing names derived from the social order not only ignores the last century of humanities and social scientific thinking, it misses the subversiveness built into acts of naming. According to some contemporary feminists, sexuality which foregrounds social roles and names erodes the foundations of patriarchy much more effectively than appeals to some natural, extra-discursive realm.[20] Furthermore, as Theweleit himself writes elsewhere, it is precisely men, such as the soldier males, with fragmented ego structures who "want a contact with the opposite sex— or perhaps simply access to sexuality itself—which cannot be *named*" (I: 205; see also 284). This contradiction in Theweleit's text results from the privileging of desiring-production as a ubiquitous and quasi-natural force.

But desire is culturally specific and neither organic nor natural. It is produced by social formations, by the very barriers which Theweleit would exile from his utopian model. We who today are facing a renewal of nationalism and fascism need to be very careful about understanding the social formations which produce such structures of desire; only by acknowledging the materiality of desire can we begin to construct alternative social formations which will oppose fascism and patriarchy. Since, in the end, all such barriers to the free flow of desire are equally oppressive in Theweleit's model, he cannot distinguish between capitalism, fascism, and communism, and he cannot propose an alternative.

While all existing hegemonic social formations may be the same in upholding patriarchal relations, patriarchy cannot be said uniquely to determine fascism, even if it provides its ground. According to Maria-Antoinetta Macciocchi, fascism builds on a particular religious articulation of patriarchy:

> [T]he seizure of power by fascism and nazism uses as levers the martyred, baneful, and necrophiliac femininity of the widows and mothers of men killed in the first world war, and the femininity of Woman as Reproducer of the Species. (68)

Macciocchi also makes clear that we cannot explain patriarchy without acknowledging women's agency in simultaneously upholding it and resisting the establishment of its barriers. Both Theweleit and Yourcenar (despite herself) have succeeded in documenting barbarism, but they will not be able to explain it until they break with psychologizing models which eliminate the interplay of phantasmic bodies with social formations. For bodies and fantasies are social formations, but social formations are not bodies, and they are definitely not fantasies. The personal is political, but the political is always more than personal.

Antipolitical posturing—whether in the name of humanism and aesthetics or anarchy—constitutes the common deep structure from which Yourcenar's and Theweleit's superficially different projects unfold. Their interrogation of fascist sexuality and their cross-gender identifications (a woman speaking as/for a soldier; a man writing like a feminist) are not ultimately subversive, but they lead us to further questions about theory and methodology. Perhaps one of the tasks for the critique of fascism in this era of resurgent nationalisms and proliferating sexualities remains the search for methodologies which understand history not as simply "incoherent" and "unstable," but—to paraphrase Benjamin—as a present-day struggle over the future with forces from the past. As long as misogyny and homophobia meet only a depoliticized and antisexual resistance, a fascist return-of-the-repressed will continue to inhabit all male fantasies.

Notes

This project would not have been possible without the advice and criticism of Jane Marcus. I am also grateful to Molly McGarry for her comments on an earlier version of this essay.
1. Unless otherwise noted, all citations from the novel given in the text in English will be from the English translation by Frick (with Yourcenar). The novel was originally translated (by the same two) into English in 1957. When I refer to the French version, I will be quoting from a later edition of Yourcenar's novel: *Alexis ou le Traité du Vain Combat* suivi de *Le Coup de Grâce*. This edition contains the 1962 preface reprinted in the English edition and crucial to my reading of the novel. Throughout, I will intersperse sections of the French text whenever the language differs significantly from the English or when I am paying particular attention to specific word use. As I hope my reading demonstrates, I am less interested in establishing an "authentic" text than in revealing the specificities of the different versions and editions of *Le Coup de Grâce*.
Theweleit's work was originally published in Germany in 1977 and 1978.
2. The work of Maria-Antonietta Macciocchi remains among the most provocative on this topic.
3. For a discussion of this contradiction in the context of Marxist and post-Marxist theory, see Rothberg.
4. For documents pertaining to the de Man case, see de Man, *Wartime Journalism,* and Hamacher.
5. This history of German feminism is taken from Altbach. Besides this helpful introductory essay, the volume also contains ample documentation from the movement.
6. Kaplan also situates her reading of Theweleit within the context of the de Man and Heidegger "scandals." Her suggestive analysis reads *Male Fantasies* alongside Art Spiegelman's *Maus,* and Duras and Renais' *Hiroshima mon amour.*
7. For documents from this debate, see Jardine and Smith. Theweleit's work

is cited as an example of "engendered male criticism" in the bibliography of Boone and Cadden.

8. See the final two chapters of Horkheimer and Adorno for an analysis of the capitalist culture industry and anti-Semitism that links these two phenomena on the basis of a critique of instrumental reason.

9. To be fair, this text, entitled "1933: Micropolitics and Segmentarity," was published in 1980, after Theweleit had completed his work, but the complexity expressed here by Deleuze and Guattari typifies their work—if not always that of their followers.

10. The French is oddly less specific here. Their eyes do not share the marker of Aryan identity; they simply have "*la même nuance d'yeux*" (143).

11. Owens also explicitly refutes Macciocchi's assertion that "the Nazi community is made by homosexual brothers who exclude the woman and valorize the brother" (223). Owens shows how, even in sophisticated feminist analysis, *homophobia* and *homosexuality* are frequently confused. The assertion of a common apparatus in the repression of women and homosexual men goes a long way to explain many of the fruitful political alliances that have been made between, for example, AIDS activists and reproductive rights activists.

12. Clearly, the notion of the "queer parallel" upon which I am playing here is specific to the English text, but as a choice for translation, it remains significant. The translators (Frick and Yourcenar) are, after all, two women living and working together during a period (the 1950s) when "queer" and not "gay" or "lesbian" was probably the dominant term of self-identification for homosexuals. See Delany's memoir of this period for a discussion of these identity issues.

13. Elaine Marks also draws attention to the connections between these passages. I will return to her important essay.

14. See Hertz for a more developed consideration of how "questions of sexual difference, of perception and of politics are rapidly brought into relation" (27) around the figure of the Medusa's head.

15. I have not been able to locate the 1957 foreword in French, but the 1962 preface is, as I noted above, affixed to the 1971 French edition. A couple of contradictions exist between these two documents, neither of which (in the English versions) are given page numbers: Yourcenar claims to have written the novel in 1939; in the second she says 1938; she claims to have heard the story directly from "Erick"; in the second she says it came from one of his friends.

16. The radio interview is with Albert Zbinden and was broadcast July 25, 1957 on Radio-Lausanne. I am grateful to Alice Y. Kaplan for supplying me with a tape of this interview.

17. In this context, I find it rather disturbing that Timothy J. Reiss, in his introduction to a special *PMLA* cluster on "Literature and the Idea of Europe," should cite Yourcenar as one of the "writers who foster a spirit that counters the historical and ever-present dark side of economic and political forces" (27). To the contrary, my reading of *Coup de Grace*, and that of Elaine Marks, situates Yourcenar specifically on that "dark side." Furthermore, what Reiss calls Yourcenar's "scathing 1940 review of Anne Lindbergh's pro-Nazi *Wave of the Future*" (27) strikes me as a shockingly ambivalent essay—one that, in any case, was not published until after her death and thus cannot be said to have advanced the antifascist cause one iota no matter how "scathing" Reiss finds it. True, Yourcenar calls the Nazi's "barbaric dogmatism" (not their barbarism!) "the most irrefutable appearance of evil." But, on the other hand, she claims that "nobody can contest that there is beauty in the passionate exaltation of the young Nazi," and that

Hitler is "in sum a man like any other" and thus must have "some more or less hidden virtues" (*En pèlerin* 61, my translation).

18. See Andrew Ross's discussion of this era.

19. For the contradictory forms of female subjectivity and agency in the Germany of this era, see the essays collected in Bridenthal et al.

20. I am thinking for example of Judith Butler's discussion of butch-femme sexuality (122–24).

Works Cited

Altbach, Edith H. "The New German Women's Movement." *German Feminism: Readings in Politics and Literature*. Ed. Edith Altbach. Albany: SUNY P, 1984. 3–26.

Althusser, Louis. *Lenin and Philosophy*. Trans. Ben Brewster. New York: Monthly Review P, 1971.

Benjamin, Walter. *Illuminations*. Trans. Harry Zohn. New York: Schocken Books, 1969.

Boone, Joseph, and Michael Cadden. *Engendering Men: The Question of Male Feminist Criticism*. New York: Routledge, 1990.

Bridenthal, Renate, Atina Grossmann, and Marion Kaplan, eds. *When Biology Became Destiny: Women in Weimar and Nazi Germany*. New York: Monthly Review P, 1984.

Butler, Judith. *Gender Trouble: Feminism and the Subversion of Identity*. New York: Routledge, 1990.

Céline, Louis-Ferdinand. *D'un château l'autre*. Paris: Gallimard, 1957.

———. Interview, with Albert Zbinden. Radio-Lausanne, 25 July 1957.

Delany, Samuel R. *The Motion of Light in Water: Sex and Science Fiction Writing in the East Village, 1957–1965*. New York: William Morrow, 1988.

Deleuze, Gilles, and Félix Guattari. *Anti-Oedipus: Capitalism and Schizophrenia*. Trans. Robert Hurley, Mark Seem, and Helen Lane. Minneapolis: U of Minnesota P, 1983.

———. *A Thousand Plateaus*. Trans. Brian Massumi. Minneapolis: U of Minnesota P, 1987.

de Man, Paul. "Autobiography as De-facement." *Modern Language Notes* 94 (1979): 919–30.

———. *Wartime Journalism, 1939–1943*. Ed. Werner Hamacher, et al. Lincoln: U of Nebraska P, 1988.

Derrida, Jacques. *Margins of Philosophy*. Trans. Alan Bass. Chicago: U of Chicago P, 1982.

Eksteins, Modris. *Rites of Spring*. New York: Anchor Books, 1990.

Farias, Victor. *Heidegger and Nazism*. Ed. Joseph Margolis and Tom Rockmore. Philadelphia: Temple UP, 1989.

Felman, Shoshana, and Dori Laub. *Testimony: Crises of Witnessing in Literature, Psychoanalysis and History*. New York: Routledge, 1992.

Freud, Sigmund. "Medusa's Head." *Standard Edition of the Complete Psychological Works of Sigmund Freud*. Vol. 28. Trans. James Strachey. London: Hogarth, 1955. 273–74. 24 vols.

Hamacher, Werner, Neil Hertz, and Thomas Keenan, eds. *Responses: On Paul de Man's Wartime Journalism*. Lincoln: U of Nebraska P, 1989.

Hertz, Neil. "Medusa's Head: Male Hysteria under Political Pressure." *Representations* 4 (Fall 1983): 27–54.
Horkheimer, Max, and Theodor Adorno. *Dialectic of Enlightenment.* Trans. John Cumming. New York: Continuum, 1972.
Jameson, Fredric. *Late Marxism: Adorno, or, the Persistence of the Dialectic.* London/New York: Verso, 1990.
Jardine, Alice, and Paul Smith, eds. *Men in Feminism.* New York/London: Methuen, 1987.
Kaplan, Alice Y. "Theweleit and Spiegelman: Of Men and Mice." *Remaking History.* Ed. Barbara Kruger and Phil Mariani. Seattle: Bay P, 1989. 151–72.
Kelly-Gadol, Joan. "Did Women Have a Renaissance?" *Becoming Visible: Women in European History.* Ed. Renate Bridenthal and Claudia Koonz. Boston: Houghton, 1977. 175–99.
Koonz, Claudia. *Mothers in the Fatherland.* New York: St. Martin's P, 1987.
Kristeva, Julia. *Pouvoirs de l'horreur.* Paris: Seuil, 1980.
Macciocchi, Maria-Antoinetta. "Female Sexuality in Fascist Ideology." *Feminist Review* 1 (1979): 67–82.
Marcus, Jane. Afterword. *Not So Quiet . . .* By Helen Z. Smith. New York: Feminist P, 1988. 241–300.
———. "The Asylums of Antaeus: Women, War, and Madness—Is There a Feminist Fetishism?" Veeser 132–51.
Marks, Elaine. "'Getting Away with Murd(h)er': Author's Preface and Narrator's Text. Reading Marguerite Yourcenar's *Coup de Grace* 'After Auschwitz.'" *Journal of Narrative Technique* 20.2 (1990): 210–20.
Marx, Karl, and Fredrick Engels. *Collected Works.* Vol. 28. New York: International Publishers, 1986. 50 vols.
Mayer, Arno. *Politics and Diplomacy of Peacemaking.* New York: Vintage, 1969.
Montrose, Louis. "Professing the Renaissance: The Poetics and Politics of Culture." Veeser 15–36.
O'Sickey, Ingeborg Majer. "Mystery Stories: The Speaking Subject in Exile." *Women's Writing in Exile.* Ed. M. L. Broe and A. Ingram. Chapel Hill: U of North Carolina P, 1989. 369–94.
Owens, Craig. "Outlaws: Gay Men in Feminism." Jardine and Smith 219–32.
Reiss, Timothy J. "Introduction: Literature and the Idea of Europe." *PMLA* 108.1 (1993): 14–29.
Ross, Andrew. "Containing Culture in the Cold War." *No Respect: Intellectuals and Popular Culture.* New York: Routledge, 1989. 42–64.
Rothberg, Michael. "Marxism after Post-Marxism." *Socialist Review* 92.1 (1992): 113–20.
Theweleit, Klaus. *Male Fantasies, Volume I: Women, Floods, Bodies, History.* Trans. Stephen Conway. Minneapolis: U of Minnesota P, 1987. 2 vols.
———. *Male Fantasies, Volume II: Male Bodies: Psychoanalyzing the White Terror.* Trans. Erica Carter and Chris Turner. Minneapolis: U of Minnesota P, 1989. 2 vols.
Veeser, H. Aram. *The New Historicism.* New York: Routledge, 1989.
Yourcenar, Marguerite. *Alexis ou le Traité du Vain Combat suivi de Le Coup de Grâce.* Paris: Gallimard, 1971.
———. *Coup de Grace.* Trans. Grace Frick, in collaboration with the author. New York: Farrar, 1989.
———. *Le Coup de Grâce.* Paris: Gallimard, 1939.
———. *En pèlerin et en étranger: essais.* Paris: Gallimard, 1989.
Žižek, Slavoj. *The Sublime Object of Ideology.* London/New York: Verso, 1989.

Alternative Modernity? Playing the Japanese Game of Culture

Andrew Feenberg

> If games both fashion and reflect culture, it stands to reason that to a certain extent a whole civilization and, within that civilization, an entire era can be characterized by its games.
> —Roger Caillois, "Les jeux dans le monde moderne"

> The writer's irony is a negative mysticism to be found in times without a god.
> —Lukács, *The Theory of the Novel*

Introduction: Games as Rational Systems

In 1938, the great Japanese novelist Yasunari Kawabata witnessed a turning point in the history of the game of Go. Kawabata was then a young reporter covering the championship Go match sponsored by his newspaper. Honnimbô Shusai, the "Invincible Master," who had reigned over the world of Go for a generation, was pitted against a young challenger. So popular was Go that

© 1995 by *Cultural Critique*. Winter 1994–95. 0882-4371/95/$5.00.

Kawabata's newspaper could offer the players substantial sums for participating and pay all the expenses of the match. These were considerable as the match lasted many months.

Kawabata felt he had witnessed the end of an era at that Go match in 1938. Many years later he brought out his old newspaper articles, added new fictional material, and published a novel called *The Master of Go* [*Meijin*]. This novel is an elegy for the world the Japanese lost as they modernized. Kawabata's rather sentimental traditionalism is not as simple as it appears at first; nostalgia is a moment in the structure of modern consciousness and, *a fortiori*, novelistic form. This is why his story has much to tell us about the nature and possibilities of modern society.

It may seem strange that Kawabata's most sustained investigation of modernity should be the story of a board game, but in fact games exemplify formally rational systems. Like markets, law, and scientific and technical research, games break loose from the continuum of social life to impose a rational order on a sector of experience. Modern institutions too are characterized by explicit rules, unambiguous measures, defined times and places of action, and equalization of participants' positions. Their game-like structure, with its predictable procedures, absence of predetermined content, and simple principles of equity are all contrasted favorably in modernizing ideology to irrational, dogmatic, and biased traditions.

We will see how Kawabata, through his narrative of the great Go match, turns the argument around and develops an implicit critique of the particularity and bias of formal rationality. He accomplishes this by the peculiar literary technique of unfolding layer after layer of meaning in the moves of the game. The apparently neutral forms of play turn out to be loaded with social, cultural, and historical content. The Go match can stand for the whole range of modern institutions invading Japan, each of which delivers far more in the way of social change than appears on the surface.

In the concluding portion of this essay, I attempt to enlarge the scope of these reflections in two directions. I will first compare Kawabata's literary technique with Lukács' early theory of the novel. Using different means derived from his own culture, Kawabata achieved a form based on the same sort of layering and double meaning Lukács analyzes in terms of the category of irony. It is this form that enables Kawabata to carry through his critique of Western modernity. Secondly, I will discuss the larger implications of Kawabata's novel for the question of modernity. Japan's cultural specificity is often mentioned as a factor in its rise to industrial power. Kawabata's novel suggests a new way of thinking about why this might be so.

The Rules of the Game

Millions of Japanese play Go much as Westerners play chess. Kawabata's novel assumes a passing familiarity with the game, and, unfortunately, we will not be able to discuss it without at least that degree of acquaintance. I must, therefore, ask the reader to bear with me for a brief description of the rules of the game.[1]

Go is said to be more difficult than chess. Although the rules are simpler, the play is more complicated if only because the board is more than four times as "big" as a chess board. Black and white stones are placed at the intersections of a grid 19 by 19 lines (Diagram 1). The number of possible moves is the factorial of 361, more than the number of atoms in the galaxy.

The aim of play is to capture territory and enemy pieces by surrounding them with one's own pieces. Once placed on the board, pieces cannot be moved; they remain where they were played until they are captured. Every piece covers the intersection of two lines, which themselves intersect with other lines at four adjacent points. Each of these points counts as an "eye" or "breathing space." Adjacent pieces of the same color share "eyes." So long as a piece or a group of pieces has at least one such "eye" uncovered by the opponent, it is "alive." Once all its "eyes" have been taken it is captured, and the space it occupied belongs to the opponent's count (Diagram 2).

Because the board is so large, it is impossible to concentrate on any one portion of it for long without losing the initiative to a more mobile adversary. Thus, contests begin all over the board, and the players periodically return to one or another of them, advancing battles toward an eventual conclusion a few moves at a time. Beginners are bewildered by the frequent interruption of these apparently inconclusive struggles, but this is the essence of the game.

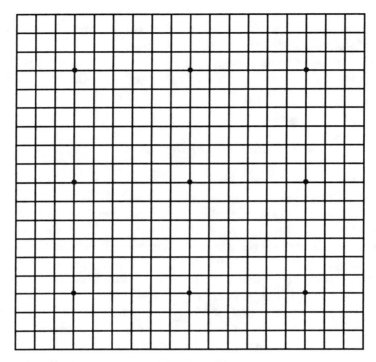

Diagram 1. From Goodell.

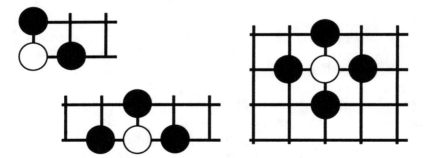

Diagram 2. From Goodell.

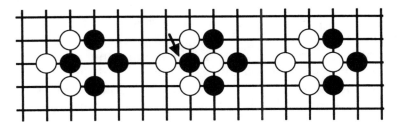

Diagram 3. From Goodell.

The game moves through roughly three phases. At first, territory is staked out by posting isolated pieces around the board. Gradually, battles emerge around conflicting claims, none of which are entirely secure in the early phase of the game. Finally, the board is filled in, the last ambiguities removed, and the captured spaces and pieces counted. Until the last phase, there are always many incomplete conquests, broken lines, lost pieces left in place, and so on. Although significant stakes ride on clearing them up properly, these housekeeping tasks are generally left till the end while the players confront more significant challenges.

The rules of Go are a model of simplicity and clarity, but they contain one logical flaw. An oscillating pattern can emerge in which both players have a disproportionately large incentive to repeat their last move. This situation occurs when the piece used to take an enemy piece is itself exposed to immediate capture, reproducing the status quo ante (Diagram 3). This situation is called a "kô," from the Sanskrit "kalpa," meaning an epoch or eternity. To prevent endless repetition, the second player is obliged to play away from the "kô" for a turn, breaking the pattern. Then the first player can fill it in. (If white plays in the space on Diagram 3 indicated by the arrow after removing the black piece, the "kô" disappears.) We will have to return later to this idea of "playing away."

The Way of Go: Autonomy and Reflection

Go was introduced into Japan from China 13 centuries ago. In Japan, it gradually evolved into a discipline, a kind of sedentary martial art. As such, Go came to be seen as a "dô," or Way of self-realization, and not primarily as a contest of strength, although obviously the best player was honored. Kawabata writes, "The Oriental game has gone beyond game and test of strength and become a way of art. It has about it a certain Oriental mystique and nobility" (117). And he compares it to the Nô drama and the tea ceremony as belonging to "a strange Japanese tradition" (118).[2] With this background in mind, one is less astonished to learn that the champion of the leading school of Go took Buddhist orders and was called the "Honnimbô."

This characteristically Japanese concept of Way has a two-tiered structure. On the one hand, for an activity to support a Way, it must be abstracted from the contingencies of everyday life and constructed as an autonomous "field" with its own logic. Then, this field must become the locus of self-transformation for the agent engaged in activity on it.

The autonomization of Go involves the following features that it shares with other board games:

1. Every move in the game must conform to an explicitly formulated, unambiguous rule.

2. Moves are stripped of semantic content and reduced to unambiguous acts that can be represented diagramatically with precision.

3. The purpose of each move and of the game as a whole is clearly defined and immanent in the rules.

4. The game discriminates between winners and losers by a precise quantitative measure leaving no room for doubt about the outcome.

5. Moves can always be clearly distinguished from other events in the social surroundings of the game, and can therefore be assigned a specific "space" and "time" of play.

6. Insofar as the rules are concerned, players' positions in the game are equivalent in every possible respect, the major and unavoidable exception being the first move.

7. The game is a collaborative performance requiring various forms of reciprocity, from the simplest (alternating and mutually responsive moves) to the most complex (attention to the competitor's state of mind or physical needs).

Two features of this list seem particularly significant. They are the evident care with which ambiguity has been eliminated from the field of play through such means as explicit rules and quantitative measures, and the artificial equalization of the players who, in everyday life, are sure to be subtly differentiated in ways the game ignores. These features of the game indicate its remoteness from the surrounding social world in which ambiguity and inequality are the rule. And by this very token, these features seem to echo strangely our modern notions of scientific and political rationality. We will return to this surprising coincidence.

Autonomy is not an end in itself, but is linked to reflexivity. Because the game can be separated from its environment, its characteristic situations can be endlessly retrieved and studied. Self-criticism, repetition, and practice can refine specialized abilities. Performance can be judged, play can be perfected, and degrees of competence measured in matches.

Reflection not only improves performance but also situates the autonomous game in the player's life process. The act of play is a practice of self-realization modifying the player through discipline. This is the core of the notion of Way; in Western societies the idea of "vocation" plays a similar role, describing the effect on the subject of its own activity in a relatively autonomous domain.

The recontextualizing practice of the game as a Way has the paradoxical effect of reinforcing its autonomy. The game is wholly absorbed in a way of life that is itself wholly absorbed in the game. As Kawabata says of the old Master, he was "a man so disciplined in an art that he had lost the better part of reality" (32).

In effect, what Erving Goffman calls "rules of irrelevance," which anchor attention on play and abstract it from the social surround, have taken over his whole life (20). This is a well-known hazard of the game. There is an ancient Chinese tale of a woodcutter who comes upon two old men playing Go in the forest and stops to watch. Eventually the game ends and the players disappear into thin air. The astonished woodcutter discovers that his own hair has turned white during the play, and the handle of his axe has rotted through. For Kawabata, the game has a demonic quality:

From the veranda outside the players' room, which was ruled by a sort of diabolic tension, I glanced out into the garden, beaten down by the powerful summer sun, and saw a girl of the modern sort insouciantly feeding the carp. I felt as if I were looking at some freak. I could scarcely believe that we belonged to the same world. (27)

No-Mind: The Structure of Conflict

The Way of the game is not about victory but about self-realization through discipline. Kawabata tells the story of two high-ranking young players who ask the advice of a clairvoyant on how to win. "The proper method, said the man, was to lose all awareness of self while awaiting an adversary's play" (42).

One immediately recognizes here the Zen concept of "no-mind" as it appears in Japanese martial arts. It describes the peculiar form of self-forgetfulness involved in effective sport or combat. But this is surely an odd application of Buddhism, a religion of ascetic detachment from the world. As Suzuki explains it in *Zen and Japanese Culture*, "non-attachment" can be extended down to the level of attentive processes, freeing the actor from inhibiting concentration on either self or other. This loosening of focus banishes hesitation and fear and improves fighting performance. "'From this absolute emptiness,' states Takuan, 'comes the most wondrous unfoldment of doing'" (Herrigel 104).[3]

This is not the place to discuss the religious implications of no-mind. What interests me more, in any case, is the structure of the concept that is derived, by a subtle transformation, from the traditional Hindu and Buddhist notion of nonduality. According to the traditional notion, conflict is illusory, as in Emerson's famous poem, "Brahma":

> If the red slayer think he slays,
> Or if the slain think he is slain,
> They know not well the subtle ways
> I keep, and pass, and turn again.
>   (qtd. in Suzuki, *Zen and Japanese Culture* 207)

Borges's story "The Theologians" reaches a similar conclusion. Here is the heavenly coda to this account of a metaphysical dispute that ends tragically with one of the disputants burned at the stake: "In Paradise, Aurelian learned that, for the unfathomable divinity, he and John of Pannonia (the orthodox believer and the heretic, the abhorrer and the abhorred, the accuser and the accused) formed one single person" (126).

These works appear to invite us to occupy a "third" position above the fray: the "I" of Brahma or the theologians' God. Presumably, if the swordsmen and the theologians could occupy this position themselves, their strife would cease, and they would be reconciled in perfect understanding.

The doctrine of no-mind agrees that apparent dualities reveal a more fundamental unity. But what makes it so interesting is the elimination of the third position. It is conflict itself which is shown to be prior to the parties it joins, an underlying unity of which they are mere projections. True nonduality, therefore, cannot be achieved by *observing* the conflicts in which others are plunged, no matter how dialectically. Such an observer would still stand in dualistic opposition to its object.

Rather, no-mind is a particular way of living duality, an existential position *within* it, and not a modality of knowledge transcending it. Hence, the Zen master's reply to the impertinent question of how the enlightened deal with hunger and cold: "When hungry, I eat, and when cold I put on more clothes" (Suzuki, *Zen Doctrine of No-Mind* 75).

This reply indicates why Zen turned out to be peculiarly available to the martial arts and, ultimately, I will argue below, to literature as well. For this doctrine, the goal is not to rise above conflict in reconciliation but to achieve total identification with the context of struggle in the very course of playing one's own conflictual role. If conflict can be transcended, it must be from within, without setting up a third consciousness above the fight.

The same point can be made in relation to Go. Insofar as the players identify completely with the situation of the board, i.e., with the "whole," they can assume their role unreservedly and carry it out apart from any concern with survival or victory. This no-mind is not a mystical unconsciousness, but a consciousness that has become one with the formal requirements of the activity frame and that sees its role within that frame as in some sense "logically" entailed rather than personally motivated.

Good play thus has nothing to do with one-sided personal aggression; at the height of the most intense competition, the players are joined in harmony in the construction of the board, much as singers respond to each other in a piece of complex choral music. Their unity, expressed in their mutually responsive moves, takes precedence over their struggle. Ultimately, they "form one single person."

The Pattern Disturbed

In Japanese culture, the pursuit of self-realization through a Way manifests itself aesthetically, in this instance as the beauty of the board on which the dance of adversaries produces a magnificent and complex pattern. Of course, the aim of Go is to win; however, Japanese commentators always note that this aim is transcended by a higher interest in the aesthetic achievement of "harmony" and pattern. Go is the collaborative production of aesthetic form through competitive play. Both moments—collaboration and competition—are equally important, for without struggle there is no beauty. The weak player who offers no resistance is incapable of collaborating in the production of a satisfying board, full of symmetry and surprise. There is thus a promise of aesthetic redemption contained in the hard-fought game; Kawabata's novel is the story of the betrayal of that promise by the modern focus on victory and defeat for its own sake.[4]

That new focus becomes apparent in the climactic move of the great match of 1938. After many months of difficult play, interrupted by the illness of the Master, the game seems perfectly poised with no advantage to either side. A struggle breaks out in the center of the board that promises to be decisive. As the day comes to an end, the challenger, Otaké, seems unsure of his course. He writes his final play of the day—move 121—on a card and seals it in an envelope, to be opened by the referees the following morning, and with that the players retire (Diagram 4).

When the seal is broken at the next session, the move is not in the central battlefield at all, but strikes at the Master far away near the top of the board. Yet it compels at least a brief response of the housekeeping sort; it resembles the move the disadvantaged player makes away from a "kô" to distract the adversary with a sharp diversionary blow. Soon the players return to the center of

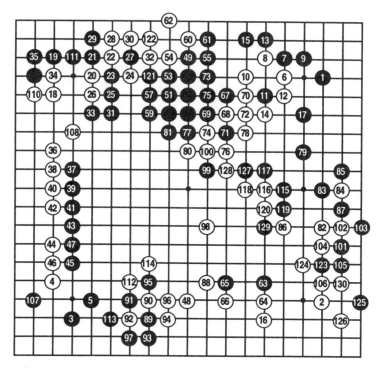

Diagram 4.

the board where the Master plays poorly, making the mistake that costs him the game.

What is the meaning of this incident? The organizers of the match granted each player 40 hours to consider their moves. Sealing the final move of the day is supposed to prevent the players from adding the time between sessions to this already generous total. But by tying the master up for a turn with his trivial sealed play, Otaké appears to have frozen the most important action so as to have a leisurely look at it overnight. The Master is convinced that Otaké used the sealed play to gain time to reflect on the difficult position in the center of the board, time he desparately needed as he was rapidly using up his allotment.

Despite the suspicious appearance of move 121, it is not certain that the challenger actually used it to gain unfair advantage. Although at one point the narrator says that Otaké "would avert defeat even if in the process he must chew the stones to bits," he is not portrayed unsympathetically (178). He is even described as reading the *Lotus Sutra* to calm himself before playing. And the narrator, who is full of admiration for the Master, also respects his challenger and, at one point, intervenes effectively to prevent him from forfeiting the match.

This ambiguous situation crystallizes the action of the novel. And because the human significance of the climactic move is ambiguous, the specificity and the concreteness of the actual play persists even after the novel appears to assign it a meaning. It remains, in fact, a permanent stumbling block to final interpretation, an ambiguous intersection of the multiple codes that structure the novel.

But whether Otaké made good use of the extra hours or not is ultimately irrelevant since the Master is so upset by the sealed play that he can no longer concentrate properly on the game. The challenger's apparent thrust toward victory disturbs the pattern and undermines the spiritual significance of the game. It is as though the delicate work of producing the board, which has as its secondary consequence victory and defeat for the players, was interrupted by a mere tug of war in which participants have no conscious relation at all to the combined effects of their labors and no purpose other than winning. The incident brings out into the open the potential conflict between collaborative and competitive dimensions of the game and thus between its roles in supporting a Way and in discriminating between winners and losers.

Because the Master is upset, his feelings come out momentarily in the presence of the reporter. Kawabata writes,

> The Master had put the match together as a work of art. It was as if the work, likened to a painting, were smeared black at the moment of highest tension. That play of black upon white, white upon black, has the intent and takes the forms of creative art. It has in it a flow of the spirit and a harmony as of music. Everything is lost when suddenly a false note is struck, or one party in a duet suddenly launches forth on an eccentric flight of his own. A masterpiece of a game can be ruined by insensitivity to the feelings of an adversary. (164)

Later the Master has his doubts or in any case is more reticent. His published account of the game, like that of the new champion, contains no criticism of this decisive move, which, despite its odd timing, is perfectly ordinary in other respects. Thus, the waves quickly cover over the suspicions that ruined the match; all rally around to protect the image of their art.

Meta-Rules: Etiquette or Equity

Modernity does not introduce rationality into social life for the first time. Every culture has domains governed by formal rules. These rules can be considered "rational" in the sociological sense of the term on two conditions: first, that they employ tests of experience or impose principles of equivalence, implication, or optimization on action, and second, that they do so with an unusual degree of precision. So it is, for example, with accounting rules designed to insure the equality of income and outgo, or legal rules that affix punishments to crimes, or the rules of Go that create a domain in which the difference between better and worse play is not open to dispute.

Although the production of such domains is not characteristically modern but essentially human, modernity can nevertheless be clearly distinguished from every other type of society. In modern societies certain of these formally rational activities are liberated from recontextualizing strategies that reconcile them with traditional rituals and social distinctions. In the case of a game like Go, potential conflicts between the requirements of the one and the other are resolved in advance by what I will call "meta-rules" that regulate the social relations of the players congruent with the requirements of play.

In the old Japan, etiquette inscribed agents' identity in all their activities without exception. The constraints of etiquette were perhaps more strongly felt in this society than one can imagine in the West. True or not, only in Japan could the story be told of the feudal general who washed and perfumed his hair before battle in case, in the event of defeat, his decapitated head were to be presented to the victor and the ladies of his court.

Etiquette recontextualizes formally rational activities to insure that they take a subordinate place in a world ordered according to quite different principles, e.g., ranking by age, which relates all human activity to the mortality of the agents and their role in family life. Deference in this context not only expresses a social prejudice but *contains* the socially dangerous equalizing potential of formal rationality.[5]

This cultural framework had completely enveloped Go in complicated quasi-religious rituals until the match of 1938. That match marks the breakdown of an older vision of the game as a spiritual discipline and the emergence of a new one in which it is essentially a test of strength. The processes of modernization that had been gnawing at traditional Japanese culture in every domain since the Meiji Restoration finally reached this odd holdout that had been ignored until then.

The modalities of this shift are linked to what I will call the textuality of Go as a board game. The decontextualized character of the play, which suits it to be a Way, also makes it possible to define the state of the game at any moment by simply recounting the sequence of moves. In fact, games resemble writing in that they produce an object that can be separated from any particular material support, such as a piece of paper or a board, and circulated as a system of signs.

The quasi-textual nature of the game suits it for dissemination through a newspaper. Like his earlier reporting, Kawabata's novel dramatizes the Go match, the twists and turns of which it follows exactly despite the poetic license he took with many human details. This exactitude is in itself significant: the narrator is a reporter, like Kawabata, and the same kinds of charts that appeared in the newspaper articles are reproduced throughout the novel.

The involvement of a newspaper in the championship match results in a significant shift in emphasis. The game, which used to be a unique spiritual performance, is reduced to a mechanically retrievable spectacle, a "match." Of course, there was always an element of show in it, but a transformation occurs when mediated mass spectatorship replaces the burdensome ritual of personally following the players to their meeting place and remaining silent in their presence. Newspaper readers are in immediate contact only with the contextless chart of the unfolding game, the thrust and parry of successive moves, the final drive toward victory, all of which can be printed exactly as played. This change, made possible by the formal autonomy of the game, eliminates its "aura," and diminishes interest in it as a Way, which now becomes a kind of folklore or ornament of the record in the press (Benjamin 224–25).

The newspaper and its readers are less interested in these traditional aspects of the game than in its fairness, so new meta-rules are introduced designed to ensure the victory of the better player. "The modern way was to insist upon doing battle under conditions of abstract justice, even when challenging the Master himself" (52). The uniformity of the game, in which nothing distinguishes the players but the color of their stones, must be reflected in their roles in play. The social institution that corresponds to this notion of equity is the contract, and the organization of the match is therefore settled contractually.

Several of these new rules are imitated from Western chess, such as time limits on play and sealed plays at the end of the day. The players are even sequestered to prevent outsiders from contributing advice. Of this code, with its cold rationalism, Kawabata says, "It later came to seem like a foreshadowing of death" (58).

One could hardly object to such conditions, especially not if, as one of the players, he wished to receive the generous rewards for playing the game under conditions that would increase newspaper sales. Yet these new rules ran roughshod over precious Japanese sensitivities in their exclusive concentration on the question "Who is the best player?"

Traditional etiquette prescribed not an equal but an unequal relationship between the older and the younger player, the champion and his challenger. Accordingly, the Invincible Master had the right to expect that his age and eminence would be recognized not merely through outward signs of respect but through obedience to his decisions about the play, the length and timing of sessions, and related matters. There is a certain conflict of interest implied in this arrangement, but the Master's position is too visible and his responsibility too heavy for him to abuse his power. Considerations of honor limit the asymmetry between the players. Was it not rude, then, to place them both on an equal footing? Was it not demeaning to the art of Go to imply, by imposing these rules, that the players are mainly interested in victory? Was finding out who plays best important enough to excuse these offenses?

In one sense, the answer is obvious. Kawabata's narrator is a good newspaperman and knows all the dirt, even on the Old Master. He does not hide from us that the Master abused his discretion to avoid a match with his challenger's teacher, Suzuki, who might well have beaten him. One of his disciples is suspected of having whispered the winning move to the Master in a previous match. And worst of all, he treated his own position as "a commercial asset" and "sold his last match to a newspaper at a price without precedent" (53). So much for virtuous old Japan!

And yet the narrator nevertheless describes the Master as "forever true and clean," which he is by comparison with slick modern players (109). Kawabata explains that the disappearance of favoritism is not the innocent gesture it appears to be, for, "New rules bring new tactics" (165). And he notes,

> When a law is made, the cunning that finds loopholes goes to work. One cannot deny that there is a certain slyness among younger players, a slyness which, when rules are written to prevent slyness, makes use of the rules themselves. (54)

The sealed play containing move 121 is an example.

Rules that claim universality in the equal treatment of all are applied in a world of particular circumstances. Far from standing above the struggle, they end up being instrumentalized in individual strategies as means to the end of victory. The shrewd grasp of loopholes in the new rules replaces the honest subtlety of the really insightful player. Thus, the ideal of fairness as a quasi-mechanical equality between players is never achieved. Once again, therefore, one must rely on the force of honor to restrain abuse. But now honor has been weakened by the alibi of conformity to the letter of the rules which takes its place in the modern mind.

There is a further unfortunate consequence of the introduction of the new rules: the loss of aesthetic values. Etiquette is, of course, extrinsic to the structure of play itself and as such may interfere with the logic of the game. But, in fact, the novel is not about the struggle between ascriptive values, such as age, and a new achievement-oriented ethos. Far from emphasizing the unfairness and distortions deference causes, the novel presents etiquette as a context of play uniquely suited to bringing out the aesthetic achievement of a truly heroic match. Meanwhile, it is the orientation toward success that is shown to distort play through introducing extraneous considerations that depend on mere technicalites. The narration thus deconstructs the opposition of ascription and achievement.

The novel lets us understand that the mere establishment of the bureaucratic framework already marked the Master for defeat. It is not just that he is bound to be less clever than a younger man at manipulating the system. No, it is more the distrust embodied in the very nature of the rules which was bound at some point to demoralize and upset him beyond endurance. Against this background some event was sure to cast doubt on the position and lead to the collapse of the Master's spirit. Kawabata writes,

> It may be said that the Master was plagued in his last match by modern rationalism, to which fussy rules were everything, from which all the grace and elegance of Go as art had disappeared, which quite dispensed with respect for elders and attached no importance to mutual respect as human beings. From the way of Go the beauty of Japan and the Orient had fled. (52)

Because etiquette privileges the collaborative over the competitive dimension of play, it opens up a space within which the aesthetic ideal of Way can flourish. But in the new Japan, the social context of play is a matter of simple fairness, abstracted from all personal considerations. Fairness projects other aspects of the game, such as equality and struggle, into the social environment. When social activity is treated as a mere competition, the structure of the game, with its clear decision between winners and losers, reaches out to simplify life itself.

Layers of Meaning

Such ideas were accessible to many Japanese writers and intellectuals, caught in the midst of a modernizing movement they lived simultaneously as a response to both the Universal—scientific truth—and the Particular—Western power. How does Kawabata develop such a dialectic in his novel? *The Master of Go* is based on multiplying codes in terms of which to interpret an apparently simple move in a game. The order and connection of meanings at each level parallels that at the other levels. The same action can be identified at all levels, unchanged except in terms of its contextualization and significance. It is not possible to order these levels causally, to explain one level by another because each has its own "logic." Such multi-layered entanglements are characteristic of formalized fields. Double or triple meanings can always be constructed around any act which has an apparently technical or formal motive in terms of its involvement with its social environment.[6]

The novel is an attempt to understand and encompass the increasingly intrusive lower levels of the dialectic, privileged by modernity, in a higher aesthetic form. The game is a formal-rational system that can be isolated from its practical context as a set of spatial coordinates, a chart. Recontextualized as a performance, the abstract chart is animated by a practice of play; it becomes *this* particular game played by these players in a definite time and place. A completely self-sufficient account of the action is possible at the level of the game, its rules, and the strategy of play, and such an account is plausibly offered in official published descriptions of the game.

Of course, there is always more going on than is deemed fit for presentation in such publications. The novel takes us behind the scenes by revealing the psychological meaning of the player's actions. At this level, the game appears as a structure of social relations, mixing respect, fairness, aggression, and anxiety in a surprisingly complicated narrative flow.

But even this description is incomplete; it abstracts from a still wider context—the social background. The players, after all, are not isolated beings but members of a society. The game is thus further encompassed in the wider practical field of social, cultural, and historical meanings animating the play. These meanings reflect the different meta-rules of etiquette and equity with their different emphases on Way and winning.

The conflict between the newspaper's rules and the old etiquette reflects a larger historical conflict dramatized in the match. The Honnimbô Shusai was not just a Go champion, but the champion of a dying civilization, the old Japan, a world in which a certain kind of aristocratic idealism and aestheticism prevailed over modern worries about success and money. For the Master, the game is the occasion for an aesthetic revelation beyond any merely personal contest. But in modern times there is no longer any "margin for remembering the dignity and the fragrance of Go as an art," and the challenger plays simply to win (52). As Kawabata writes, "The Master seemed like a relic left behind by Meiji" (63). In fact he died shortly after the finish of the match. His challenger, however decent a man, was the agent of the modern world. His victory would mean the end of the old Japan and the emergence of a new spirit, dominated by business and the media.

For Kawabata the 1938 championship match was thus emblematic of the modernization of Japan. He repeats the usual contrast between modernity and tradition familiar from Japanese literature: the struggle between ideals and interests, feeling and reason, beauty and power, etc. But despite the clichés, his narrator cannot entirely disapprove of the modern; it will bring, he says, "new vitality in the world of Go" (145).

If the narrator is ambivalent, the novel as a whole tends, as we have seen, to soften the epochal differences between its two principle characters. No doubt we are intended to discount the rumours about the Master and to believe the worst of his challenger. But the ambiguities indicate that the problem of modernization is not just about psychology or ethics; the game has different potentialities that are reflected in historically typical forms of personality. The personal level thus depends on an underlying change in the place of the game in social life.[7] A perfectly respectable move from one standpoint is an outrage from the other. The players are in effect playing different games. Their encounter must lead to a profound misunderstanding, a conflict of "doubles" in which each participant operates according to a different code.[8]

It is the journalist narrator who carries the burden of explaining these larger implications. He can do so because he embodies in his person the very ambiguity of the match. On the one hand, just as the Master reduces himself to nothing before the game, so the narrator says, "I reduced myself to nothing as I gazed at the Master" (115). On the other hand, his relation to Otaké is characterized by egalitarian affection and esteem. His doubleness reflects the doubleness of Japan itself (Pilarcik 16–17).

The profound ambiguity of the narrator's identity opens a space that encompasses all the lower fields in a sort of literary no-mind. In his Nobel Prize Acceptance Speech, Kawabata endorses such a view of his writing. He quotes the poet Saigyô: "Confronted with all the varied forms of nature, his eyes and his ears were filled with emptiness. And were not the words that came forth true words?" And he concludes, "My own works have been described as works of emptiness" (*Japan, the Beautiful and Myself* 42, 43).

Aestheticism, East and West

The Master of Go represents a type of aesthetic critique in which Japanese spirit survives outside of history, as a peculiar and quite contingent doubt haunting triumphant modernity and revealing its limits. Perhaps this is the sort of thing Tanizaki foresaw already in 1933 when he wrote his famous essay *In Praise of Shadows*. Despairing of the survival of traditional Japanese culture under the brightness of electric light, he writes,

> I have thought that there might still be somewhere, possibly in literature or the arts, where something could be saved. I would call back at least for literature this world of shadows we are losing. In the mansion called literature I would have the eaves deep and the walls dark, I would push back into the shadows the things that come forward too clearly, I would strip away the useless decoration. I do not ask that this be done everywhere, but perhaps we may be allowed at least one mansion where we can turn off the electric lights and see what it is like without them. (42)

The aestheticism of these Japanese writers has interesting similarities with the early Lukács' theory of novelistic irony as a kind of "negative mysticism."[9] The coincidence is important because it suggests a still wider context for Kawabata's critique of modernity: the novelistic tradition. Furthermore, Lukács' theory indicates a way of distinguishing Kawabata's novels, as aesthetic forms, from mere sentimental nostalgia for the past.

According to Lukács, the novel is the original and most profound critique of modernity. That critique, at least in the French and Russian novels Lukács took for typical, is aesthetic rather than moral or political. These novels are the product of an irony that is half within, half without the conflicts of the world. The novelist neither stands in polemic opposition to modern society on the ground of tradition or passion—usually exemplified in the hero— nor justifies modernization and its costs with a "grand narrative" ending in the present or leading to a shining future. Indeed, were the writer to identify purely and simply with either the world or the hero, the novel would lapse into the pamphlet or the lyric.

Novelistic irony is thus peculiarly ambivalent. On the one hand, it demystifies modernity's claim to universality by revealing the contrast between the facade and the realities of economic, political, and legal institutions. Often (in Dickens or Balzac, for example) this leads to a certain sentimentalizing of tradition. But, on the other hand, the novel's ironic structure subverts any idea of a return to the past by showing how deeply tradition has been intertwined with modernity. Indeed, tradition, like other hopeless ideals the heroes oppose to modernity, serves primarily as a marker for an impossible transcendence which can only be indicated *from within* the tensions and oppositions of society. The novelist may seem to take sides, but his irony nevertheless situates him in what Lukács calls a "transcendendental place" from which alone the whole is visible.

Formally, this ironic stance resembles the consciousness of Way, the no-mind that plays its role to the fullest while identifying with the whole to which it contributes its conflictual share. Just so, Kawabata's narrator sides nostalgically with the old Master and yet manages to depict the contradictions of Japanese tradition and Western modernity in a way that avoids tendentious polemic. He is a mysteriously neutral observer of the real struggle of the book, which produces the aesthetic patterns suitable to literary representation, the graceful move and countermove in a conflict of cultures. To depict this struggle in a "work of emptiness" is to transcend the opposition of tradition and modernity aesthetically. Lukacs' remarkable intuition of the novel's religious content is confirmed by this echo from another culture.[10]

There is, however, an important difference between Western and non-Western forms of ironic consciousness of modernity. In the West, one typical heroic type embodies ideals from the past that are doomed by social advance. But the old Master, a similar heroic type depicted in a non-Western setting, exemplifies not merely the tragedy of historical lag, but a contemporary clash of cultures. That clash takes place in the context of Western cultural imperialism in which Japan appears doomed to defeat, not so much because its time has come as because it has met a superior force that has acquired a corresponding but perhaps undeserved prestige. The later development of Japanese society shows how important it is not to overlook this difference.

Today, in a world in which Japan has become a leading industrial power, we can ask whether the continuing signs of the vitality of Japanese culture do not refute the aestheticizing pessimism of Japanese authors such as Tanizaki and Kawabata. Their position belonged to the period of cultural trauma that began with the Meiji restoration and culminated in the Occupation.

The novel prospered as a literary form during this period. It opened a space within which Western modernity could be exposed in its particularity without regression to discredited theological or ideological prejudices. Its structure was thus modern even though the surface message was often traditionalist. But if the novel, an imported form after all, could achieve such critical distance from its Western origins, why despair of the possibility that similar adaptations and amalgams might occur in other spheres, giving rise to a specifically Japanese form of modern society?

This speculation recalls a rich tradition of reflection on the possibility of alternative modernities that has been invoked since the 1930s to explain how Japan can preserve its cultural originality inside the modern project rather than through reactionary retreat (Nishida, "The Problem of Japanese Culture," and Ohashi). Despite Kawabata's despair over the apparent defeat of this prospect, it can find an ambiguous support in the underlying structure of his novel. It shows us that modernity too is a culture, or, as we will see, several possible cultures confronting each other through a process of generalized "contamination" (Vattimo 158).

Cultural Genealogy

What is meant by the notion of an alternative modernity, and is it really plausible? What I will call the "content approach" to alternative modernity emphasizes such ethnic and ideological differences as the kinds of food people eat, the role of family or religion, the legal forms of property and administration, and so on. These distinctions are weak bases for an alternative because modernization, as we have learned since Weber at least, consists precisely in erasing or incorporating such ethnic and ideological contents in a convergent model of civilization. The universalist view, which uncritically confounds Westernization and modernization, is still persuasive compared to this.

If there can be an alternative modernity, it must be based not on such contents but on deeper differences in cultural forms. Nietzsche's "genealogical" method suggests an approach because it succeeds in following the progress of a way of life from one historical period to the next. Judeo-Christianity, in this Nietzschean sense, is not a particular religion but a way of being in the world that can reappear in different ideological and institutional guises over thousands of years of history. Nietzsche would claim that this form is still active in the West as capitalism, socialism, and democracy.

Inspired directly or indirectly by Nietzsche, other philosophers such as Heidegger and Derrida have developed far-reaching models of the most fundamental metaphysical assumptions of Western culture. These philosophers tend to assume tacitly that modern institutions and technical rationality are essentially incompatible with other cultures.[11] As "postmodernity" or "multiculturalism," this view leads to a revalorization of tradition and ethnic particularity, and in the worst case collapses back into the content approach Nietzsche should rather help us to transcend.

The Master of Go practically invites such a traditionalist reading, at least to Westerners who tend to see in it a struggle between Japanese particularity and the universality of modern culture. On those terms, Kawabata would be arguing that etiquette, self-realization, and aesthetics are substantive ends that must be sacrificed for instrumental efficiency in a modern society.

This interpretation of the novel agrees with a commonplace universalist view of Japanese culture as different precisely insofar as it is still essentially feudal. These survivals presumably will dissipate as modernization proceeds (Morley 19). Of course, it is harder to believe this today than it was when the theory was originally proposed by Marxists in the 1930s. Now that Japan is the most advanced capitalist country, it seems unlikely that feudalism could be alive and well there, but the universalist view is still widely held by many observers who find Japanese culture oppressive and authoritarian.

Kawabata's novel appears deceptively compatible with the universalist framework because the old Japanese values it endorses share the pathos and fragility of the Master whose defeat marks the entry of Japan into modernity. But despite this, the novel is incompatible with the Weberian framework. Its Japanese elements are not merely substantive "contents" sacrificed to formal rationality since they include a specific strategic practice of the game. Thus, the fateful necessity of the outcome does not flow smoothly from an Enlightenment grand narrative of progress, even in Weber's disillusioned form.

In sum, it is not easy to fit Kawabata's novel into the currently fashionable paradigm of ethnic protest against totalitarian rationality. I believe that Kawabata is not so much a defender of particularity against universality as he is a critic of the pretensions of false universality. In this too he is true to the novelistic tradition as Lukács defined it.

The reorganization of Go around Western notions of fairness is not a move from particular to universal but merely shifts the balance of power in favor of a new type of player. As deference falls, it carries down with it the values of self-realization and aesthetics that flourish in the context of traditional etiquette. Henceforth, Go will be played more as a business than as a spiritual discipline. The best player, in the sense of the one who produces the most perfect game, will be replaced by the player who is best at winning—not precisely the same thing as we have seen.

Reflection on Kawabata's novel thus shows the limits of the identification of rationality with Western culture and offers starting points for a genealogy of non-Western cultural forms investing the process of modernization and altering its direction. From that standpoint, the progress of Japanese modernity would roughly parallel Western developments, which saw the emergence of new secular expressions of basic cultural forms amidst the gradual decline of the feudal-Christian tradition that had once been a vigorous expression of that same culture (Dore).

Admittedly, given the recentness of the opening and modernization of Japan, there inevitably hangs a certain ambiguity over its situation. It is difficult to decide the relative importance of survivals as opposed to the more basic cultural forms. That ambiguity emerges as a central theme of Kawabata's novel. I want to turn now to the task of unraveling it.

The Culture of Place

To this end, I will focus briefly on the category of "place" which plays such an important role in Japanese philosophy and social thought.[12] This notion underlies the concept of no-mind which we have seen at work in Kawabata's novel. As a general cultural phenomenon, it articulates an everyday experience available to every member of the society. This is the experience of seeking one's "place" in the system of social relations in which one finds oneself.

It would be easy to assimilate this category to the notion of social status and to treat it as evidence of the persistence of hierarchy in Japanese culture. This is Chie Nakane's famous theory of the *tate shakai* (vertical society) which is proposed to explain Japan's success in the modern world (Nakane). This theory has come in for much criticism because of its implicit appeal to culture to justify submission to authority (Dale 44–45). It is tempting to reject the whole notion of place as an artifact of an ideologically contaminated cultural theory, a pseudo-traditionalism in the service of rampant exploitation.

The ambiguities of Nakane's social theory are similar to those we encountered in *The Master of Go*. In both cases a quasi-feudal deference is joined to the rational manipulation of a formal system (economics, Go). But, if anything, the novelist is a more provocative observer than the social theorist. He enables us to see clearly the unique formal rationality that is already present in traditional Japanese culture. This raises the question of whether values and practices linked to that rational dimension of the traditional culture might survive the disappearance of the old deference and accommodate themselves to modern conditions.

This is not a question that occurs to Kawabata, but I would like to consider whether the logic of place may not be independent of traditional authoritarianism. It seems to be built into the structure of Japanese culture and language at a much more basic level than differences in prestige or power and signifies a far wider range of distinguishing attributes attached to the various "places" occupied by the individuals. Perhaps, like Western individualism, it is a cultural form in the broad genealogical sense capable of reproducing itself across epochal institutional changes, including changes in the distribution and exercise of authority.

There is considerable evidence for this interpretation. For example, the Japanese language (like several other Asian languages) requires one to choose pronouns, verb forms, and forms of address which reflect differences in age, gender, and status that might be signified only tacitly, for example, by dress in the West. There is a clear enough distinction between the way in which men and women speak—one of the most important differences of place— that some grammar books actually offer dialogues in both male and female versions. Masculine and feminine speech no doubt reflect gender hierarchy, but they are experienced as exemplifying the whole range of connotations of masculinity and feminity, not merely an authority relation. A similar observation applies to formal language which persists despite the rapid softening of distinctions in social rank (Miller).

Linguistic coding appears to add tremendous force to social differences or perhaps reflects an unusual force present in social reality. The Japanese belong to a culture in which you have to know your place in the social setting in order to open your mouth. This can be quite inhibiting for them when they first arrive in the West and speak a language like French or English that does not offer any obvious way of signifying place.

The notion of place does not imply unquestioning submission to the authority of social superiors. In institutions such as companies and government agencies a good deal of attention is paid to building consensus through group discussion. When things go smoothly, such consensus building is a two-way street that constrains the authorities as well as subordinates.

Naturally, things do not always go smoothly. Self-assertion is necessary in many situations, and while it is often more restrained than it would be in the West, the Japanese certainly did not have to await the arrival of Western individualism to discover it. It is already present in their own culture, but qualified and concretized by the demands of place rather than conceived, as typically it would be in the West, in universal terms as role transcendence. Place is thus not about whether one plays one's own game, but about who one is and how, accordingly, that game must be played.

Place not only shapes everyday speech and social relations but also religion and art. As we have seen, Japanese martial arts have evolved into spiritual disciplines in part under the impact of this concept, reinterpreted through the Buddhist concept of no-mind. The combatants are trained to concern themselves less with winning than with immediately and swiftly interpreting their place in the system of moves so as perfectly to fulfill situational requirements. In aesthetic terms, each gesture of combat is part of a pair, the other part of which must be and can be supplied only by the adversary. Every move in the game is in some deeper sense an element of a larger pattern produced through the collaborative competition of the players. In these artistic and religious applications of place, it is especially clear that traditional authority relations overlay a more fundamental cultural form that could perhaps survive without them.

Place and Alternative Modernity

Something like this martial approach to place is at work in Kawabata's depiction of the traditional game of Go, with its emphasis on the values of self-realization and aesthetics. He contrasts a way of life, based on playing out one's position in a larger system, with the Western focus on fairness and winning.

The difference between the two is not that one is tradition-bound while the other concentrates on the logic of play. Both are totally involved in the logic of play; both are therefore "rational" in the broad sense, although one emphasizes aspects of play most relevant to a culture of place and the other emphasizes aspects that complement an individualistic culture.

The novel shows us two alternative ways of playing Go constructed around different formal dimensions of the game. Both ways aim at victory but under different aspects. The Western emphasis on equality stems from the equivalence of "sides" in the game, which does indeed conflict with traditional deference. But the Japanese concern with aesthetics is not opposed to the formal rationality of the game; it realizes another immanent dimension of it, the essential dependence of the players exemplified in the thrust and parry of struggle.

The aesthetic values that predominate in traditional Japanese play are thus not extrinsic to the essence of the game but rather represent dimensions of it that only appear clearly in a non-Western context. Nor are these values merely particularistic. Aesthetics is usually understood as a matter of subjective taste, but mathematical and technical systems have aesthetic qualities rooted in objective rationality. A glance at any Go textbook immediately shows this to be true of games as well. The aesthetics of Go flow from the conditions of formally rational action just as rigorously as the values of the young challenger while fulfilling a very different cultural agenda.

Here modernity defeats tradition not because it is more rational, but because it is better at manipulating the new meta-rules set up to institutionalize rationality and because it is more ruthlessly oriented toward winning at any price, even if it means sacrificing the intrinsic rationality of the game, i.e., the production of a unique sequence of optimal moves in terms of the position of the pieces on the board. Kawabata reestablishes the symmetry between tradition and modernity by showing that success as such is no more rational than deference. Both are external to the inner logic of play, differing primarily in which aspects of that logic they privilege.

In sum, certain traditional values possess at least as much "universality" as the supposedly modern value of fairness. In a sense, what the novel achieves, perhaps without entirely intending it, is to present two alternative types of rationality, each of which is a candidate for modernity, although only one is triumphant, only one actually organizes a modern society.

We have here a model for thinking about alternative modernity. Japan is a good test case because it combines a very alien culture and a very familiar technology and institutional framework. As rational systems, technologies, markets, democratic voting, and so on resemble the game of Go: they too can be practiced differently in different cultural settings. In this context, Japanese culture is not an irrational intrusion but rather differs by its emphasis on different aspects of technical rationality which, as we have seen, includes self-realization and aesthetics as well as the narrow pursuit of success ethnocentrically identified with it in the West.[13] So, in Kawabata's match each move obeys the same rules but has a different significance in the different systems that invest it. Different cultures inhabit the board and influence its pattern of development.

Perhaps all modern institutions and modern technology itself are similarly layered with cultural meanings. Where a vigorous culture, whether it be old or new, manages to take hold of modernity, it can influence the evolution of its rational systems. Alternative modernities may emerge, distinguished not just by increasingly marginal features such as food, culture, style, or political ideals but by the central institutions of technology and administration.

Perhaps Kawabata's elegy was premature, and something like this is already beginning to occur in Japan. A number of experts have attempted to show that the Japanese economy draws on unique cultural resources to achieve extraordinarily high levels of motivation and effectiveness (Dore). They point to the importance in Japan of ideals of belonging, service, quality, and vocation by contrast with which the individualistic West appears ethically handicapped.

Unlike certain forms of deference which seem to be in the sort of steep decline Kawabata deplored, these ideals are not survivals doomed by the process of modernization; rather, they are the specific forms in which Japanese culture invests modernity. Indeed, the prevalence of these values may account for both the strengths and weaknesses of the Japanese model. Industrial societies too can use a maximum of vocational self-consciousness, attention to the whole, and collaborative competition. But modern political systems function best when they rid themselves of the conformism and deference that still characterizes the essentially bureaucratic ethos of the Japanese state. Hence the peculiar combination of effective economics and mediocre politics that characterizes this model (Van Wolferen).

What remains to be seen is how far the process of culturally specific modernization will go and how much transformation the Western technical heritage will suffer as Japan liberates itself more and more from its original dependency on the Western model of modernity.

Notes

1. For more on Go, see Korschelt.
2. For Kawabata's relation to this tradition, see his Nobel Prize Acceptance Speech (*Japan, the Beautiful and Myself*), and Petersen, 129–32.
3. The reader interested in the concept of no-mind should consult Suzuki (*The Zen Doctrine of No-Mind*), the chapters on swordsmanship in Suzuki (*Zen and Japanese Culture*), and Herrigel. See also Loy, especially p. 123, for the issue of the "third" point of view discussed below.
4. It is important not to miss the specific emphasis on winning characteristic of traditional play. Ritual is, of course, significant for it to a degree that differentiates it from modern play, but it would be wrong to describe it as formalistic in opposition to a modern instrumental interest in victory. One would have the same problem distinguishing formal from instrumental motives in evaluating bull fighting. And the same confusion Kawabata describes would arise, but in a ridiculous form, if a new style were introduced that consisted in shooting the bull.
5. Other recontextualizations are, of course, possible. For example, in the course of history, technical systems have frequently been incorporated into social life through guilds. Socialism might be interpreted as the demand for a similar recontextualization of modern technology in democratic forms. See Feenberg (*Critical Theory of Technology* chap. 7).
6. Cf. Latour:

> If you take any black box and make a freeze-frame of it, you may consider the system of alliances it knits together in two different ways: first, by looking at who it is designed to enroll; second, by considering what it is tied to so as to make the enrollment inescapable. We may on the one hand draw its *sociogram*, and on the other its *technogram*. (138)

"Black box" here refers to facts and artifacts produced by scientific and technological research and development. They have an inextricably intertwined social and scientific-technical logic. (The equivalent in Go would be the results of a match.) In my book, I called this a "double aspect" theory (*Critical Theory* 81–82).
7. Pilarcik offers a skillful analysis of the various ways in which characterization is used to express the epochal transition. See especially her description of the players use of time (12–13) and their strategies (14–15). Cf. Thomas Swann (105–06). But for a novel in which the same transition is treated as *essentially* a matter of changing character, compare Endo.
8. The concept of doubles employed here derives from René Girard. For more on his approach, and applications to the role of economics in the novel, see Feenberg ("Fetishism and Form").
9. Lukács:

> The writer's irony is a negative mysticism to be found in times without a god. It is an attitude of *docta ignorantia* towards meaning, a portrayal of the kindly and malicious workings of the demons, a refusal to comprehend more than the mere fact of these workings; and in it

there is the deep certainty, expressible only by form-giving, that through not-desiring-to-know and not-being-able-to-know he has truly encountered, glimpsed and grasped the ultimate, true substance, the present, non-existent God. This is why irony is the objectivity of the novel. (90)

For an extended discussion of this passage, see Bernstein (195 and ff.).

10. In the larger context of contemporary world literature, the novelistic turn is reached by different peoples at times reflecting comparable levels of development and carried out with means supplied by their cultures. Thus, behind the similarity of the Hungarian Lukács and the Japanese Kawabata, writing a generation apart, lies a deeper cause in the rhythms of modernization in different parts of the world. It is perhaps no coincidence that the Iwakura Mission, which visited Europe during 1871–1873 in search of insight into how to modernize Japan focused on the example of Hungary, a country that seemed to point the way. Their report notes: "The various nations who today are delayed in their enlightenment will be deeply impressed by studying the circumstances of Hungary" (Soviak 15). The artistic and theoretical opening made possible by the novel corresponds to a moment of critique in a process of development undergone by both countries.

11. For a useful evaluation of related issues, see Johann Arnason.

12. See Nishida ("The Problem of Japanese Culture" and *An Inquiry into the Good*), Abe, Watsuji, and Berque.

13. For more on the different moments of technical rationality, see Feenberg (*Critical Theory* chap. 8).

Works Cited

Abe, Maso. "Nishida's Philosophy of 'Place.'" *International Philosophical Quarterly* 28.4 (1991): 355–71.

Arnason, Johann. "Modernity, Postmodernity and the Japanese Experience." Unpublished essay, 1992.

Benjamin, Walter. *Illuminations*. Trans. Harry Zohn. New York: Schocken, 1969.

Bernstein, Jay. *The Philosophy of the Novel: Lukács, Marxism and the Dialectics of Form*. Minneapolis: U of Minnesota P, 1984.

Berque, Augustin. *Vivre l'Espace au Japon*. Paris: Presses Universitaires de France, 1986.

Borges, Jorge Luis. "The Theologians." *Labyrinths*. New York: New Directions, 1964. 119–26.

Caillois, Roger. "Les jeux dans le monde moderne." *Profils* 13 (1955): 26.

Dale, Peter. *The Myth of Japanese Uniqueness*. New York: St. Martin's, 1986.

Dore, Roland. *Taking Japan Seriously: A Confucian Perspective on Leading Economic Issues*. Stanford: Stanford UP, 1987.

Endo, Shusaku. *When I Whistle*. Trans. Van C. Gessel. New York: Taplinger, 1980.

Feenberg, Andrew. "Fetishism and Form: Erotic and Economic Disorder in Literature." *Violence and Truth*. Ed. Paul Dumouchel. Stanford: Stanford UP, 1988. 201–10.

———. *Critical Theory of Technology*. New York: Oxford UP, 1991.

Goffman, Erving. *Encounters: Two Studies in the Sociology of Interaction*. New York: Bobbs-Merrill, 1961.

Goodell, John D. *The World of Ki.* St. Paul: Riverside Research P, 1957.
Herrigel, Eugen. *Zen in the Art of Archery.* Trans. R. F. C. Hull. New York: Pantheon Books, 1960.
Kawabata, Yasunari. *Japan, The Beautiful and Myself.* Trans. Edward Seidensticker. Tokyo/Palo Alto: Kodansha, 1969.
———. *The Master of Go.* Trans. Edward Seidensticker. New York: Perigree, 1981.
Korschelt, Oscar. *The Theory and Practice of Go.* Trans. and ed. Samuel King and George Leckie. Rutland: Tuttle, 1965.
Latour, Bruno. *Science in Action.* Cambridge: Harvard UP, 1987.
Loy, David. *Nonduality: A Study in Comparative Philosophy.* New Haven: Yale UP, 1988.
Lukács, Georg. *The Theory of the Novel.* Trans. Anne Bostock. Cambridge: MIT P, 1968.
Miller, Roy Andrew. "Levels of Speech (*keigo*) and the Japanese Linguistic Response to Modernization." *Tradition and Modernization in Japanese Culture.* Ed. Donald Shively. Princeton: Princeton UP, 1971. 601–65.
Morley, James. "Introduction: Choice and Consequence." *Dilemmas of Growth in Prewar Japan.* Ed. James Morley. Princeton: Princeton UP, 1971. 3–30.
Nakane, Chie. *Japanese Society.* Berkeley: U of California P, 1970.
Nietzsche, Friedrich. *On the Genealogy of Morals and Ecce Homo.* Trans. Walter Kaufmann. New York: Vintage, 1969.
Nishida, Kitaro. "The Problem of Japanese Culture." *Sources of the Japanese Tradition.* Vol. 2. Ed. and trans. William T. de Bary. New York: Columbia UP, 1958. 350–65. 2 vols.
———. *An Inquiry into the Good.* Trans. Masao Abe and Christopher Ives. New Haven: Yale UP, 1990.
Ohashi, Ryosuke. *Nihonteki na mono, Yoroppateki na mono [What is Japanese, What is European?].* Tokyo: Shincho Sensho, 1992.
Pilarcik, Marlene. "Dialectics and Change in Kawabata's Master of Go." *Modern Language Studies* 16.4 (1986): 9–21.
Petersen, Gwenn. *The Moon in the Water: Understanding Tanizaki, Kawabata, and Mishima.* Honolulu: U of Hawaii P, 1979.
Soviak, Eugene. "Journal of the Iwakura Embassy." *Tradition and Modernization in Japanese Culture.* Ed. Donald Shively. Princeton: Princeton UP, 1971. 7–34.
Suzuki, Daisetz. *Zen and Japanese Culture.* Princeton: Princeton UP, 1970.
———. *The Zen Doctrine of No-Mind.* New York: Samuel Weiser, 1973.
Swann, Thomas. "The Master of Go." *Approaches to the Modern Japanese Novel.* Ed. K. Tsuruta and Thomas Swann. Tokyo: Sophia UP, 1976.
Tanizaki, Jun'Ichiro. *In Praise of Shadows.* Trans. Harper and E. Seidensticker. New Haven: Leete's Island Books, 1977.
Vattimo, Gianni. *The End of Modernity.* Trans. John Snyder. Baltimore: Johns Hopkins UP, 1991.
Van Wolferen, Karel. *The Enigma of Japanese Power.* New York: Random, 1989.
Watsuji, Tetsuro. *Climate and Culture: A Philosophical Study.* Trans. Geoffrey Bownas. Westport: Greenwood P, 1987.

Modernity and Its Vicissitudes

Joseph D. Lewandowski

I

Perhaps one of the most interesting, and certainly more problematic, aspects of modernity for cultural critics is its end:
What does the "end of modernity"—the dropping or abandoning
of the heavy enlightenment baggage of teleology, emancipation,
demythologization, subjectivity, rationality, and so on—and the
emergence of something even more peculiar, a "postmodernity,"
mean for cultural criticism? Is cultural critique still possible? desirable? tenable?

It is my suspicion that modernity contains its own critique and
that postmodernity is best understood as precisely that—as ineluctably entwined with modernity. I want to take seriously something
like Lyotard's claim that postmodernism is "undoubtedly a *part of*
the modern."[1] But for any *critical* cultural theory to emerge, we
need to *develop* more fully and clearly the ways in which the two
are bound up with one another. What is needed today is to define
and examine this entwinement of modernity/postmodernity. We
don't need to languish in, or perpetuate, the too often sterile de-

© 1995 by *Cultural Critique*. Winter 1994–95. 0882-4371/95/$5.00.

bate about the validity or defining features of postmodernity; rather, we need to bring it down to earth by realizing its *interconnectedness with modernity* and asking what relevance and significance it has for critics of cultures.

Two texts that both raise and stage this kind of entwinement are, not surprisingly, Heidegger's "Letter on Humanism" and Derrida's "The Ends of Man," texts I shall treat in some detail in what follows. My hope is that in setting a certain kind of modern discourse (in this case, Heidegger's "destruction") alongside what is now generally considered postmodern discourse (here "deconstruction"), the entwinement of postmodernity with modernity will emerge more clearly. Of course, particular maneuvers—those infinitely usable, stylized strategies of reading surface over depth, textuality over authenticity—will allow for some important points of departure and help us to pose certain questions about the "style" of deconstruction and its relation to contemporary cultural forms.

It should be made clear at the outset that neither Heidegger's nor Derrida's infinitely complex thinking can be limited to some kind of representative status, as essentially modern or the realization of the postmodern. Too often we forget that Derrida—and, for that matter, someone like Foucault or Deleuze—has not been eager to take up the banner of postmodernity. Only a few thinkers who are associated with "postmodernity"—Lyotard and Vattimo, for example—willingly accept and consistently use the term.[2] But we should remember that both Heidegger and Derrida, intentionally or not, very much "stand for" particular aspects of modernity/postmodernity. Of course, the Archimedean point of reference shifts, and modernity and postmodernity—sociohistorically and culturally constructed for various canonical, ideological, and economic reasons—are therefore not static "epochs" but rather more like tributaries in the Heraclitean stream into which one can never step twice. Still, I would suggest that the fact that these notions and their (perhaps too quick and easy) associations with Heidegger and Derrida are problematic does not invalidate or necessarily undermine an attempt to articulate their interconnectedness. Indeed, I would argue quite the opposite: since such terms are so closely meshed we are all the more obliged to clarify their relationship every time we press them into the service of critical discourse.

The issue I want to raise here and explore in this essay via Heidegger and Derrida is in many ways an extension of Albrecht Wellmer's "The Dialectic of Modernism and Postmodernism: The Critique of Reason Since Adorno."[3] Wellmer is not widely known or read in cultural studies circles in the United States (few of his writings have been translated). But his contribution to the now waning modernity/postmodernity debate should not be underestimated (or collapsed into, say, Habermas's set of criticisms).[4] Indeed, a small part of what I hope to show here is the pertinence and richness of Wellmer's thinking on contemporary cultural critique and the question of modernity/postmodernity; I am indebted to his reading throughout the body of this paper, though I shall only consider his text explicitly in my closing section. Following Wellmer, I shall try to demonstrate here that postmodernism is not a conceptual break from modern critiques of social structures and subjectivity but rather the wrestling with some of the persistent concerns and most difficult tasks of modernity—questions of the nature of community, justice, plurality, self-determination, autonomy, and so on. Such a Wellmerian reading of the "persistence" of modernity may open up the possibility of developing a distinctly *critical* perspective on our own peculiar modern/postmodern sociocultural position.[5]

II

Homelessness is coming to be the destiny of the world.
　　　—Martin Heidegger, "Letter on Humanism"[6]

If we read Heidegger as a cultural critic (and here one may defend such an approach by recalling that the later Heidegger was very much concerned with the sociocultural questions concerning technology and innovation), then he is perhaps best characterized as a reactionary for whom modern ways of thinking and being "present world crisis" (242).[7] In the "Letter on Humanism," the only text of Heidegger's I consider here, this crisis manifests itself in something he calls "homelessness." "Homelessness" for Heidegger is not of interest ontically (the displacement of thousands of war refugees is not what he is talking about here), but rather *onto-*

logically. What Heidegger does in his "Letter on Humanism" is un-couple the sociocultural question of "homelessness" from actual or ontic agents. Heidegger filters the ontic phenomenon of home-lessness through the *Seinsfrage;* he ontologizes "homelessness" and sees it as that which prevents us from making ourselves at home, from "dwelling poetically" in what he calls the "house of Being."

What Heidegger develops via an ontological analysis of "homelessness" is a rather reactionary and certainly macro-level critique of modernity: ontological homelessness is the destiny of the *world.* The general reactionary thrust of Heidegger's criticisms is very much rooted in the German Mandarin tradition out of which he emerges.[8] Heidegger does not think in terms of textuality but rather in the terms of, as Adorno not so delicately puts it, the reactionary jargon of authenticity. In Heidegger's view, authentic-ity and an authentic mode of being-in-the-world are lost and in need of critical retrieval via "Destruktion" and the posing of the *Seinsfrage:* destruction lays bare the subjective will to power that informs and infects every aspect of cultural modernity and our oblivion to the question of Being. I want to locate Heidegger's thinking about ontological "homelessness" in this text in a peculiar form of inverted (not progressive) modern thinking ("making it new" by making it old, we might say: remember Heidegger's at-traction to the ancient Greeks). While the tenor of Heidegger's critique is indeed reactionary and sounds anti-modern, he never-theless does not so much negate modernity as he reinstates certain aspects of it with his backward-looking metaphysical longings for authenticity and a "new" ground or proper place (a "home") that has somehow been foreclosed to the modern subject and with a concern for the collective "we" of the modern world.

Heidegger's critique takes as its conceptual point of departure Sartre's formulation of "existence" as it is contrasted with essence. Thinking the origin of essence—here conceived not as representa-tional or instrumental thought, but as a thinking of Being, a medi-tative thinking that "accomplishes the relation of Being to the es-sence of man" (193)—brings about or makes manifest a realization of true essences, including, especially, the essence of the human. It is because it fails to think essences in this noninstrumental, medita-tive way that Heidegger criticizes humanism, for, he argues, the "essence of man consists in his being more than merely human, if this is represented as 'being a rational creature'" (221).

Yet it is in precisely this "more than" that Heidegger, as he admits, remains within, rather than negating, the humanist tradition. Indeed, he refigures that tradition and raises the stakes: "Humanism is opposed because it does not set the *humanitas* of man high enough" (210). The historical failure of humanism, then, is to subjectivize being, making human being the lord of beings, one who is in opposition to and imposes his or her will upon the world. Developed in *Sein und Zeit,* and alluded to here, however, is human being as *Dasein*—a radicalized account of the human subject in which he or she is always and already involved in the world, is a being-in-the-world.[9] *Dasein* is peculiar insofar as it is that being which *ek*-sists or stands out in the world insofar as it can pose the question of Being. Indeed, Heidegger will often characterize such a being-there as a site of openness, a standing in relation to Being. So Heidegger does not reject the notion of an "essence of humanity" so much as he seeks to rethink radically that notion with the standing-out ("*ek*-sistence") of *Dasein.*

Heidegger then wants to ask: What does it mean to be, and what are the possibilities for, a *Dasein* in modernity? One of the things it does not mean is that *Dasein* is a privileged subject for whom language (or technology or beings) is to be used instrumentally. Rather, *Dasein* is the possible opening through which beings come to pass in their disclosive essence or Being. This coming to pass happens in language, but not in the crisis of modernity, where human beings understand language as an instrumental way in which beings, including other human beings, are mastered by humans. Such a humanistic understanding of language forces language "to surrender itself to our mere willing and trafficking, as an instrument of domination over beings" (199). Here again the problem with humanism is that it privileges the being that "has" language and reduces the disclosive power of language to the "service of expediting communication" (197).[10] Indeed, Heidegger says that

> [t]he downfall of language is, however, not the grounds for, but already a consequence of, the state of affairs in which language

under the domination of the modern metaphysics of subjectivity almost irremediably falls out of its element. Language
still denies us its essence: that it is the house of the truth of
Being. (199)

So the "fallen" state of language as instrumentalizable form of communication or mastery over "beings" is the consequence of the prevailing humanistic "domination of the modern metaphysics of subjectivity."

In contradistinction to such a metaphysical humanistic understanding of language as objectifying "actualities in [a] calcula-
tive, business-like way" (199), Heidegger gives an account of language as disclosing or unconcealing of Being:

In its essence language is not the utterance of an organism;
nor is it the expression of a living thing. Nor can it ever be
thought in an essentially correct way in terms of its symbolic
character, perhaps not even in terms of the character of signification. Language is the lighting-concealing advent of Being
itself. (206)

The *ek*-sistence of *Dasein,* as I suggested above, is not Sartre's existence in the everyday of beings, but a standing out in Being *in* (not
via) language—a way of Being *proper only to man* (204). Heidegger
thus links the neologisms ek-sistence and *Dasein* with his radicalized and ontologized notion of language as the locus where humanity's *true* essence "dwells" in order to argue that

[l]anguage is the house of Being which comes to pass from
Being and is pervaded by Being. And so it is proper to think
the essence of language from its correspondence to Being and
indeed as this correspondence, that is, as the home of man's
essence. (213)

So noninstrumental language—language as the house of Being
and "home of man's essence," a language that speaks man rather
than a language that man speaks—is the openness in which human beings "dwell" rather than construct and articulate by way of
communication, discourse, speech, and so on.

Concomitant with the ontologization of language as that

which is "pervaded by Being" and with the account of "home-lessness" as that which prevents us from authentic dwelling there persists a deep critique of reason and purposive-rational (*zweck-rational*) activity in Heidegger's "Letter." Modern rational subjects, according to Heidegger, utilize beings (*seiendes*—that which is) and thereby forget the "authentic" question of Being (*Sein*—that by which something is; that which lets beings be). Such a purposive-rational orientation represents for Heidegger both the modern imperatives of mass production and technology and the culmination of the failure of Western reason starting with Plato. Modernity *is* the fall into beings and obliviousness of Being:

> The oblivion of Being makes itself known indirectly through the fact that man always observes and handles only beings. Even so, because man cannot avoid having some notion of Being, it is explained merely as what is "most general" and therefore as something that encompasses beings, or as a creation of the infinite being, or as the product of a finite subject. At the same time "Being" has long stood for "beings" and, inversely, the latter for the former, the two of them caught in a curious and still unraveled confusion. (218–19)

Thus, the question of Being in modern thinking is reduced to a question of beings, of ontic phenomena, by way of a purposive-rational orientation that genealogically confuses the latter with the former. In modernity, human beings determine the appearance of every being as the material of labor, as a standing reserve to be put to use. Such a privileging of the human subject and its purposive-rational relation to beings misses precisely the ontological difference that Heidegger seeks to articulate in his formulation of "Being itself."

Being itself, though, is not something wholly other than reason or outside of modernity; it is

> not God and not a cosmic ground. Being is farther than all beings and is yet nearer to man than every being, be it a rock, a beast, a work of art, a machine, be it an angel or a God. Being is the nearest. Yet the near remains farthest from man. Man at first clings always and only to beings. (210–11)

That which is near in the modern world is precisely not beings, despite the proliferation of cultural commodities. Instead, Heidegger's formulation of the "still unraveled confusion" of the question of Being demonstrates that nearer than beings is Being itself: "nearer than the nearest and at the same time for ordinary thinking farther than the farthest is nearness itself: the truth of Being" (212). An important aspect of the crisis of modern thinking, then, is that it conflates what is nearest and its ownmost with beings as commodities to be produced and consumed.

The other criticism that I want to consider here is that which has already been alluded to: the ontologized "homeless destiny" that threatens modernity. The problem of "homelessness" points toward what modernity does not think and how modernity does not perceive its own condition. The "estrangement of man has its roots in the homelessness of modern man" (219). In other words, the ontic, everyday homelessness of peoples in the modern world is merely the manifestation of a *deeper* problem: the "estrangement of man." "Homelessness" is neither actual (ontic) nor textual, but rather *inauthentic*—an improper "dwelling" outside of the "true" home of *Dasein*. The "homelessness" of modern subjects serves as illustrative of a more fundamental, *ontological* question (i.e., the *Seinsfrage*) that unfolds the very destiny of modernity. Heidegger says that

> everything depends upon this alone, that the truth of Being come to language and that thinking attain to this language. Perhaps, then, language requires much less precipitous expression than proper silence. But who of us today would want to imagine that his attempts to think are at home on the paths of silence? At best, thinking could perhaps point toward the truth of Being, and indeed toward it as what is to be thought. (223)

The "everything" to which Heidegger refers here is no less than the destiny of the modern world in what he perceives as its present crisis. His thinking points toward—albeit abstractly and super-foundationally—an alternative possibility for thought, the "truth of Being" itself, and the *Dasein* that is capable of such thought. In anticipation of this alternate possibility, thinking becomes a kind of anti-intellectual and silent wandering, following a path of silence toward a "home" in language.

Still, such a silent, anti-intellectual wandering never emerges as purely a surface, anti-foundational, irrationalism of textuality and faint traces, and lack of concern for authenticity (as we shall see manifest in Derrida). Heidegger's hermeneutic that questions the nearness of Being in language intimates that the neighborhood of Being awaits *our* arrival: "Let us also in the days ahead remain as wanderers on the way into the neighborhood of Being" (224).

Hence Heidegger's "Letter on Humanism" expresses a peculiarly reactionary reading and critique of modernity and suggests a sense of the need to articulate an alternative "end." The validity of "Being itself" and its proximity in language are never questioned, nor is the notion of the "us" for whom this alternative is necessary, nor is the problematic of using anti-reason ("silent wandering") to critique reason. Instead, language as the house of Being unfolds an alternate destiny ("home") for estranged *Dasein*. The superfoundational dimensions to Heidegger's thinking—the search for and insistence on "authentic" notions, the positing of the genealogical confusion of the question of beings and Being, the proximity of Being to the openness of *Dasein*—reinvolve him in modernity's attempt to articulate authentic "ends" of humanity, of a "we." To be sure, Heidegger's level of abstraction, hypostatization of Being (as "Being itself"), and distance from any materialist concern for culture make his criticisms of modernity difficult to concretize (Heidegger himself had precisely such difficulties); his is a kind of perverse or "non-materialist cultural critique." Yet the reactionary concern for the need to transform (not simply negate) modernity cannot be divorced from Heidegger's thinking. Indeed, the "brief" (or not so brief, depending upon whom one consults) association with German National Socialism can be understood as precisely such a transformative attempt, however ill-fated and perverted.

III

His laughter then will burst out, directed toward a return that no longer will have the form of the metaphysical repetition of

humanism, nor doubtless, "beyond" metaphysics, the form of
a memorial or a guarding of the meaning of Being, the form
of the house and of the truth of Being. He will dance outside
the house.

— Jacques Derrida, "The Ends of Man"[11]

Derrida speaks, here, of Zarathustra. Zarathustra is in many
ways the aesthetic analogue of the Nietzschean *Ubermensch*—
Nietzsche's neologism for the possibility of a human existence beyond modern existence, beyond the moral imperatives of "good"
and "evil," a frame into which something other than modern, historical consciousness will fit. Precisely what that something "other"
is Nietzsche leaves open to interpretation and is beyond the scope
of this essay.[12] But for Derrida—at least the Derrida of '68, the
only one I shall be able to consider here—the "end of man" represents the emergence of a certain Nietzschean affirmation or *sich
Uberwinden,* the beginning of a non-metaphysical subject that
"awakens and leaves, without turning back to what he leaves behind him. He burns his text and erases the traces of his steps"
(152).[13] *Dasein* is, in Derrida's reading, the very embodiment of
metaphysical humanism—a "guardian of the meaning" and house
of Being. Language as the "house of Being" establishes the *raison
d'être* for Deconstruction: it is precisely *that* (linguistic) house
that needs to be deconstructed, that "subject" (*Dasein*) that needs
to be decentered. Derrida questions the Heideggerean motif of
nearness or "proximity." The metaphoric "house of Being" in Heidegger becomes the point of departure for Derrida's critique of
humanism and anthropocentrism in "The Ends of Man." For Derrida, the "ends" of man, in the equivocal sense of the word "ends,"
are in modernity unrealizable and exhausted.

What Derrida wants to do in this text is to try to succeed
where Heidegger fails: destruction did not go far enough; it still
carries the heavy metaphysical humanistic baggage of modernity.
Deconstruction introduces a particular set of technical maneuvers
(what Derrida will characterize here as "style") that Heidegger
lacks. Conceptually, Derrida presents us with a field or horizontal
paradigm rather than a vertical or depth model of thinking. But
Deconstruction also occupies a peculiar position—one can only deconstruct what has already been constructed. The *house* of Being

can only be destructured with the very same linguistic stones that comprise it and always runs the risk of reconstruction. As I have already said, postmodern discourse's conceptual positions are entwined with modern ones: their referential point—the point from which they orient themselves—is in fact modernity. From such a position, however, Derrida seeks to change or remap the "terrain" of reading, or at least undermine the Heideggerian hermeneutic that informs "Destruction's" reading and critique of modernity. But even this is problematic, since, as Derrida says, "the simple practice of language ceaselessly reinstates the new terrain of the oldest ground" (151).

Derrida begins "The Ends of Man" reflexively, by considering the political and cultural significance of an "international" philosophy colloquium and by intimating the material conditions under which such a colloquium is possible. The "inter" of this national conference suggests to Derrida's mind two things: that (1) "philosophical nationalities have been formed" (126) and (2) despite these nationalities, there is nevertheless a common element, a common language spoken among these countries that allows for an "international" colloquium. For, says Derrida, "the colloquium can take place only in a medium, or rather in the representation that all the participants must make of a certain transparent ether, which here would be none other than what is called universality of philosophical discourse" (126). What Derrida does here, I suggest, in theorizing the conditions that make "international" intellectual conferences possible, is pose a fundamental question about the possibility of subjectivity and language. Do "we"—and Derrida will close by asking, "But who, we?" (152)—still stand in the shadow of Heidegger's critique that speaks a universal language and seeks to articulate transformative "ends" for a collective *Dasein*? Are "we" hermeneutically teleological and transparent? Such a line of inquiry leads Derrida to (and away from) Heidegger's "Letter." Derrida explores the vicissitudinous readings of the notion of *Dasein* and, in turn, what is at stake in a critique that "links the *we* of the philosopher to the 'we men,' to the *we* in the horizon of humanity" (131). The question, in short, is: Once the "house of Being" is deconstructed and *Dasein* thoroughly decentered, can there be a macro-level reading of a "we"?

Yet Derrida does not simply take leave of Heidegger. Heidegger's handling of this "we" poses several problems for Derrida and the kind of "end" he wants to stake out in his text:

> [t]he thinking of the end of man . . . is always already pre-scribed in metaphysics, in the thinking of the truth of man. What is difficult to think today is an end of man that would not be organized by a dialectics of truth and negativity, an end of man that would not be a teleology in the first person plu-ral. . . . The *we* is the unity of absolute knowledge and anthro-pology, of God and man, of onto-theo-teleology and human-ism. "*Being*" and language—the group of languages—that the *we* governs or opens: such is the name of that which assures the transition between metaphysics and humanism via the *we*. (137)

Derrida senses how a "we" establishes (or presupposes) a "unity of absolute knowledge and anthropology, of God and man, of onto-theo-teleology and humanism." What is "difficult" today is to think of an "end" of humanity that is *not* organized according to the hall-marks of modernism: "a dialectics of truth and negativity" gov-erned by the relay between metaphysics and humanism and linked via a "we."

Derrida perceives the notion of *Dasein* "in" a language and thus open to the question of Being as necessarily thinking the truth of "man" in his teleological and metaphysical humanistic essence:

> The end of man (as factual anthropological limit) is an-nounced to thought from the vantage point of the end of man (as a determined opening or the infinity of a *telos*). Man is that which is in relation to his end, in the fundamentally equivocal sense of the word. Since always. (138)

Like Nietzsche, Derrida understands enlightened modern con-sciousness as essentially historical consciousness: actions, events, human life take on meaning in modernity only insofar as they un-fold temporally from the vantage point of the human subject. And it is into this teleological understanding of the human subject that Derrida situates Heidegger's reactionary account of a "homeless" "we" implicit in *Dasein* and all the subsequent humanistic readings of Heidegger done in postwar France. In Heidegger, and in post-war readings of Heidegger, the fundamental principle "proper" to *Dasein* is, as discussed earlier, its open relation and nearness to Being in language. Yet in Derrida's reading, this "general concept of proximity" allows for the aporetic relay between metaphysics and humanism. *Dasein* remains another insistence of "man" (140).

Yet it is not merely *what* Heidegger says—his readmittance of "man" vis-à-vis *Dasein*—that is in need of deconstructing, it is, more important, *how* he reads, from and with what "ends." For, argues Derrida, it is this "style of reading that makes explicit, practices a continual bringing to light, something that resembles, at least, a coming into consciousness, without break, displacement, or change of terrain" (143) that needs deconstruction. The criticism here seems to be that Heidegger remains not simply too hermeneutical and humanistic, but also stays within the realm of ideology critique, the process of unveiling or bringing to light various forms of false or distorted sociocultural practices and beliefs. Derrida reads Heidegger's hermeneutical questioning of Being as a way of reading humankind whereby "we" [he who reads others and himself, that is, the (self-)interpreting subject] are reinstated by our reading: humankind becomes *the text* to be unveiled in an ontologized reading of "homelessness." Though Heidegger appears to dissolve the modern subject by making *Dasein* "text-like" or always already involved in a world, what Heidegger goes on to do is derive a general hermeneutic from that desubjectivized text: context (being-in-the-world) becomes the text. This reinscription of the "we" vis-à-vis the proximity and presence of Being in relation to *Dasein* is telling, for

> [i]t is this self-presence, this absolute proximity of the (questioning) being to itself, this familiarity with itself of the being ready to understand Being, that intervenes in the determination of the *factum,* and that motivates the choice of the exemplary being, of the text, the good text for the hermeneutic of the meaning of Being. It is the proximity to itself to the questioning being that leads it to be chosen as the privileged interrogated being. The proximity to itself of the inquirer authorizes the identity of the inquirer and the interrogated. We who are close to ourselves, *we* interrogate *ourselves* about the meaning of Being. (142)

Here Derrida elaborates what has now become a peculiarly postmodern position: first, the critique of *Dasein* as the "good *text*" for the hermeneutic of the authenticity of "Being itself" insofar as "the reading of the text of *Dasein* is a hermeneutics of unveiling or of development" (143); and, second, the theorizing of the conditions that make an interrogation or reading of *Dasein* and, in turn, any text as exemplar possible. In Heidegger, according to Derrida, "we" interrogate or read, and thereby reinstate "ourselves" and our readability—"we" understand ourselves best. This reinstatement is the function of the equivocality inherent in Heidegger's conceptualization of *Dasein*. *Dasein* may not be human being or man, but it is nevertheless the being that we ourselves are (143); it

> is nevertheless *nothing other* than man. It is, as we shall see, a
> repetition of the essence of man permitting a return to what
> is before the metaphysical concepts of *humanitas*. The subtlety
> and equivocality of this gesture, then, are what appear to have
> authorized all the anthropologistic deformations in the read-
> ing of *Sein und Zeit*, notably in France. (143–44)

Perhaps another way of elaborating the technical maneuver here is by way of Jameson's reading in *Postmodernism* of the Frank Gehry house in Santa Monica, California (113). The "house" consists of a pre-existing 1920s structure, enveloped in a modern wrapping of corrugated metal. The old walls or wrapping of the pre-existing structure are in a sense (functionally, at least) radically refigured by the new metal wrapping: the wrapper becomes the wrapped. The "text" (the 1920s house) is no longer the same, for it has been recontextualized by the construction of a new textual frame: exteriority has become interiority—the "outside yard" is now a "room." What is of interest is not the binary question of inner-outer, but the "stylized" space between (the hyphen, the gap created by the technical wrapping), which is neither purely textual nor purely contextual. The postmodern technical move, then, could perhaps be understood as taking the form of wrapping, which is always and already itself a wrapper, whereby neither text nor context become exemplary or illustrative of any "we" or any generalizable hermeneutic observation.

This "wrapping" is, I think, something like what Derrida seeks to do when he tries to avoid a return to thinking, writing and reading "the ends of man" by suggesting two technical ("decon-structive") strategies that themselves form a kind of wrapping:

a. To attempt an exit and a deconstruction without changing terrain, by repeating what is implicit in the founding concepts and the original problematic, by using against the edifice the instruments or stones available in the house, that is, equally, in language. Here, one risks ceaselessly confirming, consolidating, *relifting* (*relever*), at an always more certain depth, that which one allegedly deconstructs. The continuous process of making explicit, moving toward an opening, risks sinking into the autism of the closure.

b. To decide to change terrain, in a discontinuous and irruptive fashion, by brutally placing oneself outside, and by affirming an absolute break and difference. Without mentioning all the other forms of *trompe-l'oeil* perspective in which such a displacement can be caught, thereby inhabiting more naively and more strictly than ever the inside one declares one has deserted, the simple practice of language ceaselessly reinstates the new terrain of the oldest ground. (151)

I quote Derrida at length here to establish how a cultural criticism grounded in something like Deconstruction would always and already be caught up in modern thinking: ceaselessly reinstating the new terrain of the previously oldest ground (the previously oldest wrapping always becomes the newly wrapped, and so on). But, however aporetic, "these effects do not suffice to annul the necessity for a 'change of terrain'" (151). Such Deconstructive criticism may be "necessary," but it is nevertheless part of the modern— neither an "absolute break" nor an "exit" is possible. Deconstruction does not destroy social structures from the outside (whereas Heidegger thought, at least in the thirties and forties, that "*Destruktion*" could). What may be possible, as Derrida intimates, is to change the terrain by introducing "a new kind of writing" and immanent form of criticism that does not inhabit "naively" that which other forms of critique claim to escape. This kind of writing will be "new" in the sense of what Derrida considers "plurality": "A new kind of writing must weave and interlace these two [a and b above] motifs of deconstruction. Which amounts to saying that one must speak several languages and produce several texts at once" (151).

This call is for specifically not a break, but for a change both in the terrain of thinking and writing. Of course, Heidegger calls for a radical kind of thinking, but the justification for that call comes in the bringing to light the exemplary text of *Dasein,* onto-logical difference, and the metaphorics of proximity of "Being itself." Derrida *attempts* something else. He "weakens" such de-structive thought with an abandonment of being-in-the-world, authenticity, and the *Seinsfrage,* and commits himself instead to a groundless superficiality and Zarathustra-like laughter and dance that would be devoid of any concern for or possibility of a "we."[14] What is needed, according to Derrida, to achieve this change of terrain, is "a change of 'style'; and if there is style, Nietzsche re-minded us, it must be *plural*" (151). In this infinitely re-usable, immanent, "stylized" critique, language is not the "house of the truth of Being"; human being is not the exemplary text to be understood—it is as deconstructable, as faint, as any other text.

IV

Its the end of the world as we know it, and I feel fine, I feel fine.
—R.E.M., *Document*[15]

In many ways, the Derrida of '68 has proved prophetic. Speaking and constructing and deconstructing several texts at once is a chief feature, not simply of contemporary criticism, but also (and more importantly) of contemporary culture. The "ter-rain" of many discourses has been altered, even leveled. Cultures become texts, the state becomes a text, consumerism becomes a text, even, as Derrida says, "we" become texts. Any "we" is suspect. *Il n'ya pas de hors-texte:* everything takes on a certain textual quality and is thus equally deconstructable: gender, truth, ethnography, law, clothing.[16] I recently came across an ad in the *Times* for a Bel-gian designer's spring clothing line entitled "Deconstruction" and another for men's jackets in *J. Crew,* which read "Totally Decon-structed." Textuality and the "stylization" of Deconstruction have become paradigmatic not simply for interpretative procedures but also and quite easily for the culture industry. Here Jameson's point is absolutely salient: postmodernism is itself a cultural mode of production (406), not of meaning, but of a stylized sign flow that *resists* meaning (91).

What such affirmative cultural production and seamlessness suggest to me is that the "end of modernity," concomitant with the "end of man," introduces a one-dimensional or leveling set of technical strategies or "styles" that are at one with cultural forms in ways that modernist critique never was (think here, for example, of Adorno's absolute scorn for jazz and the emergence of a popular culture it suggested to him). It is difficult to imagine something like "*Dasein*" emerging as a category for the culture industry of modernity/postmodernity. Modern criticism, even Heidegger's re-actionism, wanted to explode (or "destroy") cultural modernity and *reconstruct* it with the shards that remained. Deconstruction, by necessity and in Derrida's acknowledgment, *must* inhabit pre-existing (modern) social structures. The positing of norms and alternatives ("ends") is undermined in the immanent and stylized turn away from depth, foundationalism, and authenticity toward superficiality and the impossibility of any transparent "we" or "outside text" to heed the calling of something like Heidegger's *Seins-frage.*

The above epigraph, taken from a popular song published in 1987, is a text that for me crystallizes many of the ways in which postmodernity is bound up with modernity. "The end of the world as we know it" certainly preserves a kind of Heideggerian reactionism and telos, thinking "the ends of man," of "us." But the maneuver that is the refrain re- or transfigures that thinking, thereby changing the conceptual terrain that underpins any singular reading of the first half of the line: "and I feel fine, I feel fine." Here "the meaning" is not destroyed, but it does maintain a certain depthlessness and sense of play and does resist meaning in ways never present in Heidegger's reactionism (it is in fact quite difficult to conceptualize what a "Heideggerian sense" of play might be). The "end" of the world, consequently, is greeted in much the same way that the Derrida of '68 greeted it, with a wave and a laugh, "directed toward a return that no longer will have the form of the metaphysical repetition of humanism" and telos that mark the "end of the world as we know it." The line, then, serves as a referential point for, and takes on a wholly different significance in, the turn of the refrain.

The point of this seemingly digressive reading is twofold: on the one hand, I want to illustrate that postmodernity and modernity, as discourses, coexist, even in the most pervasive of cultural forms (pop music); and on the other hand, I want to demonstrate that perhaps symptomatic of postmodernity, both as a conceptual frame and a technical maneuver, is how it affords a seamless fusion with a culture that seeks only affirmation—*we feel fine, we feel fine*—in ways that modernist criticism never desired. Postmodernity seems to dance *alongside* and *with* the culture industry; indeed, tends to become indistinguishable from it. In such an immanent position, criticism collapses into a cultural form without adequately *criticizing* it.[17] Modernist critique perceived itself vocationally, as the transformer of the modern world via a transformation of modern conceptualizations of thinking, language, reason, politics, etc., though Heidegger's "errancy" in such a vocational critique should never be diminished. The stylization of Deconstruction is considerably more modest in that regard. It does not critically seek to save old worlds or build new ones. Instead, it tries to mark the superficiality of "ends" and "we's."

Still, this kind of playful reflexive questioning continually begs other questions (peculiarly modern ones): Once the question of authenticity, foundation, and a "we" has been abandoned in favor of superficiality, what is left? And, what does "superficiality" signify without an awareness of depth? Today one no longer has need of "the real thing"; indeed, even Coca-Cola, the most recognizable consumer product in the world—one whose advertising campaign was founded upon its authenticity—has abandoned its own "reality" and its utopian jingle: "I'd like to teach the world to sing, in perfect harmony . . ." Consumers now chose among Coca-Cola, Coke, Diet Coke, etc. And what remains is a second nature that becomes a nostalgia for first nature: "the real thing" of cultural modernity is now known as Coca-Cola "classic."

So perhaps we begin to see how, even in the most innocuous examples, dropping the heaviness of modernity's mode of critique is not without its transformative powers. We might also consider the boundlessness—economic, political, social—of something like the European Community and the consequent homogenization of culture into a singular, global entity (a "new world order," a "European United States"); or the sound byte technologized information systems in which "read my lips, read my hips" or "don't stop thinking about tomorrow" legitimates a presidential candidate and sufficiently motivates a voting public; where a video clip may tell "the whole story" or several stories or conflicting stories (even all three at once) on the evening news; or an institutionalized social arbitrariness whereby chance itself is planned—where the state is funded by lotteries, whose participants play the game in hopes of becoming that "one in a million" winner or that "rags to riches" story—and the stray bullet of the inner city becomes the normative standard by which everyday existence is governed. All of these are "texts" into which "we" are woven in a "sign flow that resists meaning."

Like Wellmer, I am no great critic of Derrida. Certainly we cannot and should not pin modernity's persistent sociocultural woes on Derrida or on "the postmodernists." Indeed, quite the contrary: Wellmer acknowledges, as do I, that the "style" of Deconstruction has illustrated the inherent difficulties and aporias in something like Heidegger's conceptualizations of *Dasein* and language as the disclosure of the truth of the being of *Dasein*, or, what has proved worse, the disclosure of the cultural destiny of "the German" *Dasein*. But he goes on to say that "linguistic philosophy decentres the subject, but in doing so it provides no legitimation for either hermeneutic objectivism or hermeneutic anarchism. Still less does it justify the irrational consequences that are occasionally drawn by postmodern thinkers" (70). I agree. Yet such an agreement is where I would want to begin, not "end." Cultural critique rests, to paraphrase Adorno in *Negative Dialectics,* on the texts, social formations, and institutions it *criticizes* (55). For cultural criticism, then, there remains much work to be done: "homelessness" persists, though the "house of Being" has been repeatedly deconstructed; the hauntingly familiar spectre of nationalism rises again, though *Dasein* and "man" (or "we") have reached an "end";[18] and "we" (that "we" that is now ended) have neither justice nor consensus, but emerging forms of popular illegality.[19] Such are the vicissitudes of modernity. Wellmer's point on this matter is absolutely pertinent here, and I shall close with it. He argues that when

> we bring the distinctions between reality and semblance, between truthfulness and lying, between violence and dialogue, between autonomy and heteronomy back down to earth from

heaven, so to speak—and it is only on earth that they can be located—then it would no longer be possible to assert (other than in the sense of a bad metaphysics) that the will to truth is *in itself* a will to power; that dialogue *as such* is symbolic violence; that speech that is oriented towards truth *is* terror; that moral consciousness *as such* is a reflex of internalized violence; or that the autonomous human being *as such* is *either* a fiction *or* a mechanism of auto-suppression or a bastard of patriarchy, etc. In other words, the linguistic critique of rationalism and subjectivism does provide an opportunity for thinking in new ways about 'truth', 'justice', or 'self-determination'; but at the same time it will make us suspicious of those who want to give an affirmative twist, in the manner of Nietzsche, to the psychological critique of the subject—by which I mean those propagandists of a new era which shall have cast off the burden of the Platonic heritage, and in which rhetoric shall replace argument, the will to power shall replace the will to truth, the art of words shall replace theory, and the economy of desire shall replace morality. We have quite enough of all *that* to contend with, after all, in the world as it is now. (70–71)

Notes

I am indebted throughout the body of this paper to the incisive comments and constructive criticisms of an anonymous reader for *Cultural Critique*.

1. See Lyotard's *The Postmodern Condition: A Report on Knowledge,* especially the appendix, which is entitled "Answering the Question: What Is Postmodernism?" Most generally, Lyotard tends to see postmodernism as signalling the end of "master narratives." The question Lyotard's thesis begs, obviously, is to what extent Lyotard's text is itself yet another "master narrative." This somewhat paradoxical position of narrativizing "the end of master narratives" is critically examined by Jameson in his foreword to *The Postmodern Condition* (see esp. 18–20). Here I want to consider the perhaps even more complex question of the ways in which postmodernism is "undoubtedly" part of the modern (79).

2. See Lyotard, *The Postmodern Condition,* and Gianni Vattimo's *The End of Modernity* and *The Transparent Society.* Vattimo's sense of postmodernity has been legitimately characterized as a Nietzschean reading of Heidegger: *il pensiero debole* (generally translated as "weak thought") is an attempt to "weaken" Heidegger's strong or "heavy" modernist notions of language, Being, and so on. For an analysis of the Heideggerian roots of Vattimo's postmodernity, see Barbiero's "A Weakness for Heidegger." And for a more thorough account of the Heidegger/Derrida coupling than I can give here, see Herman Rapaport's *Heidegger and Derrida.*

3. Collected in Albrecht Wellmer, *The Persistence of Modernity.* My general thesis here draws upon Wellmer's understanding of modernity/postmodernity. Wellmer sets out his basic premise in the introduction to this text:

> I shall argue that postmodernism at its best might be seen as a self-critical—a sceptical, ironic, but nevertheless unrelenting—form of modernism; a modernism beyond utopianism, scientism and foundationalism; in short, a *postmetaphysical* modernism. (vii)

4. Wellmer preserves some of the Adornian analyses of culture, the aesthetic, and history, whereas Habermas offers deeper criticisms of Adorno (though both Wellmer and Habermas see Adorno as proffering too totalizing an account of reason). Also, Wellmer offers an extended criticism of Habermas's "discourse ethics" in *The Persistence of Modernity*. For Habermas's criticisms of Adorno, see especially *Communicative Action*, Vol. 1 (339–66) and the lecture on Adorno and Horkheimer entitled "The Entwinement of Myth and Enlightenment: Max Horkheimer and Theodor Adorno" (106–30), collected in *The Philosophical Discourse of Modernity*. And for Wellmer's more Adornian affinities, see especially the essay I refer to here.

5. Jameson's *Postmodernism, or, the Cultural Logic of Late Capitalism* may be the other avenue by which to pursue such an account of modernity/postmodernity. Jameson is no stranger to the modernity/postmodernity question, though he is in many ways a peculiar kind of contributor. A detailed analysis of his position is beyond the scope of this essay, but for a fine critique, see Martin Jay's piece in *History and Theory*. Jay's discussion of Jameson's "Adornian" postmodernity points up much of what I shall only intimate here:

> If Adorno's argument about nominalism as the key to modernist aesthetics is correct, Jameson's efforts to make it quintessentially postmodernist as well seems strained. The same might be said of his claim that the turn from modernism to postmodernism is reflected in the move from symbolic to allegorical modes of interpretation, for it was precisely the privileging of the allegorical that earlier critics like Benjamin (positively) and Lukács (critically) saw as the essence of the modern. To argue that postmodernism is somehow the fulfillment of tendencies in modernism—the completion of the modernization process—fudges the issue of what is radically new in the present constellation. A mere difference in degree replaces a difference in kind. (301–02)

What Jay senses here is, in part, Wellmer's point: postmodernity is not a "difference in kind," but rather in degree.

6. This and all subsequent citations from the "Letter on Humanism" are taken from the English translation, *Martin Heidegger: The Basic Writings* (219).

7. For two exemplary readings of Heidegger's relation to critical theory and relevance to cultural critique, see Richard J. Bernstein's "Heidegger's Silence?: Ethos and Technology" (79–141) in his *New Constellation* and Thomas McCarthy's "Heidegger and Critical Theory" (83–96) in his *Ideals and Illusions*.

8. Perhaps the best, albeit most polemical, sociocultural analysis of Heidegger's thinking and politics is Richard Wolin's *The Politics of Being*. Derrida takes a very different and revealing approach to Heidegger's Nazism in *Of Spirit: Heidegger and the Question*.

9. See especially Division One, "Preparatory Fundamental Analysis of Dasein," in *Being and Time*.

10. Heideggerian inspired critiques of humanism abound in contemporary discourse (indeed, Derrida's is one such, however modified, critique). See, for example, William V. Spanos's most recent work, *Heidegger and Criticism*. Spanos

finds in Heidegger's "hermeneutics as disclosure" an emancipatory and "post"-humanist social critique.

11. This and all subsequent citations from "The Ends of Man" are taken from the English translation collected in *After Philosophy: End or Transformation?* (152). This translation is the same as the one collected in *Margins,* but I cite the afore-mentioned text because I find it particularly useful for framing what is in today's discourse very much in question: to what extent does postmodern critique signal the "end" of "philosophy" and social criticism as they have been practiced? And to what extent have critical conceptual positions been "transformed"? The collection presents both "modern" thinkers (that is, those committed to modernism as a project not yet realized of rational critique oriented toward human emancipation) and "postmodern" thinkers (that is, those who call for a "change of terrain" or an "end" to "the project of modernity").

12. The question of Nietzsche's relation to Derrida and Heidegger is, of course, not nearly so simple and is beyond the scope of this essay. But for a modern critical reading of Nietzsche, see Habermas's "The Entry into Postmodernity: Nietzsche as a Turning Point" (83–105) in *The Philosophical Discourse of Modernity;* for another perspective, see Alexander Nehamas's *Nietzsche: Life As Literature;* and for a more "post"-modern perspective, see Deleuze's *Nietzsche and Philosophy.*

13. Foucault, despite his differences with Derrida, makes strikingly similar claims in the closing sections of *The Order of Things.*

14. The notion of "weak" I borrow from Vattimo. To connect Vattimo with Derrida, one might generally conceive of *il pensiero debole* as "trace" thinking, as opposed to a depth model of thought. See also Vattimo's *The Adventure of Difference.*

15. From the song "its the end of the world as we know it (and i feel fine)."

16. I have elsewhere considered the relative merits and shortcomings of the textualization of culture. See my "Culture, Textuality, and Truth."

17. In his *After the Great Divide: Modernism, Mass Culture, Postmodernism,* Andreas Huyssen labors to articulate a genuinely critical component inhering in postmodernity. In the chapter entitled "Mapping the Postmodern," he argues that we should begin to

> explore the question whether postmodernism might not harbor productive contradictions, perhaps even a critical and oppositional potential. If the postmodern is indeed a historical and cultural condition (however transitional or incipient), then oppositional cultural practices and strategies must be located *within* postmodernism. (200)

It is precisely this *"within"* that I think tends to undermine a "critical and oppositional potential" to postmodernity. To be sure, *critical* cultural theory is "always already" within a given social structure or practice—inhabits it, as Deconstruction does—*but it can never be reduced to such an immanent position.* Adorno makes precisely this point in his "Cultural Criticism and Society" when he says that cultural criticism "must both participate in culture and not participate" (33). The point to be made is that postmodernist critique is, at best, an incomplete form of cultural criticism, and, at worst, acritical and affirmative.

18. The question of "community," of a "we," has not surprisingly become a central concern for contemporary neo-Heideggerians and Derrideans. See, for example, Jean-Luc Nancy's *The Inoperative Community* and the volume entitled *Community at Loose Ends,* edited by the Miami Theory Collective, especially Nancy's piece, and Paul Smith's more Marxian perspective on Laclau's and Mouffe's *Hege-*

mony and Socialist Strategy. However, it should also be pointed out here that Jameson realizes this problem in *Postmodernism* when he suggests that postmodern subjectivity would be "a non-centered subject that is part of an organic group" (345). The central question that such thinking poses is, to my mind: Can there be a "we" founded on a trace or absence or "non-centeredness"? Is any other notion of a "we" necessarily or ineluctably totalitarian?

19. Lyotard's call for justice without consensus is perhaps the most perplexing of his statements in *The Postmodern Condition*. Lyotard claims, in what is meant to be a criticism of Habermas, that "consensus has become an outmoded and suspect value. But justice as a value is neither outmoded nor suspect. We must thus arrive at an idea and practice of justice that is not linked to that of consensus" (66). But it is difficult to conceptualize what justice without consensus could or would be. Certainly, a once and for always and everyone consensus is not possible (nor desirable), but consensus as an idealizing presupposition for specific forms of justice agreed upon in a noncoercive public sphere seems very much desirable, especially today, when we have *neither* consensus *nor* justice. And simply inverting the equation, as Lyotard does when he calls for "disensus" and "paralogy," is woefully inadequate. Perhaps one way to begin to develop the connection between justice and postmodernity would be to turn to Levinas. In *Totality and Infinity*, Levinas argues that "language is justice" (213). Simon Critchley attempts to "use" Levinas to articulate a sense of social justice via postmodernity. See his *Ethics of Deconstruction: Derrida and Levinas*. But it remains an open question whether Levinas can provide deconstruction with some kind of ethical direction, or whether Lyotard's sense of justice is in *any* empiricohistorical sense possible. Habermas takes up Lyotard's critique in "The Unity of Reason in the Diversity of Its Voices" (115–48) in *Postmetaphysical Thinking*.

Works Cited

Adorno, Theodor W. "Cultural Criticism and Society." *Prisms*. Trans. Samuel and Shierry Weber. Cambridge: MIT P, 1981. 19–34.
———— *Negative Dialectics*. Trans. E. B. Ashton. New York: Continuum, 1973.
Barbiero, Daniel. "A Weakness for Heidegger: The German Root of *Il Pensiero Debole*." *New German Critique* 55 (1992): 159–72.
Bernstein, Richard J. *The New Constellation: The Ethical-Political Horizons of Modernity/Postmodernity*. Cambridge: MIT P, 1992.
Critchley, Simon. *The Ethics of Deconstruction: Derrida and Levinas*. Oxford: Blackwell, 1992.
Deleuze, Gilles. *Nietzsche and Philosophy*. Trans. Hugh Tomlinson. New York: Columbia UP, 1983.
Derrida, Jacques. "The Ends of Man." *After Philosophy: End or Transformation?* Ed. Kenneth Baynes, James Bohman, and Thomas McCarthy. Cambridge: MIT P, 1987. 125–58.
———— *Of Spirit: Heidegger and the Question*. Trans. Geoffrey Bennington and Rachel Bowlby. Chicago: U of Chicago P, 1989.
Foucault, Michel. *The Order of Things: An Archaeology of the Human Sciences*. Trans. Alan Sheridan. New York: Random, 1970.
Habermas, Jürgen. *Communicative Action*. Vol. 1. Trans. Thomas McCarthy. Boston: Beacon, 1984. 2 vols.

—— *The Philosophical Discourse of Modernity*. Trans. Frederick G. Lawrence. Cambridge: MIT P, 1987.

—— *Postmetaphysical Thinking: Philosophical Essays*. Trans. William Mark Hohengarten. Cambridge: MIT P, 1992.

Heidegger, Martin. *Being and Time*. Trans. John Macquarrie and Edward Robinson. New York: Harper, 1962.

—— "Letter on Humanism." *The Basic Writings*. Ed. David Farrell Krell. New York: Harper, 1977. 193–242.

Huyssen, Andreas. *After the Great Divide: Modernism, Mass Culture, Postmodernism*. Bloomington: Indiana UP, 1986.

Jameson, Fredric. *Postmodernism, or, The Cultural Logic of Late Capitalism*. Durham: Duke UP, 1991.

Jay, Martin. "Forum: On Frederic Jameson." *History and Theory* 32.3 (1993): 296–304.

Laclau, Ernesto, and Chantal Mouffe. *Hegemony and Socialist Strategy: Towards a Radical Democratic Politics*. Trans. Winston Moore and Paul Cammack. London: Verso, 1985.

Levinas, Emmanuel. *Totality and Infinity*. Trans. Alphonso Lingis. Pittsburgh: Duquesne UP, 1969.

Lewandowski, Joseph D. "Culture, Textuality, and Truth," *Philosophy and Social Criticism* 19.1 (1993): 43–58.

Lyotard, Jean-François. *The Postmodern Condition: A Report on Knowledge*. Trans. Geoff Bennington and Brian Massumi. Minneapolis: U of Minnesota P, 1984.

McCarthy, Thomas. *Ideals and Illusions: On Deconstruction and Reconstruction in Contemporary Critical Theory*. Cambridge: MIT P, 1991.

Miami Theory Collective. *Community at Loose Ends*. Minneapolis: U of Minnesota P, 1991.

Nancy, Jean-Luc. *The Inoperative Community*. Trans. Peter Connor, Lisa Garbus, Michael Holland, and Simona Sawhney. Minneapolis: U of Minnesota P, 1991.

Nehemas, Alexander. *Nietzsche: Life as Literature*. Cambridge: Harvard UP, 1985.

Rapaport, Herman. *Heidegger and Derrida*. Lincoln: U of Nebraska P, 1989.

R.E.M. *Document*. MCA, 1987.

Spanos, William V. *Heidegger and Criticism: Retrieving the Cultural Politics of Destruction*. Minneapolis: U of Minnesota P, 1993.

Vattimo, Gianni. *The Adventure of Difference: Philosophy After Nietzsche and Heidegger*. Trans. Cyprian Blamires and Thomas Harrison. Baltimore: Johns Hopkins UP, 1993.

—— *The End of Modernity*. Trans. John R. Snyder. Baltimore: Johns Hopkins UP, 1988.

—— *The Transparent Society*. Trans. David Webb. Baltimore: Johns Hopkins UP, 1992.

Wellmer, Albrecht. *The Persistence of Modernity: Essays on Aesthetics, Ethics, and Postmodernism*. Trans. David Midgley. Cambridge: MIT P, 1991.

Wolin, Richard. *The Politics of Being: The Political Thought of Martin Heidegger*. New York: Columbia UP, 1990.

Prosecuting Arguments: The Uncanny and Cynicism in Cultural History

Andrew H. Miller

> [F]ounded on the rupture between a past that is its object, and
> a present that is the place of its practice, history endlessly finds
> the present in its object and the past in its practice. Inhabited
> by the uncanniness that it seeks, history imposes its law upon
> the faraway places that it conquers when it fosters the illusion
> that it is bringing them back to life.
>
> —Michel de Certeau

In the recent conference anthology, *Cultural Studies*, there are
only four historians among the 42 participants—roughly four—
since the difficulty in counting suggests the current flux of disciplinary relations. Three of the four—Lata Mani, Catherine Hall,
and Caroline Steedman—are feminist Victorianists, and the latter
two are markedly uneasy about their inclusion in the anthology:
"Historians," writes Hall,

> have not for the most part felt it necessary to engage with a
> body of work [cultural studies] which does not appear to them
> to relate to their concerns. . . . [I]t is very striking how many

© 1995 by *Cultural Critique*. Winter 1994–95. 0882-4371/95/$5.00.

> historians do not feel obliged to investigate work which would
> relate to their own across a disciplinary boundary. . . . Simi-
> larly, many practitioners of cultural studies have little interest
> in history and rely for their 'background' on secondary
> sources which they do not scrutinize with the textual eagle eye
> that is in use for their own objects of study. (271–72)

"Theory, with a big 'T' was always privileged over history, which
ought to have been spelt with an 'e' for the dreaded empiricism"
(271). As a historian working within a cultural studies program,
Hall's professional position embodies a set of tensions common to
a broader section of those working in cultural history: that field
displays more clearly than others the lines of stress formed by the
conflict of post-structuralist theory and empirically minded history.[1] In literary and cultural studies, these theoretical tensions
were perhaps most famously signalled in the "Preface" to *Allegories
of Reading,* where Paul de Man describes his book's genesis:

> *Allegories of Reading* started out as a historical study and ended
> up as a theory of reading. I began to read Rousseau seriously
> in preparation for a historical reflection on Romanticism and
> found myself unable to progress beyond local difficulties of
> interpretation. (ix)

And, expressing an attitude that has now become widespread, the
historian F. R. Ankersmit similarly describes the "contemporiza-
tion of the historical source," the failure of evidence to "send us
back to the past" (146).[2] While there is no need, at this late stage,
to rehearse these arguments, I would like to indicate two distinct
characteristics of the theoretical domain into which they appear to
be directing the study of history and of cultural history in particular. Reading a diverse set of recent texts on culture and its past we
can see their arguments linked, first, by a tendency to recast the
philosophical dilemma of totalities in the vocabulary of the sublime
and, more specifically, the "uncanny," and, secondly, by their
shared inclination to foreground their awareness of the dilemmas
presented by the uncanniness of their topic. As they incorporate
and deploy theoretical arguments postulated by post-structuralist
theory, these texts of cultural history prosecute—enact and indict—their arguments.

The publication of Christopher Herbert's *Culture and Anomie* provides an important point of departure for these reflections; a history of the "culture-concept," Herbert's book is "a supplement and a critique" of one of the founding texts of cultural studies, Raymond Williams's *Culture and Society*. It is a supplement because, in describing the emergence of the "culture-concept" in the discourses of 19th-century anthropology, political economy, sociology, and religious thought, Herbert extends the narrowly literary scope of Williams's book; it is a critique because Williams's conception of "culture" is, in Herbert's eyes, too monolithic and coherent, its historical emergence too bland and untroubled. Against this uniform development, Herbert anatomizes the philosophical incoherence he sees characterizing the tentative formation and varied deployment of "culture," particularly as it was taken up by the emergent academic disciplines of sociology, anthropology, and political economy. This incoherence rotates around one fundamental aporia: the concept of culture

> claims to ground itself in minute observed detail yet moves in a realm of pseudoentities where "no positive terms" are to be found, but only "a relation in which visibility no longer plays a role" [Foucault, *Order* 218], and where analysis tends if rigorously pursued to take the form of infinite regress. (21)

The methods and the object of cultural studies are mismatched; from the moment its analysis came to seem valuable, culture has been observed through the wrong sort of analytical lenses. Posited as a structure or a set of relations, "a metaphysical, immaterial substance" (14), a symbolic "complex whole" (19), culture is inaccessible to empirical observation. Herbert's book thus suggests why the wariness between empirical and theoretical methods is particularly unsettling and prominent in the historical analysis of culture; other disciplinary realms and theoretical domains suffer from logically congruent disabilities, but cultural history is positioned to reveal those disabilities with particular clarity.

Having shrewdly pointed out the logical dilemma lying at the heart of their project, Herbert then catalogues the various reactions it has inspired in cultural critics. Whether dim or alarmed, the recognition of this fundamental incongruity between methods and object of study encourages a series of evasive rhetorical feints and maneuvers; the determinedly referential language of some writers and the brilliantly suasive figural rhetoric of others are both seen as reactions to the discrepancy between method and object. Not limited to the packaging and presentation of cultural criticism, this fundamental unease soaks down to influence the selection of its objects of study: among its other consequences, this methodological situation encourages cultural critics to analyze the "fantastic imagery of invisible forces" (13), "uncanny impulses and invisible frameworks" (16). The fascination of occult phenomena, of ghosts, divine presences, and "vampire-like spirits," lies, for anthropologists and sociologists, in their status as displaced representations of culture itself. And perhaps the most secure home for these unseen, uncanny representations, although Herbert's discussion here is fairly restricted, is psychology and the culture of the self:

> To grant a royal privilege to this category of invisibility as we automatically do, to define as most authentic that which is least accessible to direct observation, signals (apart from the residual influence of religious symbolism) a huge investment of prestige in various mechanisms of investigation—essential truth must be deeply hidden, otherwise what function can be performed by strenuous technologies of discovery like psychoanalysis. (255)

Herbert's primary point here is to demonstrate the pragmatic benefits to various expert systems of positing inaccessible objects of analysis, but his argument also holds that these uncanny phenomena cast up in a displaced fashion all the problems of cultural history more generally. As my epigraph from de Certeau suggests, the vocabulary of the uncanny, emerging out of one specialized "technology of discovery," serves well to describe both cultural history and its object.[3]

But, of course, *Culture and Anomie* is itself an instance of cultural studies, and perhaps the principal dramatic fascination for readers of the book lies in watching it alternately succumb to and swerve from these methodological quandaries while it points them out for us. Indeed, so strong is this fascination that it often occludes the detailed arguments Herbert has to make about past disciplinary practices. Moments of theoretical analysis and self-consciousness alternate with moments of narrative activity in abrupt fits and starts; the argument proceeds rapidly, only to be suddenly becalmed by Herbert's skepticism regarding the theoretical principles of his work. In confronting the discord between his knowledge and his performance, between his object of study and the available methods of its analysis, Herbert deploys neither of the two main techniques he notices in other writers; his argument is striking neither for its elegant, persuasively figural language, nor for its deployment of empirical evidence. Instead of opting for figure or for positivism, Herbert responds to the predicament of cultural studies and the fatal logic of his own austere argument by bold confession:

> I am simply trying to find a way to a style of history of ideas which can remain plausible or at least legible once one has become sensitized to the equivocal status of "so-called empirical observations" and systems of explanation of all kinds. If it be said that I offer a method unable to provide a rigorous self-justification, I can only reply that the lesson of much contemporary theory is that this state of theoretical disablement has become our inescapable one for the time being, and that we had better get used to it. (27)

As this theatrical collapse into pragmatism suggests, Herbert announces his own vulnerability to the charge of circularity with some calculated audacity. We are told of it on the book's opening page, and the thoroughness of this vulnerability unfolds and returns as the book develops. In an endnote, Herbert later writes:

> A Barthian concept of reading as an uncovering or an engendering of a scarcely limitable "process of equivalence" inflects (infects?) the present inquiry in ways which by now should be evident and which render it at last in a circularity bound to elude full explication, an inquiry into its own conditions of possibility. (314)

Recognizing perhaps that such circularity can just as easily demonstrate the impossibility of this project, its inability to avoid posing at least some questions which are empty or tautological, the book closes with a final confessional recognition of its conceptual predicament:

> I can only plead in my own defense that [this] is the one [logical dilemma] to which ethnographic imagination and modern consciousness itself tend inescapably, and from which no escape can for the time being be discovered. (305)

As these quotations indicate, Herbert's text is characterized by a sort of methodological pathos; I described *Culture and Anomie* to a colleague who nodded and remarked: "a long 'Dejection Ode.'"

As I have suggested, the distinctive thing about Herbert's book is that it proposes a mode of writing which foregrounds questions of its own critical viability. And at the heart of this self-reflexivity is a distinction between the performative and cognitive aspects of these texts, between what they (or their authors) know and what they do: Herbert knows that his own work is susceptible to the criticisms he levels at others, that *Culture and Anomie* is limited by the uncanniness of the object it has posited for analysis—he announces as much.[4] At the same time, while knowing this, he still does what he does, proceeding with his interpretive tasks. Slavoj Žižek has recently analyzed this shifting distance between knowledge and practice as the defining characteristic of what, following Sloterdijk, he critically calls "cynical reason": "I know very well that the theoretical principles under which I am operating are logically incoherent," one might say, "but I will continue to use them." Although Žižek unearths the operation of this "cynicism" in social theory and political philosophy, his paradigmatic illustrations come from horror movies and the films of Hitchcock, rich repositories of the uncanny; at the most general level, these cultural objects depend for their effects on our simultaneous absorption and distance, our subjection to the power of horror and our understanding that it is all "just a movie."[5] The effects Herbert describes in the work of Victorian sociologists and anthropologists as culture was first becoming an object of study have been turned into commodities and marketed through popular culture. The pleasurable experience of knowing better than one does has become a good for mass consumption. One of the achievements of Herbert's book is to have identified one particularly distinct formulation of this traditional aesthetic experience within popular culture; Anthony Trollope's analysis of class, we are told, "focuses on the paradox that people worship the doctrine of caste distinctions and key their whole lives to it to the degree that even their most private and passional experience falls under its sway, *when in fact no one really believes it at all*" (271). Once this is mentioned, one realizes that a broad range of the satisfactions Trollope provides derives from his display and enactment of this discrepancy: Trollope compliments his readers by assuming they know better than to believe in the plots he constructs—and, having received this compliment, readers can proceed to then enjoy those plots and that world. Culture, and not just its analysis, appears to be formed around the distance between knowing and doing.

This brief consideration of Trollope suggests that this attitude, as it appears in both critical and popular texts, presenting a distinctive array of reading experiences, invites its own phenomenology of reading. Such a phenomenology would catalogue experiences such as the dramatic fascination I mentioned above, the uneasy and uneven apprehension of texts as theory and as narrative, as well as a second distinctive phenomena produced by these texts, namely a fluctuating uncertainty about authorial intentions. The discrepancy between textual knowledge and action is in this light a central theoretical occasion for the destabilization of the subject in contemporary criticism: the author's inability to control the relation of knowing and doing, of constative and performative, means that readers cannot locate or accurately describe the author's positions. Reading Herbert it is clear enough that, in general, he recognizes his implication in the dynamic he is describing, but whether he recognizes this implication at this or that particular moment in his argument is less clear for the reader.

Foregrounding self-reflexive analysis, these texts cannot indicate for their readers where that analysis stops; this is an inescapable condition, one which no degree of vigilance on the part of their authors would eliminate, as Herbert—I suspect—would admit. In the case of Trollope, the publication of *The Autobiography* only exacerbated the questions—regarding his faith in the forms and methods which he employed and from which he earned a living—that are on the surface of the novels themselves. Having noticed this, we can now provide another description for the boldly confessional tactics of Herbert's book; *Culture and Anomie* is less a long "Dejection Ode" than it is a distinctly Trollopian text, and the moments of candid avowal there resemble nothing so much as those when Trollope apologizes for the failures of his narrative methods, confessing his own disenchantment with them.

Having used Herbert's book to sketch out the two central themes at play in my argument—the uncanniness of culture and consumer/critics' inevitably cynical awareness of that uncanniness—I want now to turn to several other recent works of and on cultural history in order to suggest both the prevalence of these characteristics and some significant variations taken by them. I will look initially at the visual arts, where one might suspect the disjuncture between the object of critical analysis and its circumambient culture to be sharpest. If, as Herbert argues, culture is "'a relation in which visibility no longer plays a role,'" then those disciplines designed to elucidate the visual will confront the paradoxes of the culture concept most noticeably. What was in the reading of *Culture and Anomie* an uneven narrative experience of repeated collapse and regeneration is transposed and condensed in art criticism into the ekphrastic distance between images and their cultures as represented in critics' writing. Analyzing the rhetoric of his own discipline with a "textual eagle eye," Norman Bryson reformulates the limitations of empirical analysis as predicaments for causal explanation: the causal context of a work, he notes, is inevitably supplemental and potentially illimitable; the relevant contextual details, apprehended by historical excavation, can only be circumscribed by pragmatic or polemical interests. "Once begun, the enumeration of contextual determinants knows no point of finality within its own domain" (22). Bryson extends Herbert's catalogue of the ruses by which writers attempt to escape the stark failure of their empirical methods. The illimitability of context can be finessed by appealing to any of a number of containing concepts, beginning with the text itself: the incoherence of the innumerable contextual factors is replaced by the coherence of the text; "the unity of the 'determined' object" thus "stands in for the unity of the causal account" (24). Alternatively, the potential illimitability of the causal context can be contained by reference to the "organic unity of traditions" or to the "creativity of the artist-subject." In each case, the value of a work is seen to depend on its ability to

rise above "the *mechanical* nexus of cause and effect" (26); mediocre
works can be explained by the critic through causal language;
superior works are seen as those which elude such explanation.
But all of these rhetorical maneuvers are predicated on one fundamental strategic gesture which Bryson describes as "text-stroke-
context": in order to assert the association of a particular text with
a context we must first sever them, isolating the text as an object
of study independent of its occasions. "The crucial action performed here by the rhetoric is the postulation of an interval between the text and the context, such that the two, having been
separated, may come together in a moment of proof" (31).

Having delineated these logical shifts and swerves, Bryson
himself abruptly veers into a consideration of the reception of art,
appealing to the historical effects of art as a way of escaping the
problems of their causes. "[T]he way that visual texts were apprehended by actual viewers in a given historical period . . . does a
great deal to call into question the notion of a 'timeless' response
to paintings" (31). History is best excavated not in studying the
production of texts but in their reception. Like Herbert, Bryson is
very cautious in describing the possibilities of this historical excavation, noting that the reception of cultural texts comes down to
us in conventional forms—treatises, pamphlets, catalogues, re-
views—from a very few sources. But, in a gesture that simultaneously solicits an acknowledgement of his own situation as a writer
and of the scene of aesthetic reception, he presents an image to
rectify the inadequacies of written accounts:

> So far as the historical record goes, the viewing of pictures is
> largely a silent activity. Of course it was far from being literally
> silent. I am looking at an engraving from the eighteenth-
> century, depicting an Academy exhibition. . . . The figures are
> gesticulating and craning to see, are busy talking in couples or
> in groups, are admiring or criticizing what is around them,
> are looking detached from the crowd or are quizzing the
> paintings as connoisseurs. (34–35)

The ekphrastic description given to the reader is an inversion of
the image Bryson depicts: we have it described for us verbally but
do not see the engraving which rectifies the textual record for Bryson, reminding him as he sits before his word processor of the lost

words of reception. But, of course, this rectification is itself silent; the images stand somewhere else with their mouths open but their words lost. The unfolding narratives of critical analysis are replaced by a (verbally represented) static palimpsest of images.

This silent realm Bryson designates "the reserve," and his prescriptive argument is simply that we keep this reserve in mind as we work, that the limits of what we know be a methodological familiar or companion. The reserve represents for art historians a formulation of the philosophical problem described in *Culture and Anomie* for intellectual historians: "it is well to acknowledge," writes Herbert, "the wide domain of the unknowable in the past world that we have the audacity to manufacture out of historical documents" (303). This reserve houses the ultimate object of Bryson's study, "the motility of viewing" (38), the Barthian play of wordless glances before images of the past—this "motility" serving the same role in his argument as the "scarcely limitable 'process of equivalence'" placed at the center of *Culture and Anomie*.

Sustaining a graceful and incisive analytical prose throughout his essay, Bryson suddenly waxes lyrical as he describes his guiding methodological concept, offering us again an image to arrest the narrative progression of his argument:

> The advantage of "reserve" as a concept here is precisely its negativity and emptiness. "Reserve" is dark. Once "reception" goes beyond being a discourse based on other prior discourses. and ventures out into domains where there are only viewing practices without accompanying discourse, a sudden vista appears that is that of night. A space is opened up that cannot be scanned, compounded, and generalized, for it is a space that nothing visible fills. An image of Michel de Certeau comes to mind: "a car at the edge of cliff. Beyond, nothing but the sea." (37)

Positing viewing as an experience that can be cut from previous discourses, freeing it from history, Bryson himself performs the gesture of "text-stroke-context": the viewing practice lies alone at an interval from "accompanying discourse." More specifically, however, he figures the reserve, cut off from history, as an implicitly feminine figure, something like what Julia Kristeva would call the "chora"; the reserve is a space and an image, a figure in the mind set at a distance from the analytic terms of language, a prelin-guistic, feminine space beyond rational knowledge. Given the fa-miliar gendering of the terms Bryson uses to describe this space—"dark," "fluid," "empty," "ahistorical," "silent"—it is not entirely surprising that his example of visual practices that reside in the reserve are those of women. But these examples themselves are offered without extended commentary, appearing in the text as if randomly selected: "How should we view this immense *reserve?* Above all, by remembering it is there, even when it cannot be re-trieved; and by noticing the absences in the record as much as what survives. For example . . . the absence of women" (35). Or again, but this time without the drama of the ellipses, he asks, "How is it that female spectatorship has not been, from the beginning, a pri-mary object of art-historical inquiry?" (40). The uncertainty of au-thorial intent, noted earlier as a characteristic of cultural texts at-tentive to the implications of post-structuralist claims concerning the constative and performative aspects of language, arises again: it is difficult to know how fully Bryson's repeated choice of women to exemplify the practical consequences of attending to the reserve indicates his conscious knowledge of the gendering of that cat-egory.

The lyricism of Bryson's reserve recalls Herbert's insistence that one response to the discrepancy between culture and the ana-lytical tools brought to it is figural excess; this lyricism also illus-trates Alan Liu's acute argument that the characteristic trait of recent "contextual criticism" is its substitution of rhetoric for refer-ence, its turn, anxious or enraptured, from the empirical to fig-ural. "The Real in cultural criticism," he argues, "is indistinguish-able from figure":

> How else could we understand what *is* [what Liu calls "the de-tail," the object instantiated by cultural criticism] by what *is not* except by synecdoche, metaphor, or symbol so extreme that it is catachresis? . . . We end on some cloud-wrapped Snowdon or nimbus-noumenon where any visible detail—say the way a rift in the cloud sublimes all the underlying voices of the world—marks the threshold of the visionary. (93)

As in Bryson, the visual returns to redeem the rhetorical; the stasis of an image rises to suspend critical narrative: a rift in a cloud, a car on a cliff, "sublimes" the provisionality of contextual, causal, and empirical criticism. Liu's descriptive claim, as the allusions of this passage suggest, is that current cultural criticism, which ostensibly has foresworn transcendental purchases, nonetheless remains mired in a romantic epistemological paradigm of the sublime; "contextual critics" are Romantic writers whether they like it or not. "Cultural criticism is 'first' of all an allusion to the moment when the rhetoric of empiricism confronted the early regime of the fragment: an emerging romantic rhetoric" (87). Liu's prescriptive argument is that the moment in which the critic realizes his or her position within the sublime—becomes self-conscious, aware of the radical disjuncture between the details of cliff and car and the horizonless sea of details roiling beyond—should be acknowledged and sustained.

Just as Bryson encourages us to keep the reserve in mind and Herbert announces the foundering of his method, so Liu urges critics to recognize that they repeatedly are falling into the sublime. And this process is understood, as the related process is understood in Herbert, as a failure that Liu himself does not escape:

> [W]e should be aware that we are . . . *reading*—that we are dealing with rhetoric as the facsimile knowledge or pseudo-analytic whose distinctive method is its tendency to lose its way at decisive moments, to pose a logic of detail only to thwart itself (in the essential de Manian reading) by interposing incommensurable logics. (81)

For Liu as for Herbert, cultural analysis is an inevitable process of dereliction, a Wordsworthian criticism uneasily aware that it has just crossed the Alps.

Although Liu assimilates what he calls "New Marxists" (Althusser, Macheray, Jameson) to his romantic paradigm, an old tradition of Marxist criticism has occupied itself with exactly this process of critical dereliction, of history moving forward by repeated failure: "It is almost tautological," writes Adorno, for instance, "to say that one cannot point to the concept of totality in the same manner one can point to the facts, from which totality distances itself as a concept" (10; see also Jameson 208–09). And Adorno's famous correspondence with his friend Benjamin turns on this issue, on the relation between "mere facts" and a totalizing theory. By excluding this philosophical tradition from his reflections, and by aestheticizing the incommensurability of detail and complex whole, Liu privileges the romantic and literary language of the sublime, describing the critic in terms previously used to describe the poet. Just as women occupy an uncanny place for Bryson—forcibly present but inadequately recognized—so Marxism here is present but not fully apprehended by Liu's text.

I have deferred discussing the uncanny element of Herbert's writing, but the quotations given from *Culture and Anomie* above should make it clear that this element is history itself; neatly demonstrating the way that past cultural criticism has made its object of study an uncanny phenomenon, Herbert represents the passage of time in a similarly uncanny fashion. In describing the historical development of "anomie" from its initial emergence as a boundless desire posited by Wesley and Evangelicalism to its fully developed form in the enervated restlessness described by Durkheim, Herbert sketches no progression of empirically observable events or behaviors; he does not propose to trace a history of unbridled desire and restlessness in itself. Instead he analyzes the logical and figural structures shared by a series of writers: "the congruent metaphorical structures of their texts," he writes of Wesley and Durkheim, "tell us plainly that they are participants in a single movement of thought" (72). History appears to inhabit rhetoric, emerging in the textual responses of authors to the failure of representational possibilities.

But the difficulty Herbert describes in moving from the observed particular to the "complex whole" or totality also besets this specifically historical component of his enterprise. Having delineated in his introduction the main paradox of culture study, Herbert interrupts his argument—marking this interruption with the one typographical break in the chapter—to announce: "If the concept of culture, on which so much hinges nowadays, is after all infested with logical incoherence, the question of its historical origins takes on particular interest and even urgency" (21). History suddenly rises here as the possible escape route by which the paradoxes of cultural study can be safely outdistanced. But no sooner is it sighted, however, than the possibility of this genetic "solution" to the problems plaguing culture too turns into a cul de sac. In

176   *Andrew H. Miller*

describing his attempt to study the prehistory of culture as a concept, the signs which heralded its coming before particular figures
were aware of its approach, Herbert writes:

> Like an astronomer tracking an invisible planet, by study-
> ing deflections in the orbits of visible ones, an analyst of
> nineteenth-century texts often is forced to make out the pres-
> ence of the culture-idea (always a site of disturbance in the
> intellectual cosmos) through oblique reasoning focussed on
> pieces of anomalous evidence. (24)

Instructed by Herbert himself, the reader immediately recognizes
this conceit as a rhetorical flight that masks the vulnerability of
Herbert's own methods; this absent planet is merely an astronomi-
cal version of the revenants and uncanny forces which rearrange
all that is present without themselves being fully available to perception. Rather than legitimating Herbert's project, this planetary
figure merely extends the effects of Herbert's skepticism to include
advanced science, and Herbert's move toward the historical reconstruction of the culture idea continues to suffer from the inconsistencies of cultural studies he describes. Perceiving the relations between rhetorical structures in historical texts is no more certain an
epistemological project than seeing the relation between empirically observed details and larger, complex symbolic structures. History is not conceptually prior to the emergence of those dilemmas
Herbert associates with culture, but is implicated in them. Casting
all this in a linguistic register, de Man makes this position explicit:
"The aporia between performative and constative language is
merely a version of the aporia between trope and persuasion that
both generates and paralyses rhetoric and thus gives it the appearance of a history" (131). History appears to precipitate from the
structural dilemmas of knowing and doing, cast off by the heat of
that structure's internal motion.

Again in this specifically historical guise, Herbert's text indicates a more general predicament. As Peter Novick writes, the historian's "aspiration, insofar as it transcends compiling an accurate
chronicle, is holistic comprehension" (582), but it is exactly this
move of transcendence that Herbert (like Bryson and Liu) identi-

fies and sees as a problem. And Jacob Neusner presents this well-known view of historical activity in terms familiar from Liu's essay: "For us the task is to treat the [historical] document as a cultural artifact, as evidence for the working out of a [past] social order in small detail" (138)—but the movement from evidence to social order is not so easily performed. "The written history is a story," writes Caroline Steedman, "that can only be told by the implicit understanding that *things are not over,* that the story isn't finished, can never be finished, for some new item of information may alter the account that has been given" (614). And, pithily summing much of this up, Clifford Geertz describes "the ragged Forces of History shattering the crystal Patterns of Culture" (326). One surprise of *Culture and Anomie,* given these historiographical observations, is that it does not contain a chapter on the problems of the "culture idea" in the work of 19th-century historians: one can imagine a reading of Scott and Macaulay, drawing perhaps on Lukács' work in *The Historical Novel.* But "what disappears from the product appears once again in production," and instead of taking this historical problem up as a chapter topic, *Culture and Anomie* as a whole embodies it (de Certeau 30). Indeed, what is the uncanny itself, in this context, but the return in the process of what has been lost from the product? Not present to consciousness as a memory, the repressed returns in the process of critical analysis, and what "one does" reveals what one does not always know.

But at this stage it should come as no surprise that Herbert does recognize and intermittently advertises in general terms the uncanny relation of his argument to history; one characteristic of texts which foreground the discrepancy between what they know and what they do, again, is the recognition and deflationary incorporation of their own uncanniness. "I have called my study . . . 'intellectual history,'" he writes,

> but it may hardly deserve this honorific name. It presents no very coherent narrative, indeed, hardly any consecutive narrative at all; and it leaves largely in abeyance the question of the causes of intellectual change in order to focus on uncovering sometimes intricate structures of thought and implication in particular texts. (303)

While he repeats the logic of de Man's preface to *Allegories of Reading*—announcing his turn from historical forms and analysis to close readings—Herbert also repeats his own earlier observation that the incoherence of the culture idea has given him his intellectual task. Now that he has closed that critical project, he and his readers are left where they began, looking now not to the past but to the future, waiting out the predicament of "modern consciousness," subject to an uncanny history.

I want to conclude by briefly classifying the primary responses we have seen prompted by this uneasy oscillation of knowledge and action, cognition and performance. If, as I suggested above, cynical reason encourages its own phenomenology of reading it also encourages a renewed attention to problems of evaluation. Herbert indicates as much when he addresses the charge that Trollope is a snob: "[A]ny such judgement," he writes,

> needs to notice that Trollope is at pains to advertize, rather than sweep under a rhetorical carpet, that sympathy with upper-class values means embracing a set of ideas that often seem wildly self-contradicting and morally dubious. It should notice, too, that this awkward position is nothing other than the one implied . . . by the relativistic doctrine of culture. (284)

Which is to say, to potential critics of Trollope, that the novelist has already thought of your criticism and incorporated it into his writing. "We can no longer subject the ideological text," Žižek writes, "to 'symptomatic reading,' confronting it with its blank spots, with what it must repress to organize itself—cynical reason takes this distance into account" (*Sublime Object* 30). This fundamental critical task has, to a greater or lesser degree, already been performed by the object of one's criticism, threatening to leave the reader in a sort of bemused passivity. Žižek overstates the case for the obsolescence of symptomatic criticism here. As I argued above, one cannot know with absolute certainty exactly what a text or its author knows; foregrounding its repressed blank spots, therefore, will remain one constructive critical possibility. But Žižek's general point is well taken: the value of this critical task has been attenuated by the logic of cynical reason. The limitations of knowledge and especially of its performative powers are suddenly made vivid.

The historical question which then rises—but which lies outside the scope of this essay—is why such analytical methods attentive to the performative limitations of knowledge, to all that knowledge cannot do, should be especially prevalent at this particular moment in the academy.

Beyond this ideological critique, the vocabulary of the uncanny suggests that responses to cynical reason tend to take two forms. "The recent fixation on an (an)aesthetic of the sublime," writes Dominic LaCapra, "tends to fetishize or compulsively repeat what is indeed one important and unavoidable possibility in thought" (434). The uncanny, of course, is exactly that which must be repeated (see Freud). Critics return to these uncanny analytical situations because they are constitutively incomplete, the sublime excess of culture continually escaping the empirical analysis of the critic. The uncanny structure of cultural history, the elusiveness of the conceptual problematic in the works I have been considering, encourages, both in particular texts and among various texts, what de Man called, in closing *Allegories,* the repetition of their aberration.

If this reiteration is one response prompted by the uncanniness of cultural history, the other is repression. Having identified the obsessively repetitive quality of work attentive to the sublime, LaCapra goes on to argue that the critical task before "modern consciousness" is to temper this compulsion, to explore instead

> the interaction between various dimensions of language use and its relation to practice, including the relationship between "constative" ahistorical [archival] reconstruction and "performative" dialogic exchange with the past as well as between "sublime" excess and the normative limits that are necessary as controls in social and political life. (434)

While I am sympathetic to this call, the vocabulary of the uncanny suggests that such turns from the compulsion to repeat will most easily be understood as a form of repression. Understanding the "incommensurable logics" Liu describes in disciplinary terms, for instance, Stanley Fish argues:

> In order to function in [a] discipline, the fragility of [its] identity is something the worker cannot know or at least must al-

ways forget when entering its precincts. . . . [Such] denying and forgetting are not reformable errors but the very grounds of cognition and assertion. (20)

Moving between cultural and historical analysis, in this argument, requires that one repress the provisionality of each discipline's assumptions and then proceed with a sort of blinkered methodological dogmatism. The final contribution offered to this debate by the vocabulary of the uncanny, I think, is that it encourages us to consider these two processes as somehow going on simultaneously. Fish's argument, to stay with his example, gains its persuasive force from its use of spatial metaphors: disciplines have "borders," and "property lines," across which figures may "migrate" or be "imported."

Within the imaginative field marked off by this positivist rhetoric, it appears only common sense that the interdisciplinary integration of cultural and historical analyses is difficult, for this would require that one be in two places at once. But this uncanny experience of division and duplication is exactly what recent cultural criticism posits as an intellectual norm—as Fish himself, in a qualifying endnote, seems to recognize. A colleague, he writes, has reminded him "of an experience that many of us will be able to recall, knowing while watching a horror movie that certain devices are being used to frighten us and yet being frightened nevertheless despite our knowledge. In experiences like this an analytical understanding of what is happening exists side by side with what is happening but does not affect or neutralize it." For cultural historians, this uncanny experience, as I have attempted to demonstrate, instead of being an occasional disturbance, characterizes "the time being," when an understanding of the limitations of theoretical arguments routinely accompanies their prosecution.

Notes

1. Acknowledging that the "matter-of-fact, antitheoretical and antiphilosophical objectivist empiricism which had always been the dominant stance of American historians continued to be enormously powerful" in the 1980s (593–94), Peter Novick provides a valuable discussion of competing methodological principles (see especially chapters 15 and 16).

2. Cousins provides a succinct analysis of the opposition between the "professional practice of historical investigation" (129) and philosophies of history.

3. Describing the migration of gothic images of ghosts and spirits from the external world into "the intimate space of the mind" (58), Terry Castle writes:

> By the time of Freud, the rhetorical pattern had resolved, as it were, into a cultural pathology: everyone felt "haunted." That is to say, the mind itself now seemed a kind of supernatural space, filled with intrusive spectral presences—incursions from past or future, ready to terrify, pursue, or disable the harried subject. (59)

4. While Herbert is tentative in his deployment of deconstructive reading practices, it is clear that these practices have provided a major stimulus to this recognition; in the book's concluding paragraph we are reminded of Derrida's observation in *Grammatology* that "philosophical deconstruction 'always in a certain way falls prey to its own work'" (304).

5. Sloterdijk proposes and develops the concept of cynical reason in *Critique of Cynical Reason;* more recently, Žižek's *Enjoy Your Symptom!* extensively analyzes the cynical films of Hollywood, a project begun earlier in his *Sublime Object of Ideology.* As should become clear through the course of this paper, I am less inclined than Žižek to see cynical reason as a rectifiable problem and more as a constitutive characteristic of culture and cultural criticism.

Works Cited

Adorno, Theodor. "Letters to Walter Benjamin." *Aesthetics and Politics.* Ed. Ronald Taylor. London: Verso, 1980. 110–33.

Ankersmit, F. R. "Historiography and Post-Modernism." *History and Theory* 28 (1989): 137–53.

Bryson, Norman. "Art in Context." *Studies in Historical Change.* Ed. Ralph Cohen. Charlottesville: U of Virginia P, 1992. 18–42.

Castle, Terry. "Phantasmagoria: Spectral Technology and the Metaphorics of Modern Reverie." *Critical Inquiry* 15 (Autumn 1988): 26–61.

Cousins, Mark. "The Practice of Historical Investigation." *Post-Structuralism and the Question of History.* Ed. Derek Attridge, Geoff Bennington, and Robert Young. New York: Cambridge UP, 1987. 126–36.

de Certeau, Michel. *The Writing of History.* Trans. Tom Conley. New York: Columbia UP, 1988.

de Man, Paul. *Allegories of Reading.* New Haven: Yale UP, 1979.

Fish, Stanley. "Being Interdisciplinary Is So Very Hard to Do." *Profession '89.* New York: Modern Language Association, 1989. 15–22.

Foucault, Michel. *The Order of Things.* New York: Vintage, 1973.

Freud, Sigmund. "The 'Uncanny.'" *Standard Edition of the Complete Psychological Works of Sigmund Freud.* Vol. 17. Trans. James Strachey. London: Hogarth, 1955. 217–56. 24 vols.

Geertz, Clifford. "History and Anthropology." *New Literary History* 21.2 (1990): 321–35.

Hall, Catherine. "Missionary Stories: Gender and Ethnicity in England in the 1830s and 1840s." *Cultural Studies.* Ed. Lawrence Grossberg, Cary Nelson, and Paula Treichler. New York: Routledge, 1992. 240–76.

Herbert, Christopher. *Culture and Anomie*. Chicago: U of Chicago P, 1991.

Jameson, Fredric. *Postmodernism, or, The Cultural Logic of Late Capitalism*. Durham: Duke UP, 1991.

LaCapra, Dominic. "Intellectual History and Its Ways." *American Historical Review* 97.2 (1992): 425–39.

Liu, Alan. "Local Transcendence: Cultural Criticism, Postmodernism, and the Romanticism of Detail." *Representations* 32 (Fall 1990): 75–113.

Lukács, Georg. *The Historical Novel*. Trans. Hannah and Stanley Mitchell. Lincoln: U of Nebraska P, 1983.

Neusner, Jacob. "The Historical Event as a Cultural Indicator: The Case of Judaism." *History and Theory* 30.2 (1991): 136–52.

Novick, Peter. *That Noble Dream*. Cambridge: Cambridge UP, 1988.

Sloterdijk, Peter. *Critique of Cynical Reason*. London: Verso, 1988.

Steedman, Caroline. "Culture, Cultural Studies, and the Historians." *Cultural Studies*. Ed. Lawrence Grossberg, Cary Nelson, and Paula Treichler. New York: Routledge, 1992. 613–22.

Williams, Raymond. *The Country and the City*. New York: Oxford UP, 1973.

———. *Culture and Society*. New York: Columbia UP, 1983.

Žižek, Slavoj. *Enjoy Your Symptom*. New York: Routledge, 1992.

———. *The Sublime Object of Ideology*. London: Verso, 1989.

Reforming Relativists: Debates Over Literacy and Difference

Sangeeta Luthra

It would be tantamount to blasphemy in the current political and economic climate of the United States to put under serious scrutiny the value of literacy for the individual or for modern society at large. Politicians and pedagogues alike are calling for action, not debate and reflection—"we are in a crisis, at a crossroads," they say, "and something needs *to be done!*" Of course, each program, each surge forward against the enemy is done in conference with "fact-finding missions" and expert advice on the root of the evil—illiteracy. Everyone, that is, every type of person, seems to be involved—conservative, liberal, and leftist intellectuals; the U.S. Department of Education; national and local media; and film, television, and sports celebrities. But despite the diversity of persons involved, there seems to be a singular understanding of literacy and education amongst them. The most basic aspect of that understanding is that literacy and education are ultimately, incontestably, and universally "good."

Of course, there are challenges to this uncontextualized and reified conceptualization of literacy. In this paper, I will review

© 1995 by *Cultural Critique*. Winter 1994–95. 0882-4371/95/$5.00.

some critical analyses of the term "literacy" (and "illiteracy") as well as some propositions that have been made for moving beyond a deconstruction.[1] However, to begin with we must understand the character of the obstacles that hinder attempts at critically analyzing literacy. This essay looks first at some critical attempts to redefine literacy so that literacy education and reform will recognize and respect differences based in race, class, gender, sexuality, nationality, culture, etc. The efforts of this first group of scholars originate in a concern for acknowledging, respecting, and exploring differences that get expressed through different kinds of literacy and languages in general. The respect for difference of all kinds is central.

This paper also looks at more conventional analyses of literacy, in particular E. D. Hirsch's *Cultural Literacy*, which characterize the current decline in literacy rates as an epidemic—the beginning of the end of modern civilization. In this regard, I will look at the role of anthropological theory, in particular the work of Jack Goody (for example, "The Consequences of Literacy" and *The Domestication of the Savage Mind*), in generating and continuing to support what is now the conventional and widespread definition of literacy. Juxtaposing Hirsch's *Cultural Literacy* to anthropological discourses on literacy is necessary because Hirsch begins with the anthropological thesis that literacy is a means for the "acculturation" of working-class and minority children into mainstream American culture (xvi, xvii). The efforts of this second group, as illustrated in Hirsch's work, originate in the belief that difference or "diversity" is generally antithetical to democracy and "progress" in modern societies. This group seeks to emphasize and enforce "sameness" or, as in the case of canonized anthropological theories of literacy,[2] to link literacy to other developments in Western society that place modern, Western societies at the top of a social evolutionary or developmental scale.

What Are the Stakes in Reformulating the Notion of Literacy?

In his essay "Discourse of Power, the Dialectics of Understanding, the Power of Literacy," Adrian Bennett explains, almost apologetically, that his analysis of literacy in current pedagogic practices in the United States is not meant as "an 'attack' on literacy" (19). We can see from this qualification that the stakes are high when "critique" is in danger of being conflated with "attack"—that is, when critique is viewed as destruction or annihilation. On the contrary, Bennett seeks to *augment* our understanding of literacy so that it will work better for more people than is currently the case:

> I have suggested that the discourses which we "accept and make function as true" in formal education today are typically those of the ideal texts of *essayist literacy,* and what I want to suggest now is that the constraints on truth, or understanding, associated with the discourses of essayist literacy may often act as strategies for sustaining particular relations of power. . . . [And] that wherever language is, there we will also find mechanisms (or better, strategies) of social control that make use of particular forms of discourse. (19; my emphasis)

Above, Bennett has laid out two central moves in the critique of conventional definitions of literacy. First, he points out that the word "literacy" as it is used in contemporary U.S. society is not inclusive of all the kinds of written language observable in the world. Rather, "literacy" most often refers specifically to "essayist literacy" or the "plain style of writing" that was developed in Europe during the 16th century beginning with the work of Martin Luther and later in the charter of the Royal Society of London and in the works of the British Empiricists (Olson 72–73). It is this "plain style" or "essayist literacy" that is hegemonic in current discourses (15).[3] In addition, the conflation of "essayist literacy" with writing in general is not accidental. It is a means of regulating not only writing itself, but also those who write. In other words, the absolute authority that has accrued to essayist literacy as opposed to other forms (genres) of writing, and more generally of communication, is legitimated by the association of essayist literacy with the powerful discourses and institutions of Western science.

Second, in discussing literacy, Bennett invokes power and social control. Such a move is still relatively unheard of in most popular discourses of literacy, which see it as primarily a phenomenon of foundationalist epistemology and pedagogy—entirely autonomous of politics. By inserting the issues of power, social control, and ideology, as in Elspeth Stuckey's *Violence of Literacy,* in a discussion of literacy, the proverbial first stone has been thrown and the battle has begun in the eyes of a great majority of people: academics, teachers, administrators, politicians, corporate executives, parents, and students alike. For this majority, literacy is about the Enlightenment ideal of the search for eternal and immutable knowledge, truth, and progress—all supposedly unsullied by political concerns.

By suggesting that literacy is not just a neutral *tool* through which an individual becomes a better, more intelligent, and more responsible person and through which a society can develop and become modern, we can expose in current literacy discourses a world view for what it is—one among many. Furthermore, we jeopardize its claim to exclusivity and universality. Such iconoclasm is not only a challenge to the major and minor deities of modern, Western society, which notably are as often cherished by those very groups who have been excluded from the privilege and power that flows from them. It is also a challenge to particular groups of people for whom "essayist literacy" is normative.

Most importantly, Bennett's objective is not to obliterate essayist literacy. Rather it is to validate other forms of literacy that may be working for groups other than white, middle- and upper-class, male-dominated society. In this view, the stakes for those who want to maintain monolithic conceptualizations of literacy are the preservation of a particular world view and of economic and political power for those whom that world view subsidizes. In Foucauldian terms, the conventional discourse of literacy is about the mechanics of power (131). In fact, literacy provides an especially interesting conjuncture of discourse and power because it is obviously both. It is a discourse—that is, language and communication—and it entails power as a skill and a credential through association with Enlightenment values.

While one might expect conventional articulations of literacy to involve clearly fixed meanings, this is not the case. Even for those who would ground literacy in foundationalist epistemologies and ontologies, the notion of "literacy" is ambiguous. Barbara Herrnstein Smith's analysis of Hirsch's *Cultural Literacy* highlights the ambiguity of the term "literacy" in Hirsch's work:

The verbal slippage noted above—that is, between "literate" in the sense of being able to read adequately, and "literate" in the sense of being well-read, well-educated, and, in that sense, "cultured"—is crucial to the shimmering ambiguity of the term and concept "cultural literacy". . . . ("Cult-Lit" 75)

Thus, part of what a good critique of literacy would entail is the exposure of the prevalence of the latter meaning (i.e., being cultured) and the ethnocentrism it entails, as a subtext for campaigns that claim to be concerned only with the former sense (i.e., being able to read and write). Furthermore, the conflation of the latter sense of literacy with the former is not a case of innocent confusion but is a classic case of symbolic violence through the mystification of cultural capital like literacy. Pierre Bourdieu's term for such mystification is "misrecognition" and suggests that where "misrecognition" occurs there is also the potential for symbolic violence of one group [class] against another (21, 190–97). In Hirsch's case, the misrecognition is thinly veiled since he begins with the claim that working-class children have been held back from upward mobility because of a paucity of cultural literacy in their schools (xiii–xiv). Hirsch's explanation of the current decline of American education and society elides the economic and political bases for class inequity (xi). Smith's analysis of *Cultural Literacy* seems to corroborate the element of domination that Bennett spoke of, and, as both Bennett and Smith have suggested, the stakes for keeping the term "literacy" ambiguous are high.

Although Bennett and Smith are not alone in attempting a critique of conventional notions of literacy, they still represent a small minority.[4] According to Bennett, this is because "[u]ntil fairly recently it has generally been assumed that literacy is a good thing, that in any case, it is essential to active membership in modern industrial and urban societies" (13). Bennett goes on to invoke work done in anthropology, cognitive science, sociolinguistics, and the humanities which has suggested that "the way we view the world is somehow governed by the media through which we view it and talk and write about it" (14). Although Bennett has reservations about *the extent to which* the "media" through which we perceive the world determines our understanding of it, he concludes that the work of scholars like Havelock (*Preface to Plato* and *A Pro-logue to Greek Literacy*), Ong (*Orality and Literacy: The Technologizing of the Word*), and Goody and Watt ("The Consequences of Literacy") has led to a significant shift in how literacy is understood. He says:

> There is a growing body of research on literacy from the per-spectives of anthropology, cognitive science, sociolinguistics, and the humanities that makes it difficult to view literacy any longer as an undiluted, unqualified good, or as a uniform cog-nitive skill which is neutral to the social, political, economic, and cultural conditions within which literacy takes its particu-lar forms. (14)

While I agree with Bennett's central premise that literacy must be understood within a social context, I have to disagree heartily with Bennett's conclusion that Goody and Watt have been responsible for any such historicizing and contextualizing of con-ventional and often monolithic understandings of literacy. On the contrary, in the following section, I will argue that Goody's work on literacy (and orality or nonliteracy) has only strengthened con-ventional views of literacy as having autonomous value—that is, as "neutral to the social, political, economic, and cultural conditions." The conclusions of Goody and Watt in an essay, "The Conse-quences of Literacy," and of Goody in *The Domestication of the Savage Mind* link the development of alphabetic literacy by the ancient Greeks to the development of logical, abstract, and later scientific "modes of thought" in the West.[5] The epistemology that is suppos-edly "made possible" by Greek literacy, they argue, is one that re-lies on the positing of eternal and universal knowledge and truth.[6] Ironically, it is this very epistemology that Bennett seems to be re-jecting in his critiques of "essayist literacy" and in his attempt to reformulate literacy—or, more accurately, to make it a more inclu-sive category.

Before I move on, a word on why understanding Jack Goody's work and, in general, anthropology's construction of "lit-erate" and "oral" (or, these days, "nonliterate") societies and/or "modes of thought" is important: Much of what fuels current ef-forts like Bennett's is a concern for the "illiterate" or "nonliterate"

Other; it comes as well from a concern for difference in the face of powerful and privileged ideologies that seek to debase and elide differences and diversity in order to maintain their own hegemony (see also Giroux). Moreover, it is no coincidence that in a postcolonial world very often the difference of the "illiterate" correlates with differences of race, culture, "Third World-ness," "modernness," class, and gender and that the differences of all of these correlate to the relative powerlessness of some groups in the "New World Order."

While a great deal of anthropology has and continues to explore and respect difference, there are also tendencies within the discipline, if not to efface difference, then to hierarchize it in the name of positivist science. The oral-literate dichotomy generated by anthropology is the cosmology through which a monolithic view of literacy is maintained and justified. Conversely, cultural relativist accounts of difference—also generated by anthropology, but which resist the hierarchizing tendencies of dichotomies—could be the source from which alternative understandings of literacy can be formulated and the conventional monolithic one debunked. It is from this concern for generating ways to talk about and understand cultural differences without hierarchizing them that I am led to a discussion of literacy in anthropological theory.

The Consequences of Goody's Literacy Thesis

Goody begins his treatise on literacy, *The Domestication of the Savage Mind*, with a discussion of the hazards involved in the use of certain dichotomies that have been perpetuated in anthropological comparisons of "the West with the Rest." Basically, Goody points out that the categories that constitute dichotomies like primitive-advanced, traditional-modern, precapitalist-capitalist, and simple-complex are based in the ethnocentric biases of the Western anthropologists and sociologists who originally developed these categories and, therefore, that these categories should be viewed as no longer valid for the purposes of cross-cultural comparison (1–2).

However, the above critique notwithstanding, Goody goes on to defend his own continued use of the oral-literate or "nonliterate"-literate dichotomy because, he claims, it is based in changes in "modes of communication" and can be used to gauge more "specific differences" between societies (9). He explains that "an examination of the means of communication, a study of *the technology of the intellect*, can throw further light on the developments in the sphere of human thinking" (10; my emphasis). He concludes that while the dichotomies listed above were not appropriate for comparing differences between societies, particularly between European and non-European societies, the nonliterate-literate dichotomy, reformulated as "modes of communication," can be a valid means of explaining differences in development in different societies (again, particularly between the West and the Rest)[7]:

> [D]ifferences in the means of communication are of sufficient importance to warrant an exploration of their implications for developments in human thought; and, in particular, to see whether they can give us a better account of *observed differences* than the dichotomies we have earlier rejected. (10; my emphasis)

To begin with, Goody does not problematize the "observed differences" upon which he bases his entire project. Who observed these differences? And, if the dichotomies that were developed in order to explain these differences were flawed by the ethnocentric biases of Western anthropologists, then why should the "observation" of differences in the first instance be seen as unproblematic and unmediated by the same ethnocentric biases? In other words, can we interpret the observations of colonizing and/or imperializing Europeans coming into contact with non-European societies as "proof" of either the relative "backwardness" or "advance" of non-European societies? According to historian Michael Adas, early European chronicling of the peoples they encountered in the colonial expansion was incomplete as well as unsympathetic. In his book *Machines as the Measure of Men: Science, Technology, and the Ideologies of Western Domination*, Adas argues that during the first two centuries of the European contact with non-Europeans, particularly with South Asians, Chinese, and sub-Saharan Africans, the recorded observations by Europeans were erratic and scanty and very rarely focused on indigenous scientific and technological knowledge (21–23). Thus, Goody's assumptions about "observed differences," in particular those differences pertaining to "developments in human thought," are very problematic and only serve to reproduce and reinforce the prevailing negative stereotypes about the scientific and technological (non)achievements of non-European societies.

Even if we momentarily suspend our disbelief over what the "observed differences" *really* are, we find other problems with Goody's analysis. Goody's critique of earlier attempts to explain differences between societies—as either falling into gross dichotomies of difference or of becoming "a diffuse relativism" (151) that cannot explain anything—is that they are either "non-developmental" or "simplistically so" (2). For this reason, Goody wants to bring back the notion of "development" into analyses of difference. By "developmental" analysis, Goody means an analysis that can go beyond "mere description" and can point to a "mechanism" of change or difference (16). Furthermore, such an analysis would be "interested in the further developments in these various facets of social life that seem to be associated with changes in the means and modes of communication" (19). In other words, such an analysis would be able to link the development of a particular facet of society, like the innovation of a "technology of the intellect" (151), to changes in other areas of that society like the development of science, increased individualism, the development of abstract thought, the accumulation of knowledge, and the development of history, etc. (149–50).

One problem with Goody's notion of a "developmental analysis" is that it is teleological. It assumes that understanding the conditions of production of a particular cultural innovation will also permit an understanding (or prediction) of the reception (i.e., the understandings and uses) of that particular innovation by the diverse members of that society. I would argue, however, that understanding the effects of any aspect of cultural production, even the production of a technology, requires not the apprehension of general "laws" (developmental or otherwise) that govern such effects, but rather a close and *specific* analysis of how a particular cultural production gets variously "received" or "consumed" by the various agents and/or groups within that society.

Richard Johnson, writing from the perspective of cultural studies, proposes a model of cultural production and reception using the notion of a "circuit of culture" (44). Johnson describes a circuit of culture as "a circuit of the production, circulation, and consumption of cultural products" (46). Johnson's point in describing the circuit of a cultural product is to emphasize the contingency of meaning or significance of each moment in the product's history. Goody's analysis of literacy posits specific effects of literacy, "alphabetic literacy" to be exact, without taking into account the conditions of its production or the intentions of its users.

Another critique of developmentalism can be found in Smith's *Contingencies of Value,* in which she describes the "fallacy" of developmentalism. Smith says:

> The fallacy so named here is the quite common idea of a teleologically directed "normal" maturing of aesthetic tastes and judgments and, accordingly, an ultimate "fullness" of development at which point, having moved beyond the dark glass of their "undeveloped" and "immature" likes and dislikes, now-grown children, unless innately defective, pathologically fixated, or culturally deprived or corrupted, will "recognize" the inherent value of canonical artworks and, like their erstwhile teachers and other elders, properly and naturally prefer them. (79)

We can apply Smith's discussion of the developmental fallacy to Goody's conceptualization of literacy as a "technology of the intellect" and as the means to the "teleologically directed" development of logic, rationality, abstract thought, and all of the other ingredients necessary for the maturing of science (50–51). The allusions to physical and intellectual maturity and immaturity in Smith's discussion are especially relevant given anthropology's history of patronizing descriptions of "illiterate" persons and societies as "primitive" and "childlike."

Finally, Goody's developmental analysis is also the search for a monolithic principle, in this case alphabetic literacy, to explain the complex and dynamic processes through which syllogistic reasoning and scientific thought and practice unfolded in ancient Greek and modern Western societies. To do so, Goody views literacy as a "technology" that, like its big brother science, is above the political interests of real people—the very agents doing the producing, inventing, experimenting on, and critiquing of these processes. These critiques of Goody's developmentalist approach to literacy expose important lacunae in his analysis—namely, his ignoring the effects of human intervention and intention in formulating and reformulating cultural products and processes. These critiques are also an important step in creating and legitimating alternative understandings of literacy.[8]

However, there is an important aspect of Goody's project that still needs to be addressed. Goody's project is also "to account for the Greek achievement" and "the rise of the West" and to be able to account for cultural differences beyond "merely" recognizing that cultures are different (ix). His use of a teleological notion of development to account for the achievements of the Greeks and the rise of the West reveals a major subtext in his work that is for the most part left implicit in his work: that is, the subtext of modernism and modernization. Goody's analysis and conclusions are in perfect harmony with modernist notions of Progress. His developmental view of technology suggests a kind of inevitable movement forward and seems to have the effect of re-invoking a social evolutionist paradigm at the very moment he claims to be disowning it. How else are we to understand Goody's claim that there is a fundamental shift in cognition or "modes of thought" associated with alphabetic literacy (16–18)?

More specifically, Goody's literacy thesis has an affinity with modernization theory of the 1950s and 1960s. Adas has described modernization theory as an extension of earlier programmatics of social development employed by Christian missionaries and colonial administrators:

> After World War II the modernization paradigm supplanted the beleaguered civilizing mission as the preeminent ideology of Western dominance. . . . Competing theories of dynamics and stages of the transition from "tradition" to "modernity" were debated by academics, and their jargon-laden discourse played a major role in policy formation with respect to the "underdeveloped," "developing," or "emerging" nations of the "Third World." New hierarchies of the levels of social development—the first, second, third, and (somewhat later) fourth worlds; postmodern, modern, traditional, primitive;

mature, developing, underdeveloped—replaced the civiliza-tion/barbarian/savage scale that had long served as the stan-dard. (411)

Modernization theory not only preserves a social evolutionary perspective, according to Adas, but it also preserves the earlier concerns in Europe for control or "mastery" over nature and "man's" natural environment. Ultimately, the ability "to shape the world to their own desires" (413) becomes the marker for de-termining if a particular society has achieved a sophisticated level of science and technology and of civilization.

Some modernization theorists, in particular Daniel Lerner, even describe the "modern personality" (qtd. in Adas 414). Inter-estingly, Lerner's work stresses the importance of literacy and a modern communications system in order for a society to nurture the "modern personality." Literacy and communications, ac-cording to Lerner, would enable people of traditional societies to grasp new ways of living and working that would *transform* them-selves and their societies (qtd. in Adas 414). Finally, others like Marion Levy use the principle of *efficacy* as a gauge for measuring the level of development in a society. Levy argues that a society's modernization could be gauged by "the extent to which it made use of inanimate power and employed tools 'to multiply the effect of effort'" (qtd. in Adas 414).

The parallels between Goody's conclusions about literacy and those of modernization theory are striking. We see a similar em-phasis on efficacy in Goody's conclusion that one of the effects of literacy is that it enables a society to preserve large amounts of information (37). For both Goody and Levy, efficacy means an am-plification and multiplication of effect through accumulation and mass production. In addition, Goody talks about literacy as a tool: "'Traditional' societies are marked not so much by the absence of reflective thinking as by the absence of the *proper tools* for construc-tive rumination" (44; my emphasis). Like Lerner, Goody links sci-ence and scientific thought to literacy. He says,

If we are to understand the particular contributions of Western (or any other) science[9] to the development of human thought, then we must be a good deal more precise about the matrix from which it was emerging, about the pre-existing conditions and the nature of "pre-scientific thought," . . . *it is not accidental that major steps in the development of what we now call "science" followed the introduction of major changes in the channels of communication in Babylonia (writing), in Ancient Greece (the alphabet), and in Western Europe (printing)*. . . (50–51; my emphasis)

Furthermore, Goody seems to agree with Lerner's proposition that literacy and the presence of written information *transform* the individual by creating an "awareness of alternatives" in him/her:

> Awareness of alternatives is clearly more likely to characterize literate societies, where books and libraries give an individual access to knowledge from different cultures and different ages. . . . But it is not simply the awareness of being exposed to a wider range of influences. . . . It is rather that the form in which the alternatives are presented makes one aware of the difference, forces one to consider contradiction, makes one conscious of the "rules" of argument, forces one to develop such "logic." (43–44)

Of course, most of the salubrious effects that Goody attributes to the literate form of communication, even in situations of widespread literacy, can be and have been challenged (e.g., Hoggart; Scribner and Cole). Do books, for example, necessarily provide *unmediated* accounts of difference, and do they really "force" individuals to deal with contradiction and develop logic as Goody has argued?

John Halverson in his recent essay, "Goody and the Implosion of the Literacy Thesis," argues that there is no evidence to show that literacy was necessary for the development of formal logic, syllogistic reasoning, or Western science by the Greeks (308–09). Halverson concludes that there is very little about the "consequences of literacy" proposed by Goody that can continue to be accepted when we explore the actual social "matrix" from which Greek formal logic, syllogistic reasoning, and/or Greek science were developing. Furthermore, Halverson argues that the conclusions Goody makes about the insufficiencies of oral modes of communication to sustain logical, abstract, and/or scientific thinking are simply false:

> There remains [Goody's] argument that formal, logical reason
> would never have arisen in the first place except for the histor-
> ical fact of Greek literacy, but the burden of the present cri-
> tique has been to demonstrate that this argument has not been
> made. I have tried to show, sometimes using Goody's own ma-
> terial as evidence, that many of the things deemed "impos-
> sible" in oral culture are in fact not only possible but also
> achieved in reality. I have moreover tried to show that most of
> the features of literacy on which Goody focuses—visual com-
> parison, perception of contradiction, skepticism, word-
> isolation, lists—have no demonstrable bearing on the issue,
> either theoretically or empirically. (312)

Finally, Halverson says about writing and cognition:

> The *medium* of communication—which is the issue here—has
> no *intrinsic* significance in the communication of ideas or the
> development of logical thought processes. . . . [L]anguages do
> not think, only individuals do, and the question is whether the
> assimilation of the complexities and artifices of written lan-
> guage leads to more logical thought. Certainly there is no *nec-
> essary* connection. . . . [W]ritten language in general is no more
> logical than speech. (314)

Thus far, I have tried to show that Goody's analysis of literacy
(and orality) is both analytically and empirically flawed. Perhaps
more interesting and more important than whether Goody is
"right" or "wrong," however, is asking *why* he has made the kinds
of arguments about literacy that he has. I believe that, in part,
Goody has pursued this project with such vigor and persistence
because he is working within a modernist episteme and more specifically with a Whiggish historical perspective. In addition, as I
noted earlier, because Goody rejects relativist accounts of cultural
difference as impotent, he turns to causal explanations of difference. In the next section, I will explore Goody's rejection of what
he calls "diffuse relativism." I will suggest that a relativist or "contingent" reckoning of literacy is the best way to go, both for explaining what literacy's consequences have been in various places
and times and also for developing a concept and practice that
works for more rather than less people. In other words, a cultural

relativist understanding of literacy is capable of handling difference without artificially hierarchizing it and without reducing the nature of social and cultural difference into "X causes Y" equations.

On "Diffuse Relativism"

Goody defends his use of a developmental analysis because, he says, the alternatives either reify or trivialize difference. The alternatives he is referring to are, respectively, the dichotomizing approach that has explained difference through the use of diametrically opposed binarisms and the relativistic approach that he dismisses as "diffuse" or incapable of saying anything definitive about difference or, in other words, that does not hierarchize difference. I agree with Goody's initial rejection of the impulse to dichotomize differences because such a move effectively elides the contingency of social change, which contributes to the generation of all types of difference. The dichotomies that Goody rejects have always been hierarchical and have, for the most part, privileged attributes associated with the West over those associated with the non-Western world. As I have already discussed at length, Goody does not get rid of dichotomies altogether. He preserves the oral (or "nonliterate") and literate dichotomy, and he attempts to show how that dichotomy is based in "real" differences in human cognition, which, in turn, entail different potentials for the growth and development of knowledge. By preserving this dichotomy, Goody ultimately recoups the other dichotomies he initially rejected. He also ends up recycling the discourse of "illiteracy as primitive" back into current anthropological theory.

I do not support the moves that bring Goody back to a position in which the oral-literate and, by association, primitive-civilized dichotomies get revitalized. Furthermore, I do not accede to Goody's claim that relativism is, or must be, "diffuse" or incapable of describing or explaining difference. In characterizing relativism as "diffuse" and thus analytically useless, Goody is conflating relativism with the notion of incommensurability. As a result, Goody takes an "all or nothing" approach in his critique of relativism which is no more productive or valid than the view that incommensurability between cultures and/or languages is a total and permanent state of being.

Thus far, I have argued that attempts to critique conventional, monolithic notions of literacy must include an analysis of theories of literacy and orality that have been generated by anthropology. Furthermore, insofar as attempts to devise alternative visions of literacy are based on a critique of a foundationalist epistemology, it is necessary to show how the alternative, namely relativism, is a viable and valuable epistemology *and* analytic principle.

As I stated above, Goody dismisses relativism as "diffuse" because he conflates "incommensurability" with relativism. This is a long-standing and common mistake made not only by those who support relativism in anthropological theory but also by those who have argued against it. In his essay "Anti Anti-Relativism," Clifford Geertz exposes flaws in the attacks that have been made on cultural relativism. He says:

> What the anti-relativists, self-declared, want us to worry about, and worry about and worry about, as though our very souls depended upon it, is a kind of spiritual entropy, a heat death of the mind, in which everything is as significant, thus as insignificant, as everything else: anything goes, to each his own, you pays your money and you takes your choice. (265; my emphasis)

We can see how Goody's dismissal of "diffuse" relativism is akin to Geertz's description above, particularly the phrase, "the heat death of the mind, in which everything is as significant, thus as insignificant, as everything else." Geertz goes on to cite the complaints of an anti-relativist, I. C. Jarvie, who says:

> [Relativism] has these objectionable consequences: namely, that by limiting critical assessment of human works it disarms us, dehumanizes us, *leaves us unable to enter into communicative interaction; that is to say, unable to criticize cross-culturally, cross subculturally;* ultimately, relativism leaves no room for criticism at all. (qtd. in Geertz 266; my emphasis)

Jarvie's critique and rejection of relativism are based on the belief that relativism proposes total and permanent incommensurability between "cultures" and "sub-cultures." The crux of relativism's problem, according to Jarvie, is that it "leaves us unable to enter into communicative interaction." And, it is the impossibility of communication that Jarvie labels the paradox of incommensurability. Jarvie's conflation of relativism with the notion of total and permanent incommensurability is basically the same as Goody's characterization of relativism as "diffuse." What both Goody and Jarvie seem falsely to believe, in Geertz's words, is "that if something isn't anchored everywhere, nothing can be anchored anywhere" (265).

While Geertz gives us an excellent description of the images of and reactions to relativism, he does not elaborate how these images may have developed. In particular, Geertz does not explain why relativism has caused so much confusion and crisis within anthropology. I would like to suggest that Jarvie's and Goody's understanding of relativism is not limited to them, but is rooted in a much longer tradition in cultural anthropological theory, starting from the work of anthropologist Edward Sapir and his student Benjamin Whorf and continuing, for example, in Ruth Benedict's *Patterns of Culture,* Donald Davidson's "On the Very Idea of a Conceptual Scheme," and the philosophers Michael Devitt and Kim Sterelny's *Language and Reality* (172–83, 201–03).

Edward Sapir, writing in the late 1920s and 1930s, articulates the following constructivist view of language and reality:

> [Language] powerfully conditions all our thinking about social problems and processes. Human beings do not live in the objective world alone, nor alone in the world of social activity as ordinarily understood, but are very much at the mercy of the particular language which has become the medium of expression for their society. . . . The fact of the matter is that the "real world" is to a large extent unconsciously built up on the language habits of the group. . . . The worlds in which different societies live are distinct worlds, not merely the same world with different labels attached. ("The Status of Linguistics as a Science" 209)

In this famous passage, Sapir presents an important voice of cultural relativism in anthropology.[10] Whorf develops Sapir's initial theorizations and suggests that the grammar of a language "is the shaper of ideas, the program and guide for the individual's mental activity" (212). In the following passage, he elaborates Sapir's original statement:

> When Semitic, Chinese, Tibetan, or African languages are contrasted with our own, the divergence in analysis of the world becomes more apparent; . . . *the fact that languages dissect nature in many different ways becomes patent. The relativity of all conceptual systems, ours included, and their dependence upon language stand revealed.* (214–15; my emphasis)

Eventually, the work of Sapir and Whorf was formalized into the "Sapir-Whorf hypothesis" and became part of the canon in anthropology.

While there have been many critiques and even rejections of the conclusions arrived at by Sapir and Whorf, in a subtle and yet pervasive way their work seems to have had an indelible influence on later conceptualizations of both language and culture. One characteristic of Sapir and Whorf's theory of language and culture is the principle of the wholeness or "completeness" of linguistic and conceptual systems.[11] Sapir says:

> The outstanding fact about any language is its formal completeness. This is as true of a primitive language, as of the carefully recorded and standardized languages of our great cultures. By "formal completeness" I mean [that]. . . . [e]ach language has a well defined and exclusive phonetic system with which it carries on its work. . . . [A]ll of its expressions . . . are fitted into a deft tracery of prepared forms from which there is no escape. ("The Grammarian and His Language" 153)

In this passage, we can identify a source of the notion of total and permanent incommensurability in some anthropological conceptions of culture. Sapir clearly sees continuity and completeness as normative for any linguistic/thought system. In addition, Sapir's characterization of languages and cultures as "forms from which there is no escape" suggests an incommensurability *between* forms. In the following passage, Sapir explicitly marries the notion of incommensurable wholes or systems to the notion of "relativity." He concludes his essay as follows:

It would be possible to go on indefinitely with such examples of incommensurable analyses of experience in different languages. The upshot of it all would be to make very real to us a kind of relativity that is generally hidden from us by our naive acceptance of fixed habits of speech as guides to an objective understanding of the nature of experience. This is the relativity of concepts or, as it might be called, the relativity of the form of thought. It is not so difficult to grasp as the physical relativity of Einstein, nor is it as disturbing to our sense of security as the psychological relativity of Jung. . . . It is the appreciation of the relativity of the form of thought which results from linguistic study that is perhaps the most liberalizing thing about it. What fetters the mind and benumbs the spirit is ever the dogged acceptance of absolutes. (159)

While Sapir is eloquent in arguing for relativist approaches to cultural and linguistic theory, he makes a move that seems to haunt those who came after him. In positing incommensurability between languages and cultures, Sapir makes change and/or inconsistency within a particular linguistic/cognitive/cultural system very difficult to reconcile and difficult even to recognize. Changes and/or inconsistencies are smoothed out or effaced in order to preserve the wholeness or "completeness" of the system, and the notion of incommensurability suggests a totality, closure, and impenetrability of linguistic/cognitive/cultural systems. The privileging of concepts like continuity, consistency, and totality, which we see in Sapir's work, leads to a principle of unrelenting wholeness that cannot be reconciled with the constant flux we can observe *within* and *between* languages, cultures, and societies. Indeed, to recognize such changes and inconsistencies is also to recognize the human agents behind them.

Although in this paper I will not be able to actually trace the influences of Sapir and Whorf's writings on the works of later anthropologists, it is striking that in current debates about cultural relativism the issue of incommensurability seems to be center stage.[12] In addition to Jarvie's critiques of relativism reviewed above, Melford Spiro's critique also seems to be centered on the "paradox" of incommensurability. In the essay "Cultural Relativism and the Future of Anthropology," Spiro sets himself to the task of "explicat[ing] the adverse consequences of epistemological relativism . . . for anthropological theory and research" (124). In the process of dissecting relativism, Spiro conflates "radical" cultural pluralism with cultural incommensurability (130–31). Spiro then goes on to conclude that the "adverse consequences" of epistemological relativism lie in the paradoxical nature of incommensurability for anthropological practice:

> [I]f cultures are incommensurable and if the characteristics of human nature and the human mind are predominantly culturally determined, how is it at all possible for an ethnographer to understand a group that is different from his or her own? (133)

No doubt Spiro is correct to suggest that there is a paradox in the idea of cultural incommensurability. However, Spiro's question assumes (as did Sapir and Whorf) that cultures and the people "within" them are inherently static. Incommensurability can only occur in a world that does not change and in people whose understandings and behavior are equally fixed. In other words, Spiro's critique conflates incommensurability with *immutability*. Ironically, while in the above passage Spiro claims to be discrediting the cultural determinism of relativists, his assumption of immutability is itself based in a kind of cultural determinism (130).[13]

A relativism that retains notions of the total incommensurability of experience and the wholeness of languages, cultures, and/or societies will continue to be vulnerable to critiques like the one by Jarvie and Spiro. Recently there have been critiques from within anthropology of the notion of "culture as a complex whole" that have argued against the view of culture as either impenetrable or resistant to either internal or external change or to contradiction (e.g., Clifford and Fox). In addition, there have been formulations of relativism that reject wholeness and incommensurability and that emphasize instead difference, diversity, and "scrappiness" in society (Smith, *Contingencies* 148–49).

Relativism can become the means through which difference can be described, analyzed, defended, or critiqued. Furthermore, all of this can be done without the hierarchizing that we observed in Goody's developmental method of accounting for difference. Nor is there the problem of teleology in these newer relativistic accounts of difference because they are historicized—something that has been conspicuously absent from many post-Boasian anthropological accounts of difference, particularly in the accounts of difference of "the primitive" (Clifford).

In attempts to "redefine" literacy, particularly for those, in Henri Giroux's words, "that care for the other in his/her otherness" (x), accounts of difference are central. Those who oppose difference—either by denying its existence, as in Hirsch's project of enforcing "national culture," or by denouncing difference as "divisiveness"—are themselves embroiled in ideologies that need to be constantly foregrounded. Smith points to the ideology of sameness that Hirsch tries to construct in his programmatic for educational reform:

> [A]ll the activities that Hirsch classified as "communication" and sees as *duplicative transmissions* that presuppose sameness— "common" knowledge, "shared" culture, "standardized" associations—are, in fact, always *ad hoc,* context-specific, pragmatically adjusted negotiations of (and through) *difference.* We never have sameness; we cannot produce sameness; and we do not need sameness ("Cult-Lit" 73).

We can apply the label symbolic violence to the practices and discourses through which sameness is forced upon the diversity that exists in U.S. society today (and probably has always existed in greater or lesser degrees in all societies). That is, violence and domination arise by denying the unique histories and experiences of the various groups that make up the United States, by pathologizing their experiences as abnormal and dysfunctional, and by denying them the means through which they can make their identities known.

Finally, in the context of discussions of literacy, for purposes of social and linguistic theory as well as for pedagogy and educational reform, the ideologies of modernism and modernization are probably as central as discourses of difference and sameness. The ideology of modernism is appealing to many because it simplistically links literacy in a direct way to economic and political prosperity. According to modernization discourses, the failure to become literate is seen as the failure of the individual and not the system. In other words, those who are not literate are seen as *choosing disenfranchisement,* and illiteracy is viewed as a passive-aggressive rejection of modernity itself. This ideology basically uses the "successes" of Western, industrialized nations as well as those of the elite groups of Third World nations as "proof of the pudding." The belief that modernism and modernization really do guarantee a progression to an economic and political utopia is one that is hard to shake, especially when these visions have worked *for some.* The trick, I suppose, is to show that built into the very logic of these ideologies and the systems they represent is an exclusivity. That is, we must show that modernism and modernization, like essayist literacy, will work for only a privileged few as long as they are taken as simple monolithic principles or blueprints for reform and social change and as long as reform is unresponsive to diversity and difference.

Notes

This essay has greatly benefited from discussions with Barbara Herrnstein Smith, Gaurav Desai, and Richard G. Fox. I thank them for their time and efforts.

1. It is interesting to note that the use of "deconstruction" by those who seek to analyze critically the way literacy is popularly understood is not a *destructive* move. The belief and fear behind this rejection of deconstruction are based in the erroneous notion that to deconstruct is to "de-struct"—that is, to annihilate the very thing/concept one is trying to explore. But as we see in some of the analyses and reconceptualizations of literacy below, the writers are not trying to destroy anything. They are, rather, trying to foreground the historical, epistemological, and structural constraints within which literacy is being taught, learned, and crusaded for (e.g., Bennett 24–25, 31).

2. I am referring in particular to Jack Goody's work on literacy. There are already some important critiques within anthropology of Goody's "literacy thesis," for example, Halverson, Finnegan, and Street. While I am arguing here that Goody's analysis of literacy is conventional within anthropology and also conventional among scholars and writers outside of the discipline, there is by no means a consensus within the discipline about what literacy is and what its "consequences" for society are.

3. For an extended discussion of the development of the "plain style" see Olson's essay (72–87).

4. Others who have produced radical analyses of literacy are Shirley Bryce-Heath, Paulo Freire, James P. Gee, Freire and Donald Macedo, and J. Elspeth Stuckey.

5. Like Bennett, I need to make a qualifying statement here with regard to "scientific, logical, abstract, and/or rational modes of thought." The critique that follows is not "an attack" on these modes of thought per se. It is rather an "attack"

on the developmental and teleological ways these modes of thought have been written about—as if the history of these modes of thought could have played itself out in no other way and that they, once formalized, have a life and mind of their own, autonomous of human actors. The next point in my critique is that if these modes of thought are not transcendent and autonomous of the historical contexts (and people) from which they arose, then they must be understood within the context of politics and power (see, for example, Shapin and Schaffer). Finally, I *am* skeptical of the conclusion that these particular modes of thought were originally and, more importantly, exclusively innovated in Western societies and were subsequently diffused to the rest of the world from the West.

6. Bennett describes in the following the epistemology that became the basis for "essayist literacy":

> The new epistemology, associating systematic logical progression, linear order, clarity, and certainty with the plain style of impersonal, non-metaphoric, expository prose was essentially a model of understanding. Relationships between the steps of an argument and the conclusions those steps "necessarily" led to could be made available to consciousness in the form of a sequence of explicit assertions. (16)

We will see that Goody and Watt's analysis of literacy, in opposition to orality, leads to an identical epistemology, which is, according to them, the most significant basis upon which to explain differences between "literate" and "nonliterate societies."

7. Goody does not, in this particular essay, explicitly say that he is comparing the developments of Greek alphabetic literacy and Greek methods of logical and rational thinking that were later to develop into Western science with the supposed absence of such developments in other societies. However, in an earlier essay with Ian Watt, "The Consequences of Literacy," he explicitly makes this comparison and links the rise of the West and the development of Western science to the development by the Greeks of alphabetic literacy. Furthermore, in *Domestication*, he refers to the comparison of the "West and the Rest" in a number of instances (ix, 8, 10, 51, 149).

8. The dismantling of the notion of the "illiterate primitive" (and for that matter of the "primitive") is also crucial to a project of viewing literacy, like all cultural productions, within the context in which it exists. The notion of the "illiterate, backward, simple, childlike, undeveloped, underdeveloped" primitive is particularly problematic because it has loomed large as the horrible fate of all those who never make it up that precarious peak of civilization. Finally, as Derrida has pointed out, because the notion of the "illiterate primitive" has been most elaborated upon by anthropology, any kind of deconstruction of literacy must begin with anthropology (101–40).

9. Of course, Goody never mentions "any other" science. And, his thesis seems to suggest that even the possibility of other sciences is remote except for Greek-derived, Western science.

10. Sapir's was not the only voice for a relativist view of culture in anthropology at this time. Franz Boas is generally regarded as the founder of cultural relativism (Stocking). However, Boas's relativism does not posit an incommensurability of linguistic and cultural worlds as, I will argue, Sapir's writings do.

11. A good example of the application of the principle of wholeness or completeness to theories of culture and cultural difference is the work of Ruth Benedict, particularly her *Patterns of Culture*. While the notion of culture as a "complex

whole" was articulated much earlier by E. B. Tylor, Benedict's work really established the relationship between cultural relativism and the wholeness of cultural complexes (11). This is probably because of Sapir's influence; we know that she was familiar with his work and that they were friends (Benedict 207; Handler 127–53).

12. In the above, I realize that I have not really demonstrated the effects of Sapir and Whorf's work on the understandings of later anthropologists of cultural relativism. At this point, I would not definitively say that the notion of incommensurability in later formulations of cultural relativism can be attributed primarily to Sapir and Whorf's influence. In order to do so, I would have to trace these ideas through Sapir and Whorf's students to look for their influence on later relativists like symbolic or interpretive anthropologists of the 1960s, 1970s, and 1980s. However, I do believe that it is important to explore the extent to which Sapir and Whorf have influenced current understandings of relativism both in and outside of anthropology.

13. Another angle of critique in this regard is to be found in the work of H. G. Gadamer on hermeneutics and intersubjectivity (87–139). Basically, Gadamer argues that radically different subjectivities can achieve shared knowledge and understanding (although never complete or perfect) through the creation of intersubjective spaces. That is through the force of contact or what he calls "dialectical relations between the former and the new" (138–39). This is similar to what we in anthropology have described variably as "culture contact" and/or "acculturation."

Works Cited

Adas, Michael. *Machines as the Measure of Men: Science, Technology, and the Ideologies of Western Dominance*. New York: Cornell UP, 1989.

Benedict, Ruth. *Patterns of Culture*. Boston: Houghton, 1934.

Bennett, Adrian T. "Discourses of Power, the Dialectics of Understanding, the Power of Literacy." Mitchell and Weiler 13–33.

Bourdieu, Pierre. *Outline of a Theory of Practice*. New York: Cambridge UP, 1977.

Bryce-Heath, Shirley. *Ways with Words*. Stanford: Stanford UP, 1983.

Clifford, James. *The Predicament of Culture: Twentieth Century Ethnography, Literature, and Art*. Cambridge: Harvard UP, 1988.

Davidson, Donald. "On the Very Idea of a Conceptual Scheme." *Inquiries into Truth and Interpretation*. Oxford: Clarendon, 1984. 183–98.

Derrida, Jacques. *Of Grammatology*. Baltimore: Johns Hopkins UP, 1974.

Devitt, Michael, and Kim Sterelny. *Language and Reality: An Introduction to the Philosophy of Language*. Cambridge: MIT P, 1987.

Finnegan, R. *Literacy and Orality: Studies in the Technology of Communication*. Oxford: Blackwell, 1988.

Foucault, Michel. *Power/Knowledge: Selected Interviews and Other Writings*. New York: Pantheon, 1980.

Fox, Richard. "For a Nearly New Culture History." *Recapturing Anthropology: Working in the Present*. Ed. Richard Fox. Santa Fe: School of American Research Press, 1991. 93–113.

Freire, Paulo. *Pedagogy of the Oppressed*. New York: Seabury, 1970.

———. *Education for Critical Consciousness*. New York: Continuum, 1973.

Freire, Paulo, and Donald Macedo. *Literacy: Reading the Word and the World*. New York: Bergin and Garvey, 1987.

Gadamer, H. G. "The Problem of Historical Consciousness." *Interpretive Social Sciences*. Ed. Paul Rabinow and William Sullivan. U of California P, 1987. 82–140.

Gee, James P. "What Is Literacy?" Mitchell and Weiler 3–11.

Geertz, Clifford. "Anti Anti-Relativism." *American Anthropologist* 86 (1984): 263–78.

Giroux, Henri A. "Series Introduction: Literacy, Difference, and the Politics of Border Crossing." Mitchell and Weiler ix–xvi.

Goody, Jack, *The Domestication of the Savage Mind*. Cambridge: Cambridge UP, 1977.

Goody, Jack, and Ian Watt. "The Consequences of Literacy." *Literacy in Traditional Societies*. Cambridge: Cambridge UP, 1968. 27–68.

Halverson, John. "Goody and the Implosion of the Literacy Thesis." *Man* 27 (1992): 301–17.

Handler, Richard. "Vigorous Male and Aspiring Female: Poetry, Personality, and Culture in Edward Sapir and Ruth Benedict." *History of Anthropology*. Vol. 4. Ed. George Stocking. Madison: U of Wisconsin P, 1986. 127–55. 7 vols.

Havelock, Eric A. *Preface to Plato*. Cambridge: Harvard UP, 1963.

———. *Prologue to Greek Literacy*. Cincinnati: U of Oklahoma P for U of Cincinnati P, 1973.

Hirsch, E. D. *Cultural Literacy: What Every American Needs to Know*. New York: Vintage, 1988.

Hoggart, Richard. *The Uses of Literacy*. New York: Oxford UP, 1970.

Johnson, Richard. "What Is Cultural Studies Anyway?" *Social Text* 16 (1986/87): 38–81.

Mitchell, Candace, and Kathleen Weiler, eds. *Rewriting Literacy: Culture and the Discourse of the Other*. New York: Bergin and Garvey, 1991.

Olson, D. "The Languages of Instruction: The Literate Bias of Schooling." *Schooling and the Acquisition of Knowledge*. Ed. R. C. Anderson, R. Spiro, and W. E. Mantague. Hillsdale: Lawrence Erlbaum, 1977. 65–89.

Ong, Walter. *Orality and Literacy: The Technologizing of the Word*. London: Methuen, 1982.

Sapir, Edward. "The Status of Linguistics as a Science." *Language* 5 (1929): 209–12.

———. "The Grammarian and His Language." *Language, Culture and Personality*. Ed. David G. Mandelbaum. Berkeley: U of California P, 1949. 150–59.

Scribner, Sylvia, and Michael Cole. *The Psychology of Literacy*. Cambridge: Harvard UP, 1981.

Shapin, S., and Simon Schaffer. *Leviathan and the Air-Pump: Hobbes, Boyles, and the Experimental Life*. Princeton: Princeton UP, 1985.

Smith, Barbara Herrnstein. *Contingencies of Value: Alternative Perspectives for Critical Theory*. Cambridge: Harvard UP, 1988.

———. "Cult-Lit: Hirsch, Literacy, and the "National Culture." *South Atlantic Quarterly* 89.1 (1990): 69–88.

Spiro, Melford. "Cultural Relativism and the Future of Anthropology." *Rereading Cultural Anthropology*. Ed. George Marcus. Durham: Duke UP, 1992. 124–51.

Street, B. *Literacy in Theory and Practice*. Cambridge UP, 1984.

———. "Literacy Practices and Literacy Myths." *The Written World*. Ed. Roger Saljo. Berlin: Springer-Verlag, 1988. 59–72.

Stocking, George W., Jr. "Introduction: The Basic Assumptions of Boasian Anthropology." *The Shaping of American Anthropology 1883–1911: A Franz Boas Reader.* Ed. George W. Stocking, Jr. New York: Basic, 1974. 1–20.

Stuckey, J. Elspeth. *The Violence of Literacy.* Portsmouth: Boynton/Cook, 1991.

Tylor, E. B. *Primitive Culture.* Vol. 1. London: J. Murray, 1871. 2 vols.

Whorf, Benjamin L. "Science and Linguistics." *Language, Thought and Reality.* MIT P, 1956. 206–19.

BOOKS RECEIVED

Abraham, Nicholas, and Maria Torok. *The Shell and the Kernel*. Chicago: U of Chicago P, 1994.

Allison, Anne. *Nightwork: Sexuality and Pleasure, and Corporate Masculinity in a Tokyo Hostess Club*. Chicago: U of Chicago P, 1994.

Amiran, Eyal, and John Unsworth. *Essays in Postmodern Culture*. New York: Oxford UP, 1994.

Arebi, Saddeka. *Women and Words in Saudi Arabia: The Politics of Literary Discourse*. New York: Columbia UP, 1994.

Aronowitz, Stanley. *Dead Artists, Live Theories, and Other Cultural Problems*. New York: Routledge, 1994.

Barlow, Tani E., ed. *Gender Politics in Modern China: Writing and Feminism*. Durham: Duke UP, 1994.

Bell, Shannon. *Reading, Writing, and Rewriting the Prostitute Body*. Bloomington: Indiana UP, 1994.

Bennington, Geoffrey. *Legislations: The Politics of Deconstruction*. New York: Verso, 1994.

Bhabha, Homi K. *The Location of Culture*. New York: Routledge, 1994.

Bokina, John, and Timothy J. Lukes, eds. *Marcuse: From the New Left to the Next Left*. Lawrence: UP of Kansas, 1994.

Brennan, Teresa. *History After Lacan*. New York: Routledge, 1993.

Bryson, Norman, Michael Ann Holly, and Keith Moxey, eds. *Visual Culture: Images and Interpretations*. Hanover: Wesleyan UP, 1994.

Cocks, Geoffrey, ed. *The Curve of Life: Correspondence of Heinz Kohut, 1923–1981*. Chicago: U of Chicago P, 1994.

Corbett, John. *Extended Play: Sounding Off from John Cage to Dr. Funkenstein*. Durham: Duke UP, 1994.

Craft, Christopher. *Another Kind of Love: Male Homosexual Desire in English Discourse, 1850–1920*. Berkeley: U of California P, 1994.

De Lauretis, Teresa. *The Practice of Love: Lesbian Sexuality and Perverse Desire*. Bloomington: Indiana UP, 1994.

Dienst, Richard. *Still Life in Real Time: Theory After Television*. Durham: Duke UP, 1994.

Dirlik, Arif. *After the Revolution: Waking to Global Capitalism*. Hanover: Wesleyan UP, 1994.

Dubey, Madhu. *Black Women Novelists and the Nationalist Aesthetic.* Bloomington: Indiana UP, 1994.

Elsner, John, and Roger Cardinal, eds. *The Cultures of Collecting.* Cambridge: Harvard UP, 1994.

Escobar, Miguel, Alfredo L. Fernandez, and Gilberto Guevara-Niebla, with Paulo Freire. *Paulo Freire on Higher Education: A Dialogue at the National University of Mexico.* Albany: State U of New York P, 1994.

Ferguson, Margaret, and Jennifer Wicke, eds. *Feminism and Postmodernism.* Durham: Duke UP, 1994.

Fiske, John. *Power Plays Power Works.* London: Verso, 1993.

Fraad, Harriet, Stephen Resnick, and Richard Wolff. *Bringing It All Back Home: Class, Gender, and Power in the Modern Household.* London: Pluto, 1994.

Giroux, Henry A. *Disturbing Pleasures: Learning Popular Culture.* New York: Routledge, 1994.

Goldstein, Philip, ed. *Styles of Cultural Activism: From Theory and Pedagogy to Women, Indians, and Communism.* Newark: U of Delaware P, 1994.

Goux, Jean-Joseph. *The Coiners of Language.* Trans. Jennifer Curtiss Gage. Norman: U of Oklahoma P, 1994.

Grosz, Elizabeth. *Volatile Bodies: Toward a Corporeal Feminism.* Bloomington: Indiana UP, 1994.

Gumbrecht, Hans Ulritch, and K. Ludwig Pfeiffer, eds. *Materialities of Communication.* Trans. William Whobrey. Stanford: Stanford UP, 1994.

Harrowitz, Nancy A. *Antisemitism, Misogyny, and the Logic of Cultural Difference: Cesare Lombroso and Matilde Serao.* Lincoln: U of Nebraska P, 1994.

James, Stanlie M., and Abena P. A. Busia, eds. *Theorizing Black Feminisms: The Visionary Pragmatism of Black Women.* New York: Routledge, 1993.

Kelly, Veronica, and Dorthea E. Von Mucke, eds. *Body and Text in the Eighteenth Century.* Stanford: Stanford UP, 1994.

Kerrigan, William. *Hamlet's Perfection.* Baltimore: Johns Hopkins UP, 1994.

King, Edward. *Safety in Numbers: Safer Sex and Gay Men.* New York: Routledge, 1994.

Klinger, Barbara. *Melodrama and Meaning: History, Culture, and the Films of Douglas Sirk.* Bloomington: Indiana UP, 1994.

Kopelson, Kevin. *Love's Litany: The Writing of Modern Homoerotics.* Stanford: Stanford UP, 1994.

Lee, A. Robert, ed. *A Permanent Etcetera: Cross-Cultural Perspectives on Post-War America.* Boulder: Westview, 1994.

Lunbeck, Elizabeth. *The Psychiatric Persuasion: Knowledge, Gender, and Power in Modern America.* Princeton: Princeton UP, 1994.

Mann, Patricia S. *Micro-Politics: Agency in a Postfeminist Era.* Minneapolis: U of Minnesota P, 1994.

Martin, Henri-Jean. *The History and Power of Writing.* Trans. Lydia G. Cochrane. Chicago: U of Chicago P, 1994.

Mestrovic, Stjepan G. *The Barbarian Temperament: Toward a Postmodern Critical Theory.* New York: Routledge, 1993.

Mishra, Vijay. *The Gothic Sublime.* Albany: State U of New York P, 1994.

Mitchell, W. J. T. *Picture Theory: Essays on Verbal and Visual Representation.* Chicago: U of Chicago P, 1994.

Morgan, John, and Peter Welton. *See What I Mean? An Introduction to Visual Communication.* London: Edward Arnold, 1992.

Morris, Rosalind C. *New Worlds From Fragments: Film, Ethnography, and the Representation of Northwest Coast Cultures.* Boulder: Westview, 1994.

Murphy, Timothy F., and Suzanne Poirier, eds. *Writing AIDS: Gay Literature, Language, and Analysis.* New York: Columbia UP, 1994.

Nerone, John. *Violence Against the Press: Policing the Public Sphere in U.S. History.* New York: Oxford UP, 1994.

Newcomb, Horace, ed. *Television: The Critical View.* New York: Oxford UP, 1994.

Newton, Judith. *Starting Over: Feminism and the Politics of Cultural Critique.* Ann Arbor: U of Michigan P, 1994.

Pacteau, Francette. *The Symptom of Beauty.* Cambridge: Harvard UP, 1994.

Pearce, Richard, ed. *Molly Blooms: A Polylogue on "Penelope" and Cultural Studies.* Madison: U of Wisconsin P, 1994.

Rafael, Vincente L. *Contracting Colonialism: Translation and Christian Conversion in Tagalog Society under Early Spanish Rule.* Durham: Duke UP, 1993.

Reeves, Jimmie L., and Richard Campbell. *Cracked Coverage: Television News, the Anti-Cocaine Crusade, and the Reagan Legacy.* Durham: Duke UP, 1994.

Robbins, Bruce. *The Servant's Hand: English Fiction From Below.* Durham: Duke UP, 1993.

Ronell, Avital. *Finitude's Score: Essays for the End of the Millennium.* Lincoln: U of Nebraska P, 1994.

Rose, Tricia. *Black Noise: Rap Music and Black Culture in Contemporary America.* Hanover: Wesleyan UP, 1994.

Ross, Andrew, and Tricia Rose, eds. *Microphone Fiends: Youth Music and Youth Culture.* New York: Routledge, 1994.

Shank, Barry. *Dissonant Identities: The Rock 'n' Roll Scene in Austin, Texas.* Hanover: Wesleyan UP, 1994.

Sieburth, Stephanie. *Inventing High and Low: Literature, Mass Culture, and Uneven Modernity in Spain.* Durham, NC: Duke UP, 1994.

Silverman, Hugh J. *Textualities: Between Hermeneutics and Deconstruction.* New York: Routledge, 1994.

Simone, T. Abdou Maliqalim. *In Whose Image? Political Islam and Urban Practices in Sudan.* Chicago: U of Chicago P, 1994.

Simpson, Mark. *Male Impersonators: Men Performing Masculinity.* New York: Routledge, 1994.

Spivak, Gayatri Chakravorty. *Outside in the Teaching Machine.* New York: Routledge, 1993.

Stockton, Kathryn Bond. *God Between Their Lips: Desire Between Women in Irigaray, Brontë, and Eliot.* Stanford: Stanford UP, 1994.

Torgovnick, Marianna, ed. *Eloquent Obsessions: Writing Cultural Criticism.* Durham: Duke UP, 1994.

Ulmer, Gregory L. *Heuretics: The Logic of Invention.* Baltimore: Johns Hopkins UP, 1994.

Virilio, Paul. *The Vision Machine.* Bloomington: Indiana UP, 1994.

Willemen, Paul. *Looks and Frictions: Essays in Cultural Studies and Film Theory.* Bloomington: Indiana UP, 1994.

CONTRIBUTORS

Miriam Cooke is an associate professor of Arabic at Duke University. Her research focuses on war and gender in the Arab world as seen through its literature. Among her publications is a book on *War's Other Voices: Women Writers on the Lebanese Civil War* (Cambridge). Her current research attempts to go beyond the Lebanese case to identify what has changed in warfare and its representation in the postcolonial era.

Andrew Feenberg is a professor of philosophy at San Diego State University and is the author of *Lukács, Marx, and the Sources of Criticism* (Oxford), *Critical Theory of Technology* (Oxford), and the forthcoming *Alternative Modernity* (University of California Press).

Rosemary Hennessey teaches postmodern, feminist, and gay and lesbian theory in the English department at SUNY, Albany, where she is also affiliated with women's studies. She has written *Materialist Feminism and the Politics of Discourse* (Routledge 1993) as well as various essays on feminist and cultural critique. Her current project deals with new sexual economies.

Joseph D. Lewandowski is a doctoral student in the philosophy, literature, and criticism program in the comparative literature department at SUNY, Binghamton. His current research deals with the role of language and criticism in the works of Benjamin, Adorno, and Habermas.

Sangeeta Luthra is in the department of cultural anthropology at Duke University. She is presently working on grass-roots literacy movements in India and is generally interested in subaltern perspectives and critiques on "modernization" and "development" within the context of contemporary urban Indian society.

Andrew H. Miller is an assistant professor at Indiana University and associate editor of *Victorian Studies*. His book *Novels Behind Glass: Commodity Culture and Victorian Narrative* is forthcoming from Cambridge University Press; he has essays in and forthcoming from *Yale Journal of Criticism, PMLA, ELH,* and *Genre*.

Michael Rothberg studies comparative literature at the City University of New York Graduate Center and is on the editorial collective of *Found Object*, a journal of cultural studies. His current project is "Post-Memory: Documenting Barbarism in French and American Culture After the 'Final Solution.'"

Where

you can

still

hear

people

thinking

for

them-

selves

Personal Voices on Cultural Issues

Ted Hughes on Sylvia Plath

Edward W. Said, "Gods That Always Fail"

Ross Posnock, "Roy Cohn in America"

Millicent Bell on Rodin

Margery Sabin, "The Debate in Literary Studies"

Maureen Howard on Edith Wharton

Harold Bloom, "Feminism as the Love of Reading"

Arts • Literature • Philosophy • Politics

RARITAN
Edited by Richard Poirier

$16/one year $26/two years
Make check payable to RARITAN, 31 Mine St., New Brunswick NJ 08903